WHEN THE LIONS ROARED

WHEN THE LIONS ROARED

JOE PATERNO AND ONE OF COLLEGE FOOTBALL'S GREATEST TEAMS

BILL CONTZ

TRIUMPH
BOOKS

Library of Congress Cataloging-in-Publication Data

Names: Contz, Bill, 1961.
Title: When the Lions roared : Joe Paterno and one of college football's greatest teams / Bill Contz.
Description: Chicago, Illinois : Triumph Books, LLC, [2017] | Includes bibliographical references.
Identifiers: LCCN 2017002669 | ISBN 9781629373720
Subjects: LCSH: Pennsylvania State University—Football—History. | Penn State Nittany Lions (Football team)—History. | Paterno, Joe, 1926-2012.
Classification: LCC GV958.P46 C66 2017 | DDC 796.332/630974853--dc23
LC record available at https://lccn.loc.gov/2017002669

This book is available in quantity at special discounts for your group or organization. For further information, contact:
  Triumph Books LLC
  814 North Franklin Street
  Chicago, Illinois 60610
  (312) 337-0747
  www.triumphbooks.com

Printed in U.S.A.
ISBN: 978-1-62937-372-0
Design by Meghan Grammer
Todd's Take photos courtesy of Joe Faraoni/ESPN Images

To my deceased parents, Julius Sr. and Margaret. Both provided me with the love, support, motivation, and encouragement to lead a very productive and fulfilling life.

I also dedicate this to any Nittany Lion fan or alumnus who proudly proclaims "We Are!" whenever in the presence of anyone donning anything resembling a Penn State logo. I contend that doing so reaffirms their allegiance and commitment to maintaining the highest possible standards, doing things the right way, accepting challenges head on, and finding uniquely creative ways to accomplish remarkable things.

Contents

Foreword

On January 1, 1979, I was sitting in my living room in North Canton, Ohio, watching Penn State and Alabama battle it out in the Sugar Bowl with a national championship on the line. I was a senior in high school, and the game was compelling to me for two reasons.

First, Penn State was one of several schools that was recruiting me as a quarterback and one of the four universities that I would end up officially visiting in the coming weeks. Secondly, I pondered throughout the telecast how awesome it would be to have the opportunity to one day play for a national championship in a game of that magnitude. Chuck Fusina was a brilliant senior quarterback that year for Penn State and he wore No. 14. He had led the Nittany Lions to an undefeated regular season and a shot at the title. Alabama would win the game that day, thanks to an epic goal-line stand, but something special about Penn State football resonated with me on that January day.

Shortly before I signed with Penn State, Joe Paterno sat in that very same living room on a home visit, leaned forward in his chair, looked me straight in the eyes, and said, "I think you are the quarterback that can lead us to a national championship." Exactly four years to the day of the game I had watched, wearing the same jersey No. 14, I was in the Superdome poised to lead our second-ranked Nittany Lions team against the undefeated and No. 1 ranked Georgia Bulldogs for the national championship.

The author of *When the Lions Roared*, Julius (Bill) Contz, and I arrived at Penn State together as part of the same recruiting class. We quickly developed into being teammates, friends, and ultimately comrades forever. I was from Ohio, and he was a Pennsylvania kid like many of our teammates. Our roster contained players from all over the place: New Jersey, Maryland, New York, Connecticut, Virginia, Florida, and even a tiny coal mining town in the southern tip of West Virginia. We came to Happy Valley for many of the same reasons: to play a challenging, national schedule; to play in postseason bowl games; and most of all, to be a part of a program that could compete at the highest level while never compromising the integrity of being true student-athletes.

Deep down, all of us also hoped for the opportunity to compete for and win the first official national championship in Penn State history. Julius does a wonderful job in this book of taking the reader on a journey in pursuit of this championship, focusing primarily on a 15-game odyssey that began late in the 1981 season and culminated on the night of January 1, 1983, and explaining why this team was one of the greatest in the history of college football. Although many of the facts and figures about the games are interesting and entertaining, the real beauty of *When the Lions Roared* is found with the people and the personalities that made up our team, coaching staff, and support personnel. He did an extensive amount of research and painstakingly interviewed several members of our team, and the personal tidbits and anecdotes he was able to capture and record are priceless. This book is like a backstage pass inviting readers to glimpse and grasp the heart, soul, and character of Penn State's first national championship team.

WE ARE!

—Todd Blackledge
Penn State quarterback (1979–82)

Introduction

For the better part of the 20th century, central and western Pennsylvania was known as coal country. Pale yellow clouds forming from the toxic exhaust that belched forth from 60-foot high smokestacks were a common sight growing up in the post-Vietnam era. Box-office hits such as *The Deer Hunter, Flashdance,* and *All The Right Moves* utilized this gritty backdrop to capture the essence of the area's blue-collar, shot-and-a-beer persona.

The region's economic landscape changed forever in the late 1970s with the epic collapse of the steel industry. Tens of thousands of steelworkers from Aliquippa to Altoona counted on the steady, generational employment from the steel mills and factories that lined the Monongahela, Allegheny, and Ohio Rivers. Hardscrabble, blue-collar steelworkers from different ethnic backgrounds now faced the sobering economic reality of long-term layoffs, financial hardship, and permanent relocation.

College and pro football seemed to offer a temporary respite, a distraction for these newly unemployed masses, and the quality of the local teams certainly didn't disappoint. The Pittsburgh Steelers won four Super Bowls in the '70s after decades of futility, but their dynasty did not cast too overwhelming a shadow for the two schools that reigned supreme in Pennsylvania.

Beginning in the mid-70s, the annual intrastate grudge match between Pitt and Penn State steadily escalated into every bit the equal of the more traditional Ohio State-Michigan and Auburn-Alabama rivalries. The Pitt Panthers were enjoying a grand renaissance under head coach Johnny Majors, who replaced Carl DePasqua prior to 1973. Majors wasted little time returning the school to prominence by revitalizing a moribund, left-for-dead 1–10 program in 1972 and leading Pitt to the 1976 national championship. The following season Majors returned home to his alma mater, Tennessee, affording one of his top assistants, Jackie Sherrill, the opportunity to continue to recruit nationally and keep the school ranked among the elite teams in the country.

One hundred thirty miles to the east, Joe Paterno had continued to attract attention to his program by producing undefeated—and uncrowned—teams in 1968, 1969, and 1973 while appearing in six bowl games in his first eight years as head coach at Penn State. Paterno had assumed head coaching duties in 1966 after 15 years as an assistant under Rip Engle. His Nittany Lions dominated the intrastate series with their western neighbors. However, by the time Tony Dorsett won the Heisman Trophy while leading Pitt to its first national title in 39 years, the Pitt-Penn State contest was no longer a one-sided affair.

With Majors at the helm, the stakes for this game began to climb. During a seven-year period beginning in 1976, one team—and sometimes both—entered this contest ranked among the top 15 teams in the country. Since both schools were independent (i.e. not affiliated with any major conference), scouts from virtually every major bowl routinely jockeyed for position in the home team's press box in anticipation of extending a New Year's Day invitation to the victor. The game was played on or around Thanksgiving, and each school's success turned this rivalry into must-see TV for college football fans across the country.

Both teams built depth charts full of elite players at a variety of positions. The 1980 installment of the "Battle of Route 22" showcased an array of talent rarely seen on the same field at the collegiate level. Thirteen future first-round NFL draft picks were among the roughly 180 players in uniform, including five—Jimbo Covert, Hugh Green, Dan Marino, Mark May, and Curt Warner—who would be elected to the College Football Hall of Fame.

Three others (Rickey Jackson, Russ Grimm, and Mike Munchak) would, along with Marino, be enshrined to the Pro Football Hall of Fame. In all, 29 Panthers and 34 Nittany Lions (nearly 36 percent of all players on the field that day in State College) would eventually be selected in the NFL draft.

The following year both programs again started strong. By mid-October, Penn State and Pitt had seized ownership of the top two spots in the AP poll and were on another collision course that would surely carry with it national implications.

My journey to Happy Valley began in Belle Vernon, one of a quartet of small towns that make up an area south of Pittsburgh known as the Mon Valley. Sports were very much embedded into the fabric of those towns and the area produced a handful of very prominent athletes including Stan Musial, Ken Griffey, and Joe Montana.

My mom and dad were both caring, God-fearing people who taught their kids the values of hard work and fair play as well as the clear difference between right and wrong. This book exists, to some extent, because of my mother's passion for reading and routinely dragging her three children to the Monessen Public Library on Saturday mornings to retrieve and return the various novels she had borrowed the previous week.

I had the good fortune to grow up when the Wheeling-Pittsburgh mill located across the street from that library was thriving and jobs were plentiful. Both the Pirates and Steelers won multiple championships in the 1970s, and their exploits were well-documented on the sports pages of *The Valley Independent*, which I pored over during breakfast every day. Sports were so all-consuming that I don't recall reading any other section of that newspaper until I left for college.

Most sports-crazy kids growing up before cable television spent their formative years playing whatever sport happened to be in season. When football ended in November, you played basketball or you wrestled. When basketball ended in early March, you went out for baseball, volleyball, or track. Coaches trying to convince you to specialize in a singular sport (usually theirs) or weekend travel leagues, in which parents haul their kids across state lines to face stiffer competition, were non-existent. You competed against kids from down the street or from the neighboring towns usually in multiple sports.

Filling gaps in the sports calendar meant chances to emulate Willie Stargell or Terry Bradshaw. When Little League baseball ended, the remaining days of summer were spent playing Wiffle Ball in the backyard. In the fall the occasional tackle game formed on late Sunday afternoons in a field adjacent to the cemetery across the street. When inclement weather moved us indoors, we morphed into adolescent couch potatoes, relying heavily on a magic device called a rotor, which sat perched atop the only color television set we owned. The rotor enabled us to control the direction of a giant antenna affixed to our chimney during the pre-cable era. When properly pointed we were able to get the four TV channels afforded our home and view a minimally distorted picture. To pull in the local CBS affiliate, KDKA, our antenna needed to point straight north while a northeast setting gave us access to NBC, which broadcast the overwhelming majority of Steelers games.

The majority of Sunday dinners from Labor Day through mid-December consisted of a serious batch of my mom's grenade-sized Halupkis flanked by healthy portions of kielbasa and mashed potatoes. For those of non-Hungarian descent, a Halupki is a mixture of ground meat, pork, and rice wrapped in a cabbage leaf that simmers in a tomato-based broth for several hours. Mom made sure to serve her grenades piping hot and precisely at 12:30 PM, so we could inhale several prior to jockeying for position on the sofa in time for the usual 1:00 PM Steelers kickoff.

I did not play organized football until the eighth grade in part because my parents felt the sport was too violent, but also because I exceeded the midget football league weight limit, which was around 125 pounds. Basketball was my first and far more enjoyable preference. Lacing up a pair of Chuck Taylors before finding any semi-inflated round object to launch toward the hoop attached to our detached garage was all I needed to go play. Football, on the other hand, required donning 15 pounds of body armor, and for linemen it involved fun activities such as pushing a seven-man sled around, regularly colliding into oversized dummies or each other. I wore eyeglasses for nine years, starting at the age of seven, and can attest to the fact that having those repeatedly smash down on the bridge of my nose due to an ill-fitting suspension style helmet was not a pleasant experience…at all.

My third year of organized football presented something new in the form of three-a-day preseason practices in 80-plus degree heat and stifling humidity. It didn't take long to decide that wasn't for me, so after about a week, I simply stopped showing up. My rationale was that I probably wouldn't be missed—a patently absurd thought, considering the team only had a handful of players over six feet tall or over 200 pounds.

My absence prompted head coach Jeff Petrucci to dispatch two of his trusted assistants to my house to convince me to return. I mulled the offer for a few days before returning for the final day of preseason practice. My extended leave and general lack of commitment meant I would not suit up for any varsity games that year. If I ever envisioned playing football at Belle Vernon Area, a major change in my attitude was needed.

I had been blessed with my fair share of God-given talent and began to find my groove athletically after the 10th grade. I eventually started to buy into what the coaches were teaching me on the practice field, and regular playing time soon followed. I was fortunate to be part of competitive teams in high school, playing alongside teammates who shared my contempt for losing while never backing down from any challenge. I would later come to find that this same mind-set existed at Penn State where I soon joined a team that came within a yard of delivering Paterno's first national championship.

Had I honored the first letter of intent I ever signed, I would have actually won a national championship one year earlier than I did…and would have thoroughly regretted it. College recruiters in the late 1970s were fairly aggressive salespeople, and the more convincing ones really laid it on pretty thick. Clemson got my full attention during my recruiting trip there when its dynamic new head coach, Danny Ford, handed me the keys to his Jaguar and insisted I take it for a spin. My dad had sold Fords, Lincolns, and Mercurys in Western Pennsylvania's Mon Valley region for the better part of 35 years and would bring home more family-oriented model options. Suffice it to say, this particular transportation option was decidedly different, one I couldn't resist trying out. While thermometers back in Pennsylvania hovered in the 20s, I tooled around back country roads of central South Carolina in a sleek two-door sports car, enjoying the breezy 60-degree temperatures.

Not long after I returned the car to Ford, I signed a conference letter of intent, which prohibited me from signing with other ACC schools. I figured it was the least I could do for letting me borrow his Jaguar. Plus, Ford's program was on the rise, and his ability to recruit players like an amazingly agile 300-pounder defensive tackle named William Perry resulted in Clemson winning the national championship a couple of years later. At that stage in a thoroughly confusing recruiting process, I flew back home convinced I would be heading south to play college football. Upon my return, however, my parents made it clear that Clemson would be too far to drive to attend my games. My protest gave way to the trust and respect I had for them even if I didn't comprehend their logic at the time. I still had two recruiting visits lined up with Michigan and Penn State—both of which satisfied my folks' criteria that my college choice be within a reasonable drive from Belle Vernon, Pennsylvania.

Don Nehlen was an assistant coach under Bo Schembechler at Michigan in 1978 before taking over as head coach at West Virginia in 1980. Nehlen frequently visited our home, always making sure to flash his obscenely oversized Rose Bowl ring as often as one can while not making the gesture obvious. We occasionally cross paths with people who exhibit unique behavior or character traits that endear them to us. For me, that turned out to be the case with Nehlen. Whether it was his nervous energy or the amplified acoustics in my parents' modest three-bedroom, one-bathroom house, Nehlen would routinely repeat the phrase "Do you know what I mean?" to reinforce the many virtues he believed Michigan offered me. His dogged persistence convinced me to check out the place.

I visited Ann Arbor in late January on a weekend that gave new meaning to the word frigid. The character Leonardo DiCaprio portrayed in *The Revenant*, Hugh Glass, would have been right at home in weather better suited for Eskimos or ardent frontiersmen. When I met Bo Schembechler, the Wolverines' head coach sat stoically behind an aircraft-carrier sized desk in his office. I got the impression I wasn't exactly Michigan's top recruit because he seemed distracted and called me "Bob" more than once. Bo's indifference—coupled with the fact that I also met Bubba Paris and Ed Muransky (both of whom tipped the scales at around 300 pounds) during my recruiting trip—pretty much convinced me that becoming a "Michigan Man" wasn't in my foreseeable future.

My decision against attending school in Siberia didn't leave Penn State as my only option as I continued to ponder where to play college football. Pitt was only 25 miles away and had won the national championship during my sophomore year in high school behind Heisman Trophy-winning running back Tony Dorsett. The late Foge Fazio recruited me very hard, but I felt the school's urban setting had too much of a concrete feel to it despite its strong academic reputation. I'm not sure why, but I envisioned a college campus as having mature, tree-lined sidewalks. Foge managed to do okay that year because Pitt signed the top quarterback (Dan Marino) and receiver (Julius Dawkins) in the Western Pennsylvania Interscholastic Athletic League, a year removed from signing future NFL All-Pro Jimbo Covert.

I had no real allegiance to any of the three closest major colleges that were recruiting me (Pitt, Penn State, and West Virginia). Penn State, however, had posted several undefeated seasons under Joe Paterno and narrowly missed out on winning the national title my senior year in high school. The school appealed to me because of its established national reputation for both athletics and academics and its relatively rural campus setting. Appearing in eight straight bowl games didn't hurt either.

I scheduled the last of my six official recruiting trips there the weekend after I returned from Michigan. At this point the recruiting process was becoming a real grind. Making it worse, I came down with a severe cold while in Ann Arbor, lost some weight, and generally felt miserable all week. I am pretty sure I made less than a favorable impression on Paterno when I finally met him as he sat down with my family during a Sunday meet-and-greet brunch along with other recruits at The Nittany Lion Inn. I wore an open-collared, floral shirt under my leisure suit and coughed incessantly during the meal. Joe continued recruiting me anyway, reiterating why Penn State was the right place for me. It worked since I signed a national letter of intent to play for the Nittany Lions eight days later.

My formal given name is Julius William Contz Jr., and for as long as I can remember, I went by plain old "Bill," but that came to an abrupt end in November of 1979 in, of all places, the Penn State locker room. Our head equipment manager was a salty, snarling, cowboy boot-wearing gent named Tim Shope, which we pronounced "Show Pea" just to piss him off. "Show Pea" was charged with handing out players' winter-term "pink slips," documents that listed our class schedules for the upcoming 10-week trimester. Halfway through this mundane task, Shope came across the one bearing my name. He proceeded to parade around the locker room, holding it high in the air while inquiring loud enough to anyone within earshot, "Where is Julius? Who is this JOOL-EEE-USSS Contz? Has anyone seen Jool-eee-usss?"

You can imagine what this meant to a gangly freshman, serving out a year-long sentence on the scout team and one who also was buried on the depth chart and sporting a hairstyle Anton Chigurh eventually made famous in *No Country for Old Men*. The near Contz-tant ribbing (all good-natured, I assure you) gradually subsided, and I eventually warmed up to my new identity, gaining some weird sense of notoriety among my teammates. The majority of my former Penn State teammates and coaches still refer to me as "Julius." For some unknown reason, Joe would call me "Julian" whenever he yelled at me during practice (which was often). That was something I could never quite figure out.

Over time I worked my way up Joe's depth chart. I ended up starting the final 24 games of my college career at long tackle (Penn State's terminology for the tackle that always lines up next to the tight end). When I think about it, I never really considered myself much different from any of the other players on the team. I did my best to work hard, try to do what I was told, steer clear of trouble (academic or otherwise), and make the most of my opportunities. I enjoyed contributing to successful teams and took pride in helping the ones I played on achieve some pretty lofty goals. It didn't hurt to be surrounded by other elite athletes or to avoid major injuries until I reached the NFL, where I survived long enough to start 25 games over the course of six seasons with the Cleveland Browns and New Orleans Saints.

One memory that still haunts me, though, occurred during the eighth offensive play of what turned out to be Paterno's last chance to knock off his nemesis, Paul "Bear" Bryant, when I nearly got Todd Blackledge, who was in the process of re-writing most of the Penn State passing records, killed after completely whiffing on a block. It is a mental cross I continue to bear.

Back in 1978 I helped my high school basketball team win the WPIAL championship in Pittsburgh's iconic Civic Arena, a structure that has since been demolished. Fast forward to New Year's night of 1983, I set foot onto the floor of the Louisiana Superdome (a place I would later call home for three NFL seasons) to play in the biggest football game of my life, and two rather obscure thoughts crossed my mind: you could probably fit the entire Civic Arena inside this building, and I sure as hell wasn't in Belle Vernon anymore.

Before exiting the facility that night, my Penn State teammates and I would take down our second top-ranked opponent inside of 13 months to cap an incredible 15-game stretch that began back in November of 1981. Our quarterback would intentionally empty his bladder in front of a record national television audience roughly 10 minutes before helping a former walk-on become a Penn State legend by launching the pass that would become *the* defining moment of what turned out to be an absolutely classic Sugar Bowl.

With the help of an opportunistic defense that rose up on college football's biggest stage to devour yet another Heisman Trophy winner and a prolific offense fronted by a line that transformed itself from question mark to exclamation point, the final game of my collegiate career ended with a memorable and satisfying 27–23 triumph against the Georgia Bulldogs.

The victory meant deliverance for Joe Paterno and concluded a spectacular run that culminated in the school's first national title. Hell-bent on establishing his team's national credibility since the mid-1970s, Paterno essentially orchestrated his own playoff long before one ever existed, scheduling (and beating) the best teams college football had to offer with a program that produced graduation rates consistently above the national averages. What follows is the inside story of Penn State's improbable run to the 1982 national championship as seen through the eyes of former players—along with an argument for why this team may go down as one of the best in college football history.

CHAPTER 1

Halloween Night of 1981

J ust past the halfway point in the 1981 campaign, Penn State took its 6–0 record to Miami, where dreams of an undefeated season came to an abrupt end on rainy Halloween night at the hands of Jim Kelly and Hurricanes coach Howard Schnellenberger, who had begun his career at his alma mater (Kentucky). After two years in Lexington, he moved to Tuscaloosa in 1961 to join Bear Bryant's staff at Alabama. His timing could not have been better as the Crimson Tide won their first national title under Bryant that year on the strength of a defense that allowed a paltry 2.3 points per game, never surrendering more than seven points in any single contest.

Part of Bryant's national recruiting philosophy was to attract players from other parts of the country that could add different dimensions to his program. As if to test the mettle of his newest assistant, Bryant dispatched Schnellenberger to western Pennsylvania to lure the area's top quarterback, Beaver Falls' Joe Namath, to Tuscaloosa. Legend has it that Bryant told his young coach something to the effect of "If you don't come back here with Namath, then don't bother coming back at all." Schnellenberger and Bryant's success in recruiting players like Namath would play a pivotal role in galvanizing the Alabama program. The Tide would win three national championships during the five years Schnellenberger served on Bryant's staff.

Schnellenberger left Alabama following the 1965 season and spent the next 13 years in the NFL, including two stints with Don Shula's Miami Dolphins. Schnellenberger returned to the college ranks in 1979 to resurrect the program across town in Coral Gables. One of his first moves in changing the University of Miami's football culture was to replicate what Bryant had him do two decades earlier—find a strong-armed kid from western Pennsylvania to run his offense. This time around he handed the reins to Jim Kelly from East Brady, a small town an hour's drive north of Pittsburgh.

Miami, however, was not Kelly's top choice. Like a lot of scholastic players from the area, Kelly wanted to play football for Joe Paterno and become the Nittany Lion signal-caller. "I'd always been a big Penn State fan," Kelly said. "I went to Coach Paterno's football camp during the summers before my junior and senior years of high school. I had my heart set on playing at Penn State. But then Coach Paterno called me and he told me that he'd already signed two all-state quarterbacks and that he didn't have a spot for me on the team as a quarterback. He did offer me a full ride as a linebacker. I appreciated the scholarship offer, but I wanted to go somewhere and play quarterback. That's how I ended up going to the University of Miami."

In the fall of 1979, Kelly would again visit Happy Valley—this time as a redshirt freshman for "The U." Despite ridiculously short notice, Kelly would exact revenge on Joe for not making him a Nittany Lion quarterback by engineering a stunningly one-sided 26–10 upset.

"I went into that week as the backup QB," Kelly said. "Coach Schnellenberger told me after the pregame meal that I was going to be the starter. I was shocked. But I knew it was an opportunity to show that I could play. Coach gave me that opportunity, and I made the best of it."

Two years later the stakes were even higher.

During its national broadcast, ABC aired an ominous graphic that listed four teams previously ranked No.1 in the country, and all had lost the week following their ascension to the top spot in the polls. Miami had not hosted a No.1-ranked opponent in the Orange Bowl since September of 1975. They entered this game with a misleading 4–2 mark. (Both of those losses came on the road to top 20 teams.) Their defense was holding opponents to 13 points per game while our offense was averaging a robust 37 points and 308 rushing yards per game.

Something had to give.

Revenue generation at the aging Orange Bowl facility was evidently a concern as the venue hosted an outdoor concert featuring both The Beach Boys and the Commodores the night before the game. While not uncommon at more modern facilities with synthetic turf, the event would wreak havoc with the natural grass playing surface. "When we came out to warm up the next day, we found shards of glass out of the field," recalled former Nittany Lions running back Jeff Butya. Strong storms would arrive shortly after intermission and turn the field into a near-quagmire.

Injuries also played a pivotal role in our upset loss on All Hallows' Eve. Weeks earlier junior tailback Curt Warner had scorched Nebraska for 238 yards in a key road win. Three games later he dazzled an overmatched Syracuse defense with a school-record 256 yards rushing in the Carrier Dome. Warner literally established himself as the greatest show on turf a full quarter century before the "other" Kurt Warner led his high-flying St. Louis Rams offense to victory in Super Bowl XXXIV. During the first five weeks of the '81 season, Curt had quietly become a serious contender for the Heisman Trophy (eventually awarded to USC's Marcus Allen) by rushing for 838 yards on 115 carries, a gaudy 7.3 yards per carry that led the entire country.

But Curt tweaked his hamstring in practice the week before the West Virginia game, and the injury severely limited his effectiveness. Warner played sparingly against Miami, picking up just 21 rushing yards. (In addition, our senior co-captain and inspirational leader on defense, linebacker Chet Parlavecchio, missed the entire contest with an injury.) The aggressive Hurricanes defense had every intention of shutting down our running game by crowding the line of scrimmage. That strategy, along with the fact that Curt wasn't close to 100 percent, were key reasons why we trailed for the entire game.

We self-destructed, missing four field goals while turning the ball over three times in the final quarter, including twice in the final three minutes. Joe also committed a rare strategic error by failing to call his final timeout with the ball on the Miami 2-yard line at the end of the first half. Make no mistake, it was mission accomplished for a stingy Miami defense that included seven future NFL draft picks and stifled a running attack that had been cranking out more than 300 yards per game.

Enter Todd Blackledge, who had been somewhat inconsistent in his first full year as our starter. Time and again, Blackledge rose to the occasion against Miami. Despite enduring a fierce pass rush, he almost single-handedly pulled the game out by throwing for more than 350 yards and breaking several Nittany Lions passing records while outplaying Kelly. Trailing 17–0 going into the final period, we mounted a furious comeback and nearly pulled the game out before losing 17–14. If there was any consolation in this frustrating loss, it was that Todd's performance served notice that our offense was no longer one-dimensional and had quick-strike potential.

Following the upset loss to Miami, we lost again two weeks later at home to the one coach and team Joe could never figure out—Bryant and his vaunted Crimson Tide. This was Alabama's inaugural trip to Happy Valley and the first game played between the two schools since the epic 1979 Sugar Bowl. Nearly three years removed from that contest, Bryant had assembled yet another tough and talented team that would finish the 1981 season ranked sixth in the AP poll.

Alabama broke open a tight contest by scoring 17 straight points to take a 24–3 halftime lead. We took the second-half kickoff and drove to the Tide 1-yard line. However, in a sequence eerily similar to the '78 Sugar Bowl, Alabama's defense rose up to prevent us from scoring any points despite running seven plays inside the 5-yard line. The Tide complemented their wishbone option with speedy wide receivers who got behind our secondary on several occasions. Any chance at redemption or an outside shot at the national championship slipped away as the Bear's mastery over Joe continued in a 31–16 Alabama win.

With a record that stood at 7–2 and a top bowl bid now very much in the air, our remaining schedule included a home game against Notre Dame followed by the annual battle with the Panthers in Pittsburgh. Pitt had taken over the top spot in the polls after our unexpected loss in Miami, and the Panthers were beating the absolute tar out of everyone they played.

CHAPTER 2

Football Royalty and a No. 1 Rival

November 21, 1981
Notre Dame (5-4) at No. 13 Penn State (7-2)

U nder first-year head coach Gerry Faust, Notre Dame visited Beaver Stadium for the first time in its program's storied history. Despite being ranked in the top 10 in both major wire services at the start of the season, the Fighting Irish were scuffling after close losses to Florida State and USC, both of whom were nationally ranked.

Curt Warner's nagging hamstring injury meant Joe would revert back to starting sophomore Jonathan Williams at tailback, a move that had worked well earlier in the season when Jon ran for 140 yards against West Virginia. Williams, along with sophomore Harry Hamilton, electrified an already pumped up crowd in the game's first minute. Hamilton took the opening kickoff back 50 yards followed by Williams exploding for 40 yards on the first play from scrimmage. We scored two plays later to take a 7–0 lead less than 60 seconds into the contest. In only his second career start, Williams roasted a Notre Dame defense for 192 yards on 27 carries. Jon happened to be the latest from what seemed to be a plug-and-play, next-man-up stable of NFL-caliber running backs that Paterno managed to stockpile that season, including Warner, Joel Coles, and Mike Meade.

Despite its misleading 5–4 record, Notre Dame built a 21–17 lead midway through the fourth quarter. Then an improbable play shifted the game's momentum in our favor.

Notre Dame quarterback Blair Kiel dropped back to pass inside our 35-yard line and attempted to hit one of his running backs circling out of the backfield. What the Irish signal-caller could not have possibly imagined was reserve nose tackle Greg Gattuso dropping back into coverage and running step for step with the Notre Dame receiver. Gattuso reached over his shoulder to make an off-balance, one-handed interception...15 yards downfield. Nearly every player on our sideline had to blink two or three times at what had just happened. We literally could not believe our eyes as we watched a 255-pound defensive lineman pick off a pass that far downfield.

Todd's Take

The interception occurred at such a critical point in the game and it not only showcased Greg's athleticism, but it also displayed the creativity of our defensive coaching staff. As I cover college football today for ESPN, I see zone blitz coverages all the time where defensive backs or linebackers rush the quarterback while defensive linemen drop into zone pass coverage. However, in 1981 that was not a common practice at all. It was a great call, at the perfect time, and as big as Greg was, I'm sure the Notre Dame quarterback, Blair Kiel, had no idea where he came from to make the play.

But Gattuso was a pretty accomplished athlete, having played fullback at Seton LaSalle High School in Pittsburgh while helping lead his team to the WPIAL championship. It probably didn't hurt that one of his high school teammates was a guy named Jim Sweeney, who would go on to play at Pitt and for 15 NFL seasons with the New York Jets, Seattle Seahawks, and Pittsburgh Steelers. Like most Panthers offensive linemen coached by the late, great Joe Moore—a list that includes Russ Grimm, Mark May, Jimbo Covert, and Bill Fralic—Sweeney played with near flawless technique, had excellent feet, and great strength and leverage. It was a rare occurrence to see any Pitt offensive lineman surrender a sack.

Weather permitting, in late spring we would play pick-up basketball outside the dorms in South Halls on the asphalt courts to stay in shape. Penn State recruited its fair share of multi-sport athletes, and we had no shortage of talented basketball players on the football team (John Luton, Jeff Hostetler, Mark Fruehan, Kevin Baugh, and Blackledge, to name a few). In addition Curt Warner and Kenny Jackson ran track, Ron Heller had a 3–0–1 record in a brief stint as a Penn State varsity wrestler, and Steve Sefter went on to become an NCAA heavyweight wrestling champion. Suffice it to say, there were some pretty gifted athletes on campus in the early 1980s.

One of the biggest surprises—to me, anyway—was how agile Gattuso actually was on a basketball court. For someone playing the interior of the defensive line at close to 260 pounds, he was a damn good ballhandler and shooter who could make it rain field goals from deep. His sensational defensive play kept Notre Dame off the scoreboard and jump-started our offense. Blackledge culminated a lengthy scoring drive by going over from a yard out with less than three minutes left, giving us a hard-fought 24–21 win.

After our stirring fourth-quarter comeback against a gritty and stubborn team, we found ourselves playing the role of spoiler against Pitt. While that wasn't exactly what we had in mind at that stage in the season, the opportunity to knock off the No. 1-ranked team, not to mention the bitter rival that had beaten us in each of the past two seasons, guaranteed we would be ready to play.

November 28, 1981
No. 11 Penn State (8-2) at No. 1 Pitt (10-0)

Much has been written about the outcome of this contest, and it remains one of the darkest days in the history of the proud Panthers' football program. A Pitt victory and another against Georgia in the Sugar Bowl would have delivered the Panthers' second national championship in six seasons. Instead, a lopsided 34-point loss only further infuriated loyal Panthers followers, whose collective loathing of Penn State and Joe Paterno may have already been at an all-time high. The consensus among most former Panthers seems to be that had these teams played 10 times Pitt would have won eight or nine of them. The outcome of this contest is a shining example of why you actually play the game because anything can—and in this case did—happen.

Todd's Take

 Even though I was an Ohio kid, I loved playing in this rivalry game because you could feel the energy ramp up during the week with so many Pennsylvania players who knew each other—and in many cases played with each other—during high school. I have been fortunate in my 25 years of broadcasting college football to cover all of the major rivalry games at least once: Ohio State-Michigan, Alabama-Auburn, Texas-Oklahoma, USC-UCLA, Notre Dame-USC, Florida-Georgia, Florida State-Miami, Michigan State-Notre Dame, LSU-Ole Miss, Alabama-Tennessee, and Army-Navy. I would put Penn State-Pitt, during my four years in Happy Valley, right up there with the best of all rivalry games in terms of intensity, passion, history, and the assembled talent on the field.

Pitt entered the contest, having won its previous 17 games under Jackie Sherrill, who had chalked up a 52–9–1 record in five seasons at Pitt. That mark solidified his reputation as a top recruiter and gameday strategist. A few years earlier, Joe had infuriated Panthers fans with a comment about not "leaving college football to the Switzers and the Sherrills" in reference to the steady decline of ethics and morality in college football. Joe never intended the remark to go public. He had made it during his regular Friday chat with Penn State beat writers. Those sessions were strictly off the record and a chance for the media to sit down with Joe in a more relaxed setting. The comment made it into print because a reporter at one of the chats did not know it was off the record and ran with it.

Our outspoken senior linebacker, Chet Parlavecchio, threw some gasoline on the already smoldering rivalry a few days before the game. Parlavecchio, appearing on a Pittsburgh sports broadcast, made it quite clear that Pitt's perfect record did not impress him. "Pitt's No. 1," he said. "They played that tough schedule—Rutgers, Temple, and Thiel. Now they're going to be in a real football game."

Thiel?

"Ricky D'Amico had a friend named Kevin who went to Thiel and had visited Penn State earlier that fall," Parlavecchio said. "When Rick introduced us, I didn't even know Thiel was a college." An annoyed Sherrill shot back, saying the linebacker "didn't have the class to get into Pitt." The opposing coach and player would end up having a closer encounter during the game.

What's odd is I can't recall Paterno ever chastising Chet in public or any team meeting about his comments. Perhaps Joe secretly concurred with his co-captain. Suffice it to say, the overwhelming majority of Panther fans in attendance wanted Chet's head on a platter. *How dare any Nittany Lion insult us? We're the No. 1 team in the country! Why isn't Paterno disciplining that kid? Who does this Parlavecchio think he is?*

Truth be told, Parlavecchio may have relished calling attention to what he truly felt was a distinct advantage we had after playing a much more difficult schedule. I am not sure even Chet knew how prophetic his rather bold and obnoxious pregame inference would turn out to be, but his comments defined him to the core.

Chet did more than just take a poke at Pitt. The confidence that bordered on cockiness also reflected the high expectations Penn State players had in the early 1980s. Freshmen like me, who had arrived on campus in August of 1979, joined a squad that was eight months removed from the narrow 14–7 Sugar Bowl loss to Alabama. The '78 Penn State team was Joe's first to ever enter a bowl game ranked No. 1 in the country and it finished literally one yard shy of Joe's fourth perfect season in 13 years as head coach and the school's first national championship.

Returning seniors that fall entered camp with a chip on their shoulder. The group included Lombardi Award winner Bruce Clark; Matt Millen, who went on to win four Super Bowl rings with three different NFL teams, as well as future NFL players Irv Pankey; Matt Suhey; Lance Mehl; and Mike Guman. Most of those dudes came back pissed off and regularly took out their frustration on freshmen on the scout team. As one of those scout teamers I learned a valuable lesson that fall. Getting pounded by Clark and Millen taught me that I had to get a lot bigger, faster, and stronger if I was going to have even a remote chance to compete at this level.

My experience as a typical freshman at a major college program wasn't much different than others, something that was not lost on the Penn State coaching staff. "Until you see the reaction of a high school All-Star to getting knocked down, you really don't know how successful you are in recruiting," assistant coach Dick Anderson said. "That's especially true with offensive linemen. They are usually the biggest kids on their high school teams and can get away with certain things because of their size, their athleticism."

I was no exception. At Belle Vernon Area High School, I was the heaviest player on the team, weighing in at a robust 220 pounds. "In college all of a sudden they are challenged and in a couple of ways. One is getting into the proper condition. Big guys generally have a difficult time adjusting to the conditioning, to really getting in shape," Anderson said. "Then there's the competitive aspect, getting knocked around for the first time and so on. Most all freshmen have that deer in the highlights mentality. Am I good enough? Can I really compete here? I don't think there is anyone who doesn't go through that. It is important for coaches to understand that freshmen are just different than everybody else. They are just like every other college student in terms of emotional make-up. They are experiencing things they have not done before, and at times it's difficult." The transition from high school to D-1 football is indeed a challenge for most. It absolutely was for me.

Two years later Penn State featured another talented and strong-willed senior class.

Along with Parlavecchio, Sean Farrell, Ed Pryts, Rick D'Amico, Matt Bradley, Jim Romano, Mike Munchak, and Leo Wisniewski comprised a very confident set of leaders. All seemed to play and practice with a mean streak. To this day, I contend it was these seniors' swagger and self-assuredness that played a central role in a great deal of the success Penn State enjoyed in the '80s. Every one of those guys put on a football helmet with a "Hey, I plan to kick your ass all day" mind-set.

"Most of the seniors on that team, especially the ones on defense, would argue and fight amongst each other constantly," D'Amico said. "The language we used wasn't very flattering either."

Wisniewski cites one example of that group's arrogance that confirmed D'Amico's claim. "We were playing N.C. State in Raleigh in 1981," Wisniewski said. "An official comes over to our defensive huddle during a timeout and says, 'I am hearing too much profanity, and if I hear any more, I will call an unsportsmanlike conduct penalty!' No sooner did the word 'penalty' leave his mouth than Matt Bradley, standing in the back of the huddle, yells out, 'Ah fuck you!' The ref looked up at us, shook his head, turned around, and walked away."

D'Amico still laughs about the incident. "Can you imagine what the other team's offense must have thought of all of the on-field quarreling going on in our huddle?" he said. "The guys in my recruiting class were all my friends, but there was not a lot of compassion. We celebrated toughness. When I got hurt and missed some time, I felt like a fifth wheel. It was perceived as a weakness. At times you got absolutely skewered and had to develop a warrior mentality."

* * *

Parlavecchio, more than anyone, embodied this confidence and swagger. He would lead the team in tackles in both his junior and senior seasons despite missing two full games due to injury in 1981. That Chet became a force at "Linebacker U" is a story in itself. Near the end of the first week of practice in 1980, Joe juggled his defensive depth chart (a fairly common occurrence during the preseason) and moved Chet, a junior, to the second team behind a talented sophomore, Walker Lee Ashley. Back then the color of your practice jersey identified your status on the depth chart, and some shade of blue was a good thing. A light blue jersey meant you ran with the first-team offense while a navy blue practice jersey meant you were with the first-team defense.

When Chet arrived at his locker and found a bright-red jersey, he was absolutely livid. He stomped into the coaches' locker room and demanded an explanation. Joe, along with Jerry Sandusky, Chet's position coach, met with Chet in a small room adjacent to where the coaches dressed—a room where the late J.T. White, a longtime assistant coach and Paterno confidant, would occasionally play Crazy Eights with some of the players.

Chet voiced his frustration and was anything but diplomatic about it. "In my 10 years on Joe's staff I had never ever been part of any meeting like that before where a player was absolutely furious, pointing fingers, veins popping out of his neck," said former longtime assistant Fran Ganter.

The meeting didn't last long, and Chet stormed out of it with Ganter in close pursuit. Despite Fran's best efforts to get him to return, Chet refused and went to his dorm room still furious and convinved he had played his last down for Penn State. "Jonesey and Bobby Blade [1980 team captains Greg Jones and Bob Jagers] later came to my room to get me to reconsider, but I had my bags packed. I was ready to leave," Parlavecchio said. "They talked me out of it."

What happened after Chet's blow-up took Ganter by complete surprise. Upon returning to the coaches' dressing room, he found a very composed Paterno preparing to head to the field for practice. "Just relax," Paterno told his assistants. "I know where he's coming from. Chet's a competitor. He wants to win. I like that. We need more players like him. I'm just afraid he may be gone for good and that he'll transfer."

Ganter was astonished. "I expected Joe to be pissed, and instead he was incredibly calm about the whole thing," Ganter said. Fellow assistant coach Dick Anderson offered his perspective on how Paterno handled disgruntled personnel. "Joe believed that, while he couldn't treat all his players equally, he would treat them all fairly," Anderson said. "Chet was an intense competitor. Joe recognized that, but he also understood those types of players because he grew up around guys like that in Brooklyn."

A day later Chet had cooled off and asked Joe to reinstate him to the team. Joe called a team meeting before practice to address Parlavecchio's insubordination. A talented but emotional player quitting the team over a demotion was a very serious transgression. Sensing an opportunity to unify his young team, Paterno exited the room and left it up to his players to decide Chet's fate.

Jones and Jagers were both respected leaders. They took control of the meeting and solicited input mostly from the team's upperclassmen. After an overwhelming majority of players lobbied for Chet's return, an obscure walk-on stood up halfway through this open forum.

"Hey guys, if this was about a walk-on who quit, the team we wouldn't even be having a meeting," running back Jeff Butya said.

The room immediately went silent. You literally could have heard a pin drop. As we all looked around incredulously to see who had the stones to utter such a ludicrous comment, the "Legend of The Loose BOO-tay" was born.

The running backs at Penn State in the early '80s were an unusually entertaining group and especially creative when it came to both locker-room banter and nicknames they assigned each other. Initially nicknamed "The Elusive One" for his attempt to avoid the daily punishment inflicted on most scout teamers, Butya's moniker was shortened then merged with his last name to form "BOO-tay."

Jeff meant no ill will toward Chet with his proclamation. But his status on the depth chart coupled with the fact that he had been on the team for only a few months did not endear him to many people in the room. Butya, in one bold stroke, managed to hang a giant bull's-eye on himself. Word of

Jeff's comment quickly got back to Chet. "Rick D'Amico came running out of the meeting as soon as it ended and told me exactly what went on and who my new main adversary now was," Chet recalled.

It was the ultimate betrayal and from a most unlikely, yet readily accessible, source. Butya instantly became Parlevecchio's personal scout team rag doll. "Everyone voted Chet back on the team except one guy," Leo Wisniewski recalled. "It would set off pressure cooker-type rage that Chet would routinely unleash on BOO-tay."

To properly understand Chet's advantage, consider the hedges surrounding the practice field. In the early 1970s, those eight-foot tall hedges had been planted just inside the fence that surrounded the practice fields, effectively discouraging any onlookers, or possible spies, from sneaking an extended peak at Joe's practices. These hedges were about seven to 10 yards beyond the nearest sideline and well past where any player would normally come into contact with them. Anyone who ever served as a scout teamer referred to the hedges as "rose bushes"—not so much because we ever saw flowers in bloom but due to the sharp thorns that would stick to your uniform (and skin) whenever you encountered them.

The scout team was made up of true freshmen and players who are below the fourth team on the depth chart. Their marching orders were to execute plays the upcoming opponent was expected to run in an effort to give the guys, who are likely to play, a good look. They were issued practice jerseys with numbers on them to resemble the uniform numbers of the upcoming opponent. They were worn like a red badge of courage, an inglorious reminder to all of one's status on the roster.

The opponent's plays were drawn up on 10 x 13-inch cards and held aloft by a graduate assistant. Once all scout teamers saw their assignment, they waited a few seconds to allow the defense to call its own signals. They then broke the huddle intent on trying to execute the play as close to what appeared on the card but usually at around three-quarters speed. If the defense reacted swiftly and properly, the offense and defense moved on to the next play. If, however, any position coach was dissatisfied with the reaction or technique used by his players, he could demand to run the same play again.

Knowing what play will be called is a huge advantage to defensive players as they can now anticipate where the point of attack will be. Provide this advantage to an aggressive Parlavecchio hell-bent on maintaining his status with the starting defensive unit, then factor in a walk-on with an "I-better-go-all-out-or-Joe-will-throw-me-off-the-team" outlook, and you have a recipe for true crime, punishment, and abuse. "I remember seeing Chet throw Butya like a Frisbee," Ganter said.

Butya taking flight and ending up in the hedges as the result of a hard hit from Parlavecchio and his entourage became a regular sight. It was common for his fellow scout teamers to help untangle Jeff from the hedges and get him back to the huddle. To his credit Jeff always found the resolve to soldier on without complaint. "I'd always get up smiling, which would make [Parlavecchio] so mad," Butya said. "But I was having the time of my life. I was there to get them ready. I knew my role. My gameday was Tuesday. It was a blast."

D'Amico's attempts to reign in the abuse did little to offset Parlavecchio's stubbornness. "After a while I remember us going to Chet, saying, 'Can you please give this kid a break?' I mean it was brutal," D'Amico said. "I recall several occasions where Chet hit him so far out of bounds they went through the hedges and rammed into the cyclone fence. We would come back to the huddle and get a little chuckle, but there were many times we told Chet, 'Hey, you're gonna kill the guy.' Chet had his own agenda. It was a relentless pursuit of making someone's life miserable. There were times we thought we were real close to him agreeing to give him a break, but he would always go back to the dark side. He'd come back with, 'Hey, it's a violent world. Sometimes it just felt good to unload on a guy.'"

Butya's backfield brethren recognized the abuse he absorbed—as well as his inner resolve. "As a scholarship player, you had a greater appreciation for the guy's effort, what it took for him to even be in that room," said running back Jon Williams. "Jeff was part Energizer Bunny and part Timex watch—he had a ton of energy, took a licking, and kept on ticking."

Joel Coles echoed Williams' sentiments. "Butya may have been stumpy, but he was one of the toughest kids on the team," Coles said. "Our defense just teed off on him. Those guys knew full well who was getting the ball, where the play was going, and would take out their frustrations on BOO-tay."

Practices for bowl games were sometimes held outdoors regardless of conditions. One of these gave Butya the chance to leave a slightly different impression on his teammates. "It snowed pretty heavily the night before, but Joe still had us outside on the turf," Parlavecchio said. "The snow was shoveled off to the side in big piles. One time we hammered Jeff so hard into a snowbank you couldn't see him. It looked like a cartoon cutout."

Things came to a head in a practice, leading up to our bowl game against USC. Following another typically aggressive Parlavecchio encounter, Jeff sprang off the ground and rifled the ball he was carrying at Chet's head. The ensuing fight that erupted had in reality been building for months and got both players ejected from practice. "Everyone else was still on the field finishing practice, so it's just me and Chet in the locker room," Butya recalled. "After we peel off our uniforms and start to walk toward the showers, he turns to me and says, 'Enough's enough, that's it!'"

And just like that, their personal War of the Roses came to an end.

* * *

The '81 seniors inspired a lot of people, myself included, to take their game to a higher level. Ten-win seasons and top 10 rankings were the norm around here. I was getting a chance to play on a regular basis that year, and my main goal was to do well enough, so none of those seniors got in my face to "discuss" my substandard play.

Given the upcoming opponent (Pitt), where the game would take place (western Pennsylvania,) and what was at stake (a rivalry game against the No. 1-ranked team in the country), playing lousy football would obviously fall short of those guys' expectations. The game was a homecoming for those of us who grew up in western Pennsylvania. Bragging rights were absolutely at stake. I hadn't played very well the previous week against Notre Dame and had serious doubts on how I could match up against a defensive line that included Bill Maas, Dave Puzzuoli, J.C. Pelusi, and Chris Doleman.

Hostile does not begin to describe the overflow crowd that crammed into

Pitt Stadium on a raw day in late November. Pitt fans fully expected to see their top-ranked Panthers take down the Nittany Lions for a third consecutive season, something they had not done since around World War II. Pitt had averaged more than 43 points a game in three lopsided wins leading up to the contest—albeit against somewhat suspect competition. Our fall from the top spot earlier in the season only added to Panthers fans' enjoyment. Just like the previous year in State College, there was no shortage of talent on the field for this game, as 36 of the 44 offensive and defensive starters were later selected in the NFL draft.

Just prior to kickoff, Joe chose to only send our three co-captains (Leo Wisniewski, Sean Farrell, and Chet Parlavecchio) out for the coin toss while the remainder of the squad stayed in the locker room. It was a subtle yet strategic ploy on Joe's part to reinforce the us-against-the-world mentality he felt we needed to survive this environment. The crowd that day smelled blood, and after the game's first 15 minutes, it appeared they were on the verge of seeing some.

Pitt owned the first quarter as Dan Marino picked our secondary apart. He threw two absolute darts for touchdown passes, staking his Panthers to a quick 14–0 lead. We didn't help matters by generating a grand total of minus-one yards of total offense in the first period. We were being thoroughly outplayed in all facets and on the verge of being completely embarrassed (on national TV, no less). A rout, it seemed, was imminent.

Early in the second quarter, the presumptuous Parlavecchio clotheslined a Panthers receiver several yards out of bounds on the Pitt sideline—and well after the whistle had blown, promptly drawing a 15-yard unsportsmanlike conduct penalty. From my vantage point on the opposite sideline, it appeared that Chet was also using the opportunity to "discuss" his rather pugnacious play with an absolutely livid Jackie Sherrill. Joe rarely condoned such behavior. However, if he was upset, he sure didn't show it, possibly sensing that Parlavecchio's aggression may just give us the spark we so desperately needed.

Shortly after Parlavecchio's sideline encounter with Sherrill, a seismic momentum shift occurred. Cornerback Roger Jackson, who had picked off a Marino pass in the back of the end zone on the previous Pitt possession, belted All-American wide receiver Julius Dawkins in mid-air, resulting in another interception. "Roger hits Dawkins, and the ball pops up right into my hands," said safety Mark Robinson. "They could have gone up 21–0. At that point we decided it was time to start playing Penn State football. Pitt receivers got short arms awful quick."

Junior wide receiver Gregg Garrity concurred. "I remember watching Marino throw his second touchdown thinking, 'Oh man, here we go.' I thought if they scored another one we were in trouble," he said. "After that hit [by Jackson], their receivers wanted nothing to do with going anywhere near the middle of the field."

Julius Dawkins grew up in Monessen while I grew up in the adjacent town of Belle Vernon. We competed against each other in both football and basketball in high school, were each selected (along with Marino and Jeff Hostetler) to play in Pennsylvania's prestigious Big 33 All-Star Game, and eventually chosen in the 1983 NFL Draft. As previously mentioned, my formal given name is Julius William Contz Jr. What are the odds that two guys named Julius would grow up roughly five miles apart from each other, compete against each other at both the high school and college level, and then go on to play NFL football? Probably as remote as spotting the No. 1 team in the country 14 points on its home field then coming back to win the game in an absolute rout.

Following the Dawkins-Jackson collision, Todd Blackledge began finding receivers roaming free in the Pitt secondary. He led us on two long second-quarter scoring drives to knot the game at 14 going into halftime.

The visitors' locker room at Pitt Stadium was a dimly lit dungeon with small, damp cubbyholes to store your belongings. Spartan conditions, to say the least. The drab surroundings did not stop us from coming out for the second half sky high, confident, and with momentum on our side. "At half-time Joe comes in and says, 'We got 'em, right where we want 'em,'" defensive tackle Greg Gattuso said. "To me that negated any remaining uncertainty in the room. I said to myself, 'Hey, if the old man says it's so, then who are we to say otherwise?'"

Pitt continued turning the ball over, which set us up with great field position. Twice during the third quarter, Blackledge found Roger Jackson's younger brother, Kenny, wide open for easy touchdowns. We proceeded to score the next 34 points to win going away in what ended up being one of the worst defeats ever suffered by a No. 1-ranked team. It got so bad for Pitt that our final two touchdowns came when Farrell, the All-American guard, recovered a Curt Warner fumble in the end zone, and Robinson picked off yet another Marino pass and ran it back 91 yards for a score...with one shoe on. "Their receiver ran a short turn-in route, and I was in perfect inside position. I remember looking Dan right in the eye," Robinson said. "He thought he could throw it anywhere and tried to fit the ball in there. I stepped right in front, then just took off. One of their linemen tore my shoe off around the Pitt 35-yard line, and from then on, I couldn't get much traction. Worse, my sock was coming down, and I'm thinking, *Man, if someone caught me from behind, I would have been teased about it for the rest of my life.* Ninety-two yards later, I get to the end zone, and one of the first guys to greet me was Daryl Smith, a buddy from my hometown. Daryl was 6'5", played at North Carolina, and had hopped over the wall to congratulate me. When you watch the play on YouTube, you see this big dude in a sleeveless winter vest bear-hugging me."

Other on-field exchanges, especially between hometown acquaintances, weren't quite as cordial. Rick D'Amico and Marino graduated from Pittsburgh's Central Catholic High School a year apart. Following another Marino incompletion early in the final quarter, Rick grabbed his former Central teammate as the punt teams come onto the field and couldn't resist saying, "Yo, Danny. You're fucking throwing them to everyone else...what about me?"

Marino's "kiss my ass" response only made D'Amico, Parlavecchio, and Chet's band of instigators laugh even harder as the game had become a mismatch of near-epic proportions.

"That game was so much fun because there were so many kids you knew, played with and against, worked out with, on the other side of the field," said cornerback Dan Biondi, who had played at Penn Hills High School in suburban Pittsburgh. "We changed our defense after the first quarter and started dropping nine guys in the secondary while rushing just two guys. It seemed like they never adjusted their gameplan and just kept throwing the ball. I never understood why they didn't try and run the ball more."

Gattuso recovered several fumbles that day. "I tell [Pitt center] Emil Boures whenever I see him that I intimidated him into those fumbles, which I'm sure makes him mad," Gattuso said. "D'Amico claims that Emil pancaked me 15 yards downfield, and I happened to fall on the ball. It was a pretty amazing day for those of us who grew up around Pittsburgh."

It was also a significant day for fellow sophomore receiver Kenny Jackson, who established a new Penn State record with 158 receiving yards. Meanwhile, Blackledge's second lights-out performance inside of a month allowed him to outplay a future NFL Hall of Famer on his home turf. "As a competitor, you want to play well, but quite honestly I didn't really compare myself to him," Blackledge said. "The numbers [Marino] put up during his junior year were just ridiculous. I didn't consider myself to be in the same class with Dan. Coming into the game, I didn't expect a shootout. Our offenses were really different that year, and I felt he was a notch above me. When we met again the following year, I felt we were on equal footing. I just wanted to play well and capitalize on the opportunities their defense gave us. Pitt made the determination they were gonna stop the run so they blitzed a lot and played zero [man-to-man] coverage with no free safety help. Once we got on track in the second quarter, we just blasted them with big plays. They must have felt we wouldn't find time to locate open receivers in a secondary that included guys like Tim Lewis and Tom Flynn. They took a gamble and lost."

The outcome of the game would impact Pitt's recruiting, including its pipeline from nearby Youngstown, Ohio. The Panthers had cultivated this area regularly, luring the likes of Matt Cavanaugh and the Pelusi brothers (John and J.C.) to Pitt. Michael Zordich, who ended up picking Penn State over Pitt, was one of the most coveted players from that area and a high school senior in 1981. Along with a handful of other top recruits, Mike was invited to watch this game from the Pitt sideline. "It went from complete euphoria to dead silence by the end of the game," Zordich said. "Those guys were just devastated. The other recruits and I had to walk back through their locker room after the game. Some of their coaches didn't know what to say to us. To call the mood in there somber would have been a massive understatement."

USA TODAY chose the contest as its Game of the Year. It was an absolutely sweet and satisfying win, especially for Nittany Lions players hailing from this part of the state. It ended Pitt's two-year mastery over us and cost them the chance to win the national championship. It made our earlier losses to Miami and Alabama seem like distant memories. Blackledge celebrated the win against rival and No. 1 Pitt over a dinner at Klein's Seafood in Pittsburgh with his family and Warner.

The game would not be the final interaction between Parlavecchio and Sherrill. Chet met up with the Pitt coach in an airport on their way to the East-West Shrine game in Palo Alto, California. "I figured after that Pitt game all I was gonna do was hold for field goals and extra points," Chet said, "but Jackie comes up to me and says, 'Hey, let's just put all this behind us.' I thought that was classy. I end up being the game's defensive MVP, and as we're running off the field, he yells, 'Hey, I'll bet Paterno never got you an MVP!'"

CHAPTER 3

The Fiesta Bowl

January 1, 1982
No. 7 Penn State (9-2) vs. No. 8 USC (9-2)

We headed west for the second straight year, but this time we were teeing it up against the USC Trojans in the Fiesta Bowl. After coming from behind to beat Notre Dame and dismantling Pitt, our confidence going into this newly minted New Year's Day game was extraordinarily high.

Bowl games afford its participants an abundance of extra time to prepare—and more than enough idle time to get into trouble. Had Joe found out about Gregg Garrity's mechanical bull mishap five days before the game was played, Todd Blackledge would have been without one of his starting wide receivers. "I think the place was called 'Cowboys,'" Garrity said. "It was some huge, warehouse-sized building with multiple bars. A lot of other players were taking their turn on the mechanical bull. I got hurt because I was squeezing my legs so tight, trying not to fall off. I felt a pop and fell off the thing. It was pretty intense pain, and I had a hard time walking. I got back to the hotel and immediately went to the hospitality suite, which was set up as a mock after hours training room. I told 'Hoch' [trainer Jim Hochberg] what happened, and he replied, 'I appreciate you being honest with me. Okay, we'll have to tell Joe something else, so here's what we're gonna do. We'll tell him it happened in practice.' He was so cool about it!"

* * *

Jim Hochberg was a punter and a quarterback for Penn State before graduating in 1956. He joined the Penn State staff in 1959 as an assistant trainer with the football team. In 1997 he was appointed coordinator of sports medicine and the head trainer for the team. To us players, he was plain old "Hoch." I don't think any of us ever fully realized the clout he carried in the program. But he was the one guy in Happy Valley to whom Joe Paterno always had to listen.

Tim Bream, who joined the program in 1981 as a student trainer, said discussions between Hochberg and Paterno regarding injuries would sometimes get heated. "Hoch was on the staff when Joe was an assistant, so there was an autonomy factor there," said Bream, who is now the Nittany Lions' head football trainer. "Joe had to get clearance from Hochberg for a guy to play and, while it may have pissed him off, Joe had to abide by Hoch's decision. Hoch had the absolute final say as far as injuries. There was one time Scott Radecic was having recurring stingers. Hoch deemed Radecic healthy enough to practice. However, he was to be held out of contact drills. Joe went nuts when he found out and demanded an explanation. Without blinking an eye, Hoch told Joe, 'Hey, if you want him for this Saturday, then that is all he can do. End of story.' And it was."

Bream gained early insight into their difference of opinion regarding nutrition during one of his first away trips. "On trips where we would bus to games, the team would usually stop at Ed's Steak House in Bedford for dinner," he said. "I am eating next to Hoch, and Joe sits down right next to me. He starts complaining to Hoch about the ice cream being served for dessert, claiming it would slow down his players the following day. In mid-sentence Hoch interrupts Paterno and says, 'Just relax, Joe. It ain't gonna hurt 'em.'"

Hochberg's lone vice was the object of occasional satire. "Hoch loved to smoke his pipe, usually before practice when he taped ankles in the training room," Bream said. "The entire room would reek of Captain Black. Joel Coles was notorious for waltzing in, taking Hoch's pipe out of his mouth, and dispensing his own expert medical opinions to any backfield personnel within earshot: 'Williams, you're not hurt. Get taped up, you're a full go today. Todd, put another ice pack on your shoulder. Curt, take another day off.' You couldn't help but laugh."

While Hoch kept Joe in the dark about Garrity, the latter did very little other than light jogging for a day or so after his mechanical bull mishap. "As gameday approached, I really didn't think I would be able to play," Garrity said. "I had the thing taped up pretty heavily on the day of the game but didn't shoot it up. That may have occasionally gone on behind closed doors [at Penn State], but I never saw it."

Todd's Take

We believed we were as good as any team in the country at the end of the season. We had proven it convincingly in Pittsburgh and now we had one more opportunity to prove it against a national program like USC. To add to our incentive (particularly our senior-laden defense), the Trojans featured the Heisman Trophy winner, Marcus Allen. I also remember sensing that USC wasn't approaching this game with the same tenacity and focus that we were. Perhaps they were disappointed to not be playing in the Rose Bowl against a Big Ten opponent. They were an extremely talented football team but not as motivated as the guys in the plain white uniforms.

With regard to our upcoming opponents, assistant coach Tom "Scrap" Bradley noted a rather obvious "air of confidence" with some of the seniors on defense one day when he walked past a meeting room. "I hear those guys laughing out loud, really carrying on," Bradley said. "I opened the door, and

Chet, Eddie Pryts, Leo, and some of the others were watching film on USC. I asked them, 'Hey, you guys really think you're that good?' Without hesitation Chet goes, 'Yes, we do.'"

Bradley wasn't the only coach concerned. "During one film session, one of the coaches got upset, turned the projector off, and says, 'That's it; this meeting is over.' I go to the team dinner that same night and see Chet, Leo, and Rick all sitting together," defensive backs coach John Bove said. "I go over and ask why they were laughing in the film room, and D'Amico chirps up saying, 'Bovie, did you watch their film? They got a couple of guys flopping all over the place like fish out of water!' I said, "Rick, you should be focusing on how the USC tight ends are blocking not their other guys!' Rick just laughs, pats my hand, says 'Bovie, we are gonna kick their ass.'"

Dick Anderson shared his fellow coaches' angst in spite of such bravado. "We were really concerned a few days before the game," he said. "I was personally upset because we had guys sitting in meetings giggling at Southern Cal. The defensive coaches said the same thing. Where were our heads at? We went out to Tempe to prove a point, to finish on a high note. Some of those guys were just so cocky, so confident, so sure of themselves."

They had good reason to be, as it turned out. Our defense saved its best for last by playing its finest game of the year and completely shutting down Marcus Allen. The Heisman Trophy winner came into the game averaging more than 200 rushing yards per game behind an offensive line that featured future first-round draft picks in Roy Foster, Bruce Matthews, and Don Mosebar. He managed just 85 rushing yards against us.

On the game's first play, defensive tackle Dave Opfar stripped the ball away from Allen. It popped directly into the hands of Roger Jackson, setting the tone for what had to be a very frustrating day for the future NFL Hall of Famer. USC's offensive line had no answer for Opfar or Leo Wisniewski, who won Defensive Player of the Game honors after registering several tackles behind the line of scrimmage in the first quarter alone.

Following Allen's fumble, a healthy Curt Warner found the end zone from 17 yards out to give us an early lead. Warner used the game to remind the national audience that his record-breaking efforts against Nebraska and

Syracuse were no fluke. He spent his afternoon in the desert demonstrating that he was every bit the equal of Allen.

USC All-American linebacker (and my future Browns teammate) Chip Banks accounted for the Trojans' lone touchdown by returning an errant Blackledge throw 20 yards to tie the game early in the second quarter, but the Trojans never really threatened after that. Later in the same period, a heavily taped Garrity made an acrobatic catch on a slightly underthrown pass from Todd and scored untouched to give us a lead we would never relinquish.

Despite missing two field goals and getting stopped at the Trojans 1-yard line as time expired in the second quarter, we led 17–7 at halftime and held a decided edge in total yardage (257 to 113). Both gaps widened after we took the second-half kickoff and marched right down the field for another score. Warner finished the 80-yard drive by sweeping around right end virtually untouched for 20 yards to put the game out of reach at 24–7. Dave "the Mad Paff" Paffenroth blocked a USC punt out of the end zone for a safety in the second half while Wisniewski continued to spend most of his day in the USC backfield. In all, our defense registered five sacks, three interceptions, and two fumble recoveries. "Turned out that Southern Cal just couldn't compete with us that day," Anderson said. "They couldn't mount an offense because they couldn't block Leo. He was too quick and too strong, too explosive. As a coach you hope your younger players look at that type of performance and say 'Wow,' then take that with them when they become the guys that step out onto the field."

Garrity ended up playing well despite the injury. His long touchdown catch complemented Warner and the running game, which helped keep Allen and the USC offense on the sidelines. The 26–10 victory was our second-straight double-digit win over a Top 10 opponent. After withstanding Dan Marino's first-quarter aerial assault, our defense had surrendered just three points over the final seven quarters and against the No. 1 and No. 8-ranked teams in the country. It also closed the books on a season where we ended up third in the final Associated Press poll.

One poll, the Dunkel Index, actually identified us as its 1981 national champion. Before the Associated Press created a poll from votes cast by sportswriters, Dick Dunkel Sr. authored one of the most accurate yardsticks for rating college football teams, a complex statistical formula that proved to be a very accurate measurement when applied to the performance of one team versus another. His index was one of the few known formulas to incorporate the strength of a team's schedule.

The top eight college football teams in 1981, according to the Dunkel Index were:

1. Penn State 104.2
2. Washington 102.5
3. Clemson 102.3
4. Pittsburgh 101.2
5. Georgia 100.7
6. Michigan 100.3
7. Miami (Florida) 100.1
8. Nebraska 99.7

Several other entities use their own method to quantify rankings based on schedule difficulty. *USA TODAY's College Football Encyclopedia* published its toughest schedule leaders with rankings going back to 1953 while the NCAA published their toughest schedule program from 1977 to 2008. Along with the Dunkel Index, these two ranked Penn State's schedule as the most difficult in the country in 1981. "We didn't realize how tough that schedule was. We just went out and played," D'Amico said. "I remember someone writing an article at the end of '81, emphasizing it and that the games against Alabama, Pitt, Nebraska could have been considered New Year's Day bowl games being played in October or November."

Another comprehensive website, sports-reference.com, calculates a metric called Strength of Schedule (SoS) for every college football team going back to 1872. The 1981 Nittany Lions' SoS (11.86) was not only the highest in the country by a wide margin but is the third highest *ever* among teams that managed to win at least 10 games while playing the nation's most difficult schedule. Furthermore, it marked only the second time in the history of college football that a team posted a 10-win season against the toughest schedule in the country, according to this metric.

The following April, 10 Penn State players were taken in the NFL draft, including four (Mike Munchak with the eighth overall pick, Sean Farrell with the 17th pick, Wisniewski with the 28th pick, and Jim Romano with the 37th pick) in the first two rounds. The 1982 draft marked the first time in Penn State's illustrious history that six Nittany Lions were taken in the first three rounds.

CHAPTER 4

From Basketball Star to Quarterback

The national high school graduating class on 1979 included marquee names like Elway, Marino, and Kelly. That same class included a strong-armed prep signal-caller from North Canton, Ohio, who felt college basketball was in his future until a revelation at a prep All-Star camp the previous summer opened his eyes. "Basketball was my favorite sport to play in high school," Todd Blackledge said. "I was an inside player, but at 6'4", wasn't quite big enough to play there at the college level. I went to the B/C All-Star Basketball Camp in Milledgeville, Georgia. The camp invited around 250 of the top players in the country." The overall experience helped crystallize what sport Todd would choose for his future. "I had to guard Ralph Sampson a few times," Blackledge said. "I came up to his navel. I never saw guys 6'8" or 6'10" that could do the exact same things skill-wise that I could do. I left that camp thinking football wasn't such a bad thing and the better way to go."

Pundits agreed. Football analyst and computer scientist Dr. Charles Howell published his National 100 list of the top high school football players. Blackledge was 77th on that list. "I wasn't being recruited [for basketball] the same way I was in football," Blackledge said.

Football was a way of life in the Blackledge household. Todd's father, Ron, played tight end at Bowling Green University and then coached college football at Cincinnati and Kentucky. "My dad was the head coach at Kent State my senior year," Todd said. "I thought about going there and playing for him, but his situation was a little tenuous there at the time."

The criteria Blackledge would use to make his decision wasn't all that complicated.

"I wanted to go somewhere where I could throw the football but also to a place that was gonna compete at a championship level versus winning two to three games a year," he said. "It also couldn't be too far away from home, so my parents could enjoy the experience of me playing. I narrowed it down to Tennessee, Notre Dame, Penn State, and Michigan State. The basketball program at one of them helped elevate the school to the top of that list. My first visit was to Penn State. I had a good time there but probably liked Michigan State a little better. Their head coach was a guy named Darryl Rogers and liked to throw the ball all over the place. During my visit I also attended a Michigan State basketball game when they had Greg Kelser and Earvin Johnson. That was pretty exciting."

Program stability was a pivotal factor, and keen parental advice proved prophetic. "My dad felt that Darryl Rogers was kind of a warm weather guy and might not be there long," Blackledge said. "Sure enough, a year later he went to Arizona State. The deciding factor for me was that I wasn't sure how long Darryl Rogers would be there, and I knew Joe wasn't going anywhere at Penn State. The stability of his program was the key for me."

Blackledge's freshmen class spent their first two weeks on campus crammed into the long-ago-torn-down military dorms located adjacent to the indoor ice rink and a stone's throw from the practice fields. By the fall of 1982, these barracks would eventually be converted into single occupancy dorm rooms, but in August of 1979, Paterno decided to wedge his players in two to a room, a possible penalty for losing to Alabama in the Sugar Bowl the previous January.

The rooms were roughly the size of a modern day walk-in closet and made for a rather intimate setting for players to get further acquainted. A lone desk was wedged in between two closets accompanied by standard-size, cast-iron bunk beds built to accommodate normal-sized people. Players over six feet tall learned to sleep curled up at night primarily because dangling your feet over the edge of your bed would cause undue pain and suffering to feet and ankles, already sore from the two-a-day practices, when anyone pushed open the door to enter the room.

"The one thing I remember was how close those barracks were to the locker rooms," Blackledge said. "I'm not sure if Joe was trying to save money, but they were not spacious living conditions by any means."

The conclusion of preseason camp meant vacating the cramped accommodations and moving into more spacious dorm rooms elsewhere on campus. The change in scenery would prove especially challenging for Blackledge. "After we broke preseason camp, my first roommate was Dick Maginnis, and we were as opposite as opposite could be," Blackledge said. "Joe's philosophy was to try and pair guys who were opposites. After a while I almost quit and went home. It was really difficult."

Maginnis had grown up in State College, and his rather laid-back lifestyle presented another challenge for Blackledge. "Dick had a lot of local redneck type friends that chewed, drank beer," Blackledge said. "I listened to R & B, soul music and hung out with a lot of the black guys on the team. Dick and I clashed in a lot of different ways, but the biggest one involved a little divine intervention. A few weeks into the season, Dick gets a pet Python. Now I hate snakes to begin with, but he decided to keep it in our dorm room in a little aquarium. I remember him having to put this big glove on to feed the python small mice."

Housing pets in a 9 x 12 dorm room meant there aren't many places for reptiles (and their prey) to hide. "The mice were always getting loose in the room," he said. "Worse, the snake got loose a few times. One time it wound up curled up under my covers. That kind of put me over the edge. I went to Joe a couple of times. Part of it was that I was hurt. [Blackledge broke his hand his freshman year and redshirted] and wasn't playing. I was feeling sorry for myself and actually contemplated going home. Joe called Maginnis into his office. After that Dick and I had a come-to-Jesus meeting. He was visibly upset and told me he didn't want to lose his scholarship."

The upcoming holiday season would spell doom for the python. "The dorms were closed around the holidays, and Dick had to take the snake home during Christmas break," Blackledge said. "The problem was that his mom wouldn't let him keep it in the house, so he kept the snake up in the attic where it froze to death so it never came back after Christmas."

The python's utter and untimely demise did not deter Maginnis' attempts to turn his dorm room into *Wild Kingdom*. "Things were okay for a while," Blackledge said, "but later in the winter term, I went home for the weekend, came back, and Dick was in our room along with a Saint Bernard. I came in and the dog was laying on my bed just drooling all over it. It was the last straw. He was ready to live with somebody else and so was I."

Another freshman from the same recruiting class also gave second thoughts to making a change. "My first roommate my freshman year was Lou Bartek," Curt Warner said. "Personally, I liked Lou, but we really didn't blend as roommates. He was a great teammate, but I needed to go in a different direction. It just wasn't the right chemistry. At some point Ledge asked me to be his roommate, and I said, 'Sure, why not?' Todd was a good guy; we liked the same music. Academically, Todd was a cut above most of the other players, very smart. I learned quite a bit as far as studying and preparing for class from him. He had a great family, went to the same bible study. We formed a great relationship and are still good friends to this day."

CHAPTER 5

The 1982
Preseason

In the summer of 1982, around 25 to 30 players remained in State College to take classes and work out—a pretty rare occurrence in college football at the time. It may have set a precedent after other programs witnessed how strong our passing attack looked to start the season. "That was the only summer I stayed up there," Blackledge said. "We knew we had some rebuilding to do with some guys that hadn't played a whole lot, but we also knew we had quite a collection of talent at the skill positions. I don't know if staying on campus in the summer was commonplace at the time, but now it's almost a rule."

Blackledge organized informal 7-on-7 workouts most weekday afternoons that summer and clearly understood their importance. So did his teammates. "It was totally unsupervised but really helped us get our timing down," Gregg Garrity said. "There were enough defensive backs up there that summer to do regular pass catching and route running. We had everything in place: veteran quarterback, quality running backs. By early August confidence was very high."

That Garrity was even at Penn State is quite a story in itself. He played running back and defensive back during his senior year at North Allegheny

High School in suburban Pittsburgh. He also played basketball and ran track. His 440-meter relay team still holds the school record. Despite his scholastic exploits, no Division I school offered him a scholarship. "I was too skinny," Garrity said. "The Syracuse people loved my films, but when the recruiter came to my high school, his jaw dropped when I met him. 'You're too small,' he said. We went down to our outdoor track, and I ran a sub-4.4 40. To cover his ass, the guy said, 'Well, half our team can run that fast.' I started to doubt myself a little after hearing, 'You're just not big enough' a few times."

One of Joe Paterno's very first recruits was Jim Garrity, Gregg's father, and Joe would later acknowledge that the elder Garrity was "one of the greatest athletes I had seen in my life." The two stayed in touch over the years. "My dad and Joe were very good friends. About a week after National Letter of Intent day, he called Joe and said, 'I honestly think he can play up there.' As a courtesy to my dad, Joe invited us up to visit the campus," Garrity said. "I had gone to Penn State's summer football camps for the three previous years, so we knew our way around, but Joe personally escorted us through the facilities. I remember us walking into the weight room while Bruce Clark and Matt Millen were in there working out. Those guys were specimens, man. I said to myself, *Holy shit, these guys are huge.*"

After the brief tour, the trio returned to Paterno's office. "Joe told us they would bring me in as a preferred walk-on and that no one would know any different," Garrity said. "I distinctly remember him saying, 'You will be treated the same as the other players on scholarship. If you can prove you can play Division I football, you'll be offered a scholarship.'"

Joe's promise evidently carried a lot weight with the impressionable Garrity. "One thing about Joe is that he was always a man of his word," Garrity said. "If he tells you something, then you can hold him to what he says. He didn't care if you were on scholarship or a walk-on, if you were a five-star or a no-star. The best player played. On our drive back home, we stopped at Clarion University. The head football coach offered me a free ride on the spot, saying, 'I think you are a blue-chip player. If you go up there [Penn State], and it doesn't work out, you can always play here.'"

Penn State receivers coach Booker Brooks recalled Gregg's early days on campus. "Initially the coaches decided Garrity was gonna be a defensive back, but our secondary coach John Rosenberg didn't think he'd work out there," Brooks said. "I liked his quickness and suggested we move him to wide receiver. I think he struggled to get on the field early on, but somebody got hurt, which gave him the opportunity. Once he began playing, he never gave up the spot. Gregg worked hard to become not only an excellent receiver, but a good blocker too."

Not long after reporting to campus in the summer of 1979, Garrity discovered he had the skillset necessary to play at the Division I level. He also found out firsthand that another fellow freshman had similar, if not superior, attributes. "On my second or third day there, they ran a shadow drill where you had to try to get around the guy across from you without them touching you," Garrity said. "I made it all the way to the finals and went up against some kid named 'Curt.' The next thing I knew, he was by me. This guy was 10 times quicker than I was. I called home that night and told my dad, 'Hey, keep an eye on a kid named Curt Warner. He is something else.'"

Garrity's observation was spot on as Warner wasted no time making an impact. In his very first collegiate contest, Warner accounted for nearly 300 yards of total offense, including 100 on the ground while catching two passes for 71 more. He scored three touchdowns in the second quarter alone. "I didn't expect to do much other than return kicks," Warner said. "I had a decent freshman training camp and was surprised I got called on early in the game. I had told parents and friends not to expect much, that I may not play a lot. All of a sudden, a couple series into the game, and Fran [Ganter] says, 'You're in.'" The performance turned out to be the best ever by any freshman in Penn State's proud, 92-year history. It took Warner exactly one game to do it.

Up until the spring of 1980, Garrity had never played wide receiver at any level. He proved to be a quick study, and by 1982 he, along with Kenny Jackson and Kevin Baugh, gave Blackledge three very reliable targets. "That '82 group worked very hard in practice." Brooks said. "And they got better every day. It's like watching a tree grow—you don't notice the change day to day, but six months later, it's obvious the tree has grown. They reminded me a lot of the previous group we had with Bassett, Cefalo, Fitzkee, and Shuler."

Without question our interior run blocking was *the* biggest question facing the offense in 1982 due to the losses of Mike Munchak, Sean Farrell, and Jim Romano. Although that meant our offensive line would be a work in progress, scoring points was not expected to be a big problem with the variety of weapons Todd had at his disposal. Dick Anderson was entering his second year as offensive coordinator after coaching the offensive line for 10. "The staff always began by identifying the best football players on the team and then tried to see if we could get them all on the field at the same time," he said. "We had to determine how would they fit together, if they were compatible, the best possible scenarios. Joe started a lot of the discussions relative to moving players around—not all but a lot of them—with: 'I see this kid playing here, I think we need to move this guy here.' Joe was a master at that, really very good in that facet."

Joe and his staff tinkered with the line after concluding that tight end Ron Heller would be a better fit at offensive tackle. "In '82 the obvious choices to play tackle were long, rangy guys like [Contz] and Heller. Ronnie didn't run all that well and had some limitations getting down the field," Anderson said. "You take that athleticism, move it to tackle, and it now becomes a factor. We liked Mark Battaglia's competitiveness, his smarts. The obvious place for a small but quick, tough guy like Mark was at center. [Pete] Speros and [Dave] Laube had both played tackle, but with their size, we were better off moving them inside."

Anderson understood that cohesion is a critical component to the success of any offensive line. Graduation takes its toll at the collegiate level virtually every year, and a developmental phase occurs prior to the group truly becoming a solid unit. Certain qualities and the players who possess them like Battaglia, a fifth-year senior, would need to emerge if we were to exploit the weapons we had at our skill positions. "There was a standard, a certain level of play you were expected to perform at, and I wanted to uphold my end of the bargain," Battaglia said. "I added a certain likeability factor while also contributing unselfishness and team focus. We had a lot of good football players who were also good athletes returning. Their lack of significant playing time could be offset with some other attributes."

Playing to the level from the previous year would be a formidable challenge, but Anderson cited other factors as reason for cautious optimism. "The '82 line wasn't as talented as the previous group, but we had a bunch of very good players," he said. "You took what we had in terms of talent then combine it with the intangibles—the character of the kids, their work ethic, the *want* to be good, and you have the makings for what goes into a championship team. So much of a football team is the chemistry and how the players mesh. Those are some of the intangibles you really just can't measure. The '82 team had a lot of that."

Anderson felt the 1982 group were a lot like the standout 1973 and 1978 teams. "All three were very similar in terms of their willingness to work at it, to get along with one another, to work with each other," he said. "In my judgement that is what makes the difference as far as who can win when the chips are down and recover from adversity. I have coached more talented groups that did not reach the goals the '82 team did."

Joe made his own lofty goals clear in letters he sent to the players during the summer:

THE
PENNSYLVANIA
STATE
UNIVERSITY

June 7, 1982

Dear Squad Member:

All of you have your summer conditioning programs and should be in the
aerobic running part of the program. It is absolutely vital that in order
to be in top condition and in order to get stronger so you can increase your
speed and quickness, you do aerobic training. Furthermore, this part of your
program will help to eliminate pulls and other nagging muscle injuries when you
start your intensive work.

Again, I cannot emphasize too strongly just how vital it is to have this squad
come back in great physical condition. Although we made progress in the spring,
we still, have a long way to go to be a really good football team. If we have
to go at a slow pace because we aren't conditioned to go at a fast pace, we
will not be able to accomplish what is absolutely necessary in pre-season
practice. This will be a very difficult pre-season practice and we will
practice longer than we have in the last couple of years.

We all have personal and team goals--very high goals--and to achieve them will
take completely dedicated, hard working people. And when I think of this,
I realize that we have to push literally year-round, so faithfully follow
your summer conditioning program.

Have a good summer. If you have any problems, don't hesitate to call your
position coach or me. Please give my very best to your family.

Sincerely,

Joseph V. Paterno
Head Football Coach

JVP:cmn

FOOTBALL OFFICE
INDOOR SPORTS COMPLEX
UNIVERSITY PARK, PA 16802
TELEPHONE 814-865-0411

His correspondence in early June warned us about his plans to hold longer, more demanding preseason practices and the need for every player return to campus in peak physical condition. For the first time in my four years there, Joe would employ two different running tests, and we had to successfully complete both before being allowed to set foot on the field. Every senior knew these tests were serious business since Joe had stripped Matt Millen of his captaincy three years earlier when he failed to complete one of the tests.

Offensive linemen were required to complete two half-mile (880 yards) runs. The first one had to be finished in less than two minutes and 45 seconds, and after a two-and-a-half minute breather, the second had to be finished in under 2:50. On the second of these two runs, you would be near exhaustion and running on pure adrenaline. If you didn't train for this test during the summer, you would really struggle to complete it. "That summer Tom Bradley had to stay after me and Joe Hines regarding our running tests," Greg Gattuso said. "I guess Joe was worried we wouldn't be able to make the 880s, so he had "Scrap" [Coach Bradley] drive to Pittsburgh to time me in the 880 run, then drive up to Cleveland to time Joe Hines at least once a month because we were gonna be in the D-line rotation. I took that test at least five times during the summer and passed it every time. I played hoops all summer to stay in shape and could run, so I never had a problem with it. I also had a summer job. Scrap shows up on a day I was working and missed the chance to time me. He drives up to Cleveland, misses timing Joe Hines, drives back to Pittsburgh to time me, then back to Cleveland to time Joe, then back to State College. I always felt that was amazing dedication from the staff to make sure we were doing what we were supposed to do."

One of my more enduring memories from that preseason occurred the day after we reported for practice when I observed something I consider to be one of the greatest athletic achievements ever performed by any plus-sized individual in the 20th century. Laube and I had been part of the same 1979 recruiting class. Dave was an absolute bear of a man, a take-no-prisoners type from Fair Lawn, New Jersey, with a bit of a mean streak. His normal playing weight was around 255 pounds, making him one of our heavier players on the team. Dave reported to camp in August weighing at least 20 pounds more than his assigned playing weight…and proceeded to ace *both* of his 880 running tests. I can vividly recall how tight my chest felt and barely being able to catch my breath at the start of the second run. Yet the much-heavier-than-he-should-be Laube passed both with flying colors.

The only other thing I can compare Dave's performance to occurred prior to the start of the New Orleans Saints' 1987 training camp in sultry Hammond, Louisiana. Offensive tackle Stan Brock, all 6'6" and 295 pounds of him, completed a mile-and-a-half run test in less than 10 minutes, finishing *ahead* of several Saints linebackers and tight ends.

Not satisfied the 880s proved his team was in shape, Joe called for a second set of running tests the following day, a series of 15 40-yard sprints. "After striding out 40 yards, players had 30 seconds to jog back to the starting line," said former Penn State strength coach Chet Fuhrman. "We were trying to simulate the time between a play, the rest and the recovery before you ran the next [play]. It was a pretty grueling test because guys' legs were rubbery from running 880s the previous day. I never really liked [the 880s] because they didn't simulate any football activity."

This second set of conditioning runs weren't the only tricks Joe had up his sleeve as he pushed us hard during the preseason with up-tempo, physical practices, sensing that what he had to work with could be pretty special. He saw his '82 squad as a rough-cut diamond that required a combination of polish and stress testing if it was to stand up to the challenges a second straight ultra-tough schedule would present.

Not only did Joe face the task of replacing three interior offensive linemen, he had also lost an entire set of linebackers—Ed Pryts, Chet Parlavecchio, Matt Bradley, and Rick D'Amico had all graduated—as well as an underrated cornerback in Paul Lankford. Scott Radecic entered camp as a strong candidate to fill one of the inside linebacker positions and incurred some of Joe's stress testing early on. "One day in camp, we're running a half-line drill on one of the Astroturf fields nearest to the locker room, and the offense is just running all over the defense," Radecic said. "Joe blows his whistle to stop practice, and I'm thinking, *Okay something is wrong, but hey, I'm doing all the right stuff, so yeah, Joe, you tell those guys who the problem is.* He walks up to our huddle, points his finger directly at me, and in that high-pitched voice says, 'You wanna know what the problem is? YOU! You're the problem!'"

Like countless others before him, Radecic was beginning to realize how dramatically his world had changed after being elevated to starter status. "That absolutely shocked me. It was such a traumatic thing," he said. "You're playing linebacker up there, and the first few years were fine, but that all changed when you put the blue jersey on. It becomes this real big frigging deal. Reporters start asking me about the legacy of linebackers at Penn State. I mean, I'm just a kid playing football. Do I know the history around here, about the guys who played the position before me? Well, no, not really. Up until that point, I probably didn't have the right mental attitude."

Paterno chastising Radecic had the desired effect. "I had to have a real heart-to-heart with myself after practice," he said. "That was horrible to be singled out in front of your teammates. I was determined to work hard enough to never let these guys down, to never be the one they point at and say, 'He's the reason why we're not being successful.'"

Radecic would emerge as a linchpin for our defense and make several game-changing plays in the second half of the season. Joe's reprimand of him at practice may have set him on a path to a breakout season. "That was a real game-changer for me mentally and emotionally," Radecic said. "It really changed my attitude of what it meant to go out every day in practice to try and get better. We all came from successful programs in high school, we all knew how to win. Joe was teaching us how to win games that would change the momentum of the season. That stuff probably happened every day in practice, but you don't recall it if it didn't happen to *you*. When it did, you remember it *forever*."

CHAPTER 6

The Start of an Epic Season

September 4, 1982
Temple (0-0) at No. 8 Penn State (0-0)

Most major preseason publications had Pitt as the No. 1 team in 1982. *Sports Illustrated's* first ever "College and Pro Football Spectacular" rated the Panthers as their top team, citing the fact that Pitt returned 18 of 22 starters, including future first-round NFL picks Dan Marino, Jimbo Covert, Bill Maas, and Tim Lewis. *SI* had slotted us way down at No. 9. That didn't sit well with us for two reasons: we had hung nearly 50 points on our in-state rivals in their backyard the previous November and we had great skill position players in Todd Blackledge, Curt Warner, Jon Williams, Gregg Garrity, Kenny Jackson, and tight end Mike McCloskey.

The offensive line was the biggest question mark, and among the moving parts with this group, Ron Heller's transition from tight end to short tackle may have been the most intriguing development. It also had been the most frustrating one, at least for Heller—who had never played on the offensive line, going back to his midget league days—and came to camp expecting to be the second team tight end behind McCloskey. Those expectations changed as soon as he finished his 880 running test. "I ran with the tight ends and linebackers and ran well," Heller said. "Right after I finish, I'm bent over, completely exhausted, and Paterno walks over to me. He says, 'Hey, Ron, I gotta talk to you. We don't have a lot of depth at tackle and we're in a bit of a jam. I wanna move you there. Do you have any problems with that?' Honestly, I was just glad he knew my name. I just wanted to play, to get on the field. My first thought was the second-team tight end plays a lot more than a second-team tackle, so I asked Joe, 'If I don't end up becoming the starter, can you switch me back to tight end?' He said, 'Yes, no problem.'"

Curiosity would then get the best of Penn State's newest offensive lineman. "So I then asked, 'When did you know you wanted to move me to tight end?' And Joe goes, 'Oh, months ago, right after spring ball. I countered with, 'Well, then why did you make me do the running test with the tight ends?" Then he started yelling at me, 'Ahhh nuts Hellah! Is that all you guys ever think about?'"

He was yet another victim of a cruel Paterno mind game.

"I will never forget my very first one-on-one pass protection was against Walker Lee Ashley," Heller said. "I wound up on my butt and thought to myself, *These guys are relying on me to do this? If so, then we're in big trouble.* Walker Lee was a beast, but by the end of camp, I blocked him a few times and started believing I could actually play."

"Early on I recall him being really nervous," guard Pete Speros said, "so I tried to get him to relax by telling him, 'Hey man, take it from me. Short tackle is easy. All you do is cut-off blocks.'"

Heller would pay Speros' words of encouragement forward later in camp. "I remember sitting down next to Mike Zordich during a break in one of the preseason scrimmages in the stadium," Heller said. "Mike was an incoming freshman. He was visibly upset so I asked him about it. He said something to the effect of: 'I am in way over my head and I'll never play here.'"

Joe Diange was our assistant strength coach and grew up near my hometown. One day he told me, 'Hey, they wouldn't have recruited you unless they knew you could play here. I always remembered that, so I just told Mike,

'Hey, I don't know if you'll [play here] or not, but I felt the same exact way as you did when I first got here. He looked at me and said, 'Really? You felt like that?' I said, 'Absolutely.' Mike ended up playing a lot that year as a true freshman, then had a long career in the NFL."

Any concerns Joe had about the offensive line didn't stop him from cutting Blackledge loose in our season opener. The hard work Todd put in with his receivers during the summer was evident as he threw three first-quarter touchdown passes before the Temple Owls finished their final verse of the national anthem. While we ended up cruising to a 31–14 win, we scored all of our touchdowns through the air.

The newly constructed offensive line failed to knock anybody off the ball or control the line of scrimmage as we posted mediocre numbers on the ground. Afterward Curt was gracious enough to deflect any criticism away from the line. However, we knew how terribly disappointed he was in not playing much of a role in the opening win. It was obvious we lacked continuity, and developing the type of ground game that could eat clock would take some time.

Watching game film the following day only confirmed our pedestrian effort. Afterward Speros and Battaglia organized a "linemen only" meeting. We used it to air any grievances and collectively conclude our performance was nowhere near Penn State standards. The expectation was that you went out and pounded the ball on the ground against teams like Temple. We didn't come close. Individually, we committed to getting a little bit better every single day. We were determined that our group would not be this team's weak link.

A few night's prior to our second game with Maryland, I joined a few teammates for an adult beverage to watch No. 1 Pitt kick off its season in a primetime game at Three Rivers Stadium. It surprised us to watch Marino toss four interceptions and his vaunted offense ring up less than 200 total yards while struggling to score against North Carolina. Pitt came from behind to prevail 7–6, but we left that establishment sufficiently lubricated (we didn't want to cramp up on the short walk home) and convinced that if our line could get its act together, we would pose major problems for virtually anyone we would face, including Pitt.

September 11, 1982
Maryland (0–0) at No. 7 Penn State (1–0)

A relatively unknown quarterback named Norman brought his untested Maryland Terrapins into Beaver Stadium to renew a long-standing rivalry after a one-year hiatus. Junior Boomer Esiason, new head coach Bobby Ross, and a defense featuring future NFL players Mark Duda and Pete Koch ended up giving us all we could handle on a muggy afternoon.

Esiason kept our defense off balance most of the afternoon, connecting on touchdown passes of 50 and 60 yards, the second of which staked his club to a 24–23 lead midway through the third quarter. "Maryland had this quarterback no one ever heard of who burned us a couple of times in the third quarter," defensive end Steve Sefter said. "After their second long touchdown pass, the defense comes off the field, and Joe is screaming at Radecic about what happened. Scott tells him, 'I got picked,' and Joe yells right back, 'Well, run *through* the pick!'"

Joe kept us fresh by regularly substituting players, and our second unit provided some much-needed relief by putting together two scoring drives in the second half. We eventually won 39–31, wearing down a team that would finish its season 8–4 and ranked in the top 20.

Todd Blackledge delivered a second consecutive lights-out performance, shredding the Terps' secondary for four touchdowns in an aerial showcase between two future NFL quarterbacks. Our running attack struggled for the second straight week, averaging less than four yards per attempt against Maryland's wide-six tackle alignment. The jury was definitely still out on the ground game, but overall we were happy to be 2–0.

September 18, 1982
Rutgers (0–1) at No. 8 Penn State (2–0)

Unlike our previous two contests, we got off to a relatively slow start against the Scarlet Knights, a team we usually handled pretty easily. Our running game continued to sputter while our secondary surrendered another long pass play for the second straight week. This time it was a 65-yard bomb to speedy wide receiver Stephen Baker "the Touchdown Maker." Our special teams bailed us out big time as Mark Robinson returned a punt 92 yards for a touchdown to give us a 21–14 lead at intermission.

Joe Paterno lit into us pretty good at halftime, and it worked. Todd Blackledge threw three touchdown passes in the second half, bringing his season total to 12 through just three games. It appeared we were on the verge of becoming BYU East after the 49–14 win. "It's like night and day around here," wide receiver Kenny Jackson told reporters of our more aggressive offensive attack.

Other things were changing, too. Todd Blackledge was attracting attention as a legitimate Heisman Trophy contender while Curt Warner's hopes of winning the coveted award were rapidly fading. Through three games it seemed as though Joe had given Todd the keys to a brand new Ferrari with instructions to open it up. The aerial circus everyone had anticipated in Pittsburgh had stalled out and instead shifted 125 miles east with no end in sight. Blackledge had transformed into Dan Fouts without the Grizzly Adams beard, Jackson was John Jefferson sans goggles and close-to-the-vest Paterno had morphed into Don Coryell. To old school Nittany Lion fans this Chargers-like, pro-style passing attack was a nuclear weapon in the age of trench warfare. We also were 3–0, relatively healthy, and headed into the biggest game of our young season.

Todd's Take

Through no fault of his own, Curt Warner's Heisman hopes were dashed in the first month of the season. Curt was my roommate and best friend and was the best player I ever played with—at Penn State or in the NFL. Nobody worked harder or prepared more diligently during the summer leading up to the 1982 season than Curt. He was a tremendous leader in the weight room, on the field, and in the locker room. He was in terrific shape when the season started, but unfortunately for him, our running game was behind our passing game when September rolled around.

Curt never complained, never stopped grinding, and always put the success of the team first. He did whatever we needed him to do. He was a very good receiver out of the backfield and worked to become an effective pass blocker. Living with him I could see some of his hurt and frustration, especially with reporters constantly probing about causes to his slow start. He even briefly lost it in a postgame interview after one of those early games. My heart ached for my friend, and he did his best to enjoy the success I was having, but it was tough at times. Curt handled things like a champion and always promoted the team first.

CHAPTER 7

Agony and Ecstasy

September 25, 1982
No. 2 Nebraska (2-0) at No. 8 Penn State (3-0)

In 1979 our administrators had agreed to a four-year, home-and-home series with traditional powerhouse Nebraska. The Cornhuskers had taken the first two games of the series rather convincingly by the time we traveled to Lincoln for our second game of the 1981 season. We ended up winning a hard-fought, back-and-forth game behind Curt Warner's incredible 238 rushing yards and five field goals from senior Brian Franco. In my opinion this was one of the true signature wins in Penn State history. We ended up beating an opponent consistently ranked in the top 10 that we had never defeated. And we beat them at their place by playing their game of smashmouth football.

One year later Nebraska brought its own formidable arsenal of offensive weapons to Happy Valley to face off against Blackledge and a downfield passing game firing on all cylinders. Huskers quarterback Turner Gill led a prolific offense that featured running backs Roger Craig and Mike Rozier, wide receiver Irving Fryar, and center Dave Rimington. The Cornhuskers came in averaging 55 points per game while we had racked up 31, 39, and 49 points in three contests. Suffice it to say, a defensive struggle was not in the forecast.

The night before the contest, senior co-captain Ken Kelley would do his best Nostradamus impression during an outdoor pep rally on a soccer field adjacent to Beaver Stadium. "It's not that we might beat Nebraska; we're *gonna* beat Nebraska," Kelley emphatically told the delighted crowd. Kelley had traveled a long and winding road to becoming a co-captain of the Penn State football team. He had been a standout quarterback, safety, and line-backer at Sterling High School in Stratford, New Jersey. He beat out future teammate Chet Parlavecchio, among others, for New Jersey Player of the Year honors as a senior but didn't have a clear-cut position at the next level. "I was recruited as an athlete, not necessarily a quarterback," Kelley said. "I weighed around 205 pounds in high school and was considered a tweener. During my first few years at Penn State, I played several positions on defense, including middle linebacker, outside linebacker, and defensive end. I put on some weight, got up to around 220 but had alternated with a younger player, Harry Hamilton, at the Hero position my junior year. I really wasn't given any explanation why. The Hero is essentially an oversized defensive back that plays the run and the pass equally, so I wasn't given a real shot to play outside linebacker until my senior year."

Kelley's status as a fifth-year senior and quiet, workmanlike practice habits set the proper tone with his defensive teammates. His prediction at the Friday night pep rally—chiefly the supremely confident manner in which he delivered it—was inspiring. It had everyone on the team believing we were more than ready for Nebraska.

The game was moved to late afternoon to accommodate a national TV audience. Temporary lighting was set up outside the stadium for the first time, adding to an already electric atmosphere. The additional lights, as it turned out, only further illuminated what many still consider the most exciting finish in Beaver Stadium history.

We cranked out more than 500 yards of total offense as Todd Blackledge repeatedly found open receivers in Nebraska's secondary. Warner broke loose for several long runs in the first half, including his first rushing touchdown of the season, but struggled with leg cramps in the third quarter. Our ground game didn't miss a beat as our running-back-by-committee approach, which included underclassmen Jon Williams, Tony Mumford, and Skeeter Nichols, helped us pile up more than 200 yards rushing.

Our defense found ways to frustrate the potent Huskers offense for most of the game. In the trenches nose tackle Greg Gattuso battled two-time Outland Trophy winner Rimington to a draw. "My very first career start was the Rutgers game the week before, and I didn't play real well," Gattuso said. "Now Dave Rimington and his Outland Trophy comes to town with Dean Steinkuhler lined up right next to him. Both those guys ended up being first-round picks. Rimington was *the* strongest guy on the planet and got off the ball very quickly but didn't have very long arms, which meant he would snap the ball from up under his chin. I lined up really tight to him, almost facemask to facemask, to never give him any space. He was a big legwhip guy too, and my legs were black and blue after the game. I ended up holding my own against him. It was a war."

Rimington would repeat as the nation's Outland Trophy winner in 1982 while Steinkuhler would win it the following year. Neither the hardware nor caliber of players intimidated Gattuso. "People asked how I did that. I said it's because of going up against Romano, Munchak, and Farrell every day in practice," Gattuso said. "I assure you, butting heads with an ornery Jimmy Romano was no picnic, but it made you a lot better football player. Our practices made sure you never had to fear anyone you went up against in actual games."

We maintained the lead from the outset despite missing three field goals, but late in the third quarter, control of the game started to slip from our grasp. Right around that time (near dusk), the temporary lights went out for about 10 minutes. I'm sure I wasn't the only one on the field who thought playing a few series in near darkness was more than a little strange. It reminded me of the scene in the movie *Airplane!* where all the lights on the runway suddenly go out with the culprit being a guy in the air traffic control tower holding a power cord and uttering "just kidding" prior to plugging it back in. For a second I thought some up-to-no-good Nebraska fan had snuck into the press box and sabotaged what was turning out to be a pretty good football game.

When the lights came back on, so did the Nebraska offense. The Cornhuskers scored 10 unanswered fourth-quarter points to take a 24–21 lead with 1:18 left in the game. The mood in the stands turned somber. "I was in the 10th grade and selling Cokes in the north end zone," said Pete Allen, whose family had moved to State College in 1976. "I got done selling at the end of the third quarter and wanted to stick around to watch but couldn't find a seat because the stadium was full. I ended up sitting down on the steps in between the sections. Turner Gill scored right in front of where I was sitting, and it cast such a pall over the entire stadium. We had all gone through such heartbreak before back in 1978, and the fans could not believe that Nebraska was gonna beat us since we were winning the whole game."

What the fans couldn't have known was that Gill's quarterback sneak for a touchdown merely set the stage for a fantastic finish. The genesis of the final drive actually occurred as our offense stood on the sideline watching Gill methodically march his team down the field for the go-ahead touchdown. As we waited to re-enter the game, I vividly recall Mark Battaglia reiterating two things: "There still is a lot of time left," and "They haven't stopped us all day long." There was this indescribable sense of calm standing there at that moment with no one panicking despite the chaos and relatively dire circumstances. Everyone seemed fully aware of the task at hand. Each of us realized we had our own job to do.

Todd's Take

I don't remember exactly what I said, but I do recall feeling we have played too well. I just believed we were destined to win. That's not to take anything away from Nebraska because they were a great team, but we led at halftime despite having two TDs called back on penalties and missing three field goals. We were moving the ball at will but didn't have as much as we should have to show for it.

Ron Heller still needed a little convincing that we could pull out the game. "As we jogged onto the field I'm thinking, *There's no way; there's just not enough time left,*" he said. "We get in the huddle, and Blackledge is just so confident in the way he spoke: 'Here's what we're gonna do and how we're gonna do it.' I became a believer right then and there all because of what he said in that huddle. Just uncanny poise and leadership."

We caught a huge break on the kickoff as Nebraska was flagged for a personal foul penalty, giving us good field position on our 35-yard line. Blackledge called two plays in the huddle, and on the first one, Skeeter Nichols advanced a screen pass 15 yards to midfield. With a little over a minute left, Todd drilled Kenny Jackson on an out route to get us deeper into Nebraska territory. However, the Huskers defense stiffened, leaving us with a fourth and 10 at their 33-yard line with 25 seconds left in the game. On the drive's most critical play, Blackledge delivered an absolute bullet to Jackson for 11 crucial yards, but a questionable spot had officials calling for a measurement.

At that point we were all dead tired, so the brief stoppage to bring out the chains helped us catch our collective breath. I remember looking over at the sideline and thinking stadium security had either decided to go home early or were too busy watching the action. It turned out to be a gorgeous night in Happy Valley, and there were people in street clothes lined up five or six rows deep around the south end of the field. Unbeknownst to us, Beaver Stadium was minutes away from complete bedlam.

A short Blackledge scramble out of bounds left just 13 seconds on the clock. On second down Todd again dropped back and fired a pass to McCloskey who ran a route toward the Penn State side of the field. McCloskey caught the pass, but replays later showed that he hauled it in after he was out of bounds. "I'm standing alongside the guys I usually hung out with—Carmen Masciantonio, Doug Strang, Scott Carraher, and John Walter," said reserve safety Mike Suter of his vantage point from the Penn State sideline. "We all leaned out onto the field to watch the play, and we all agreed Mike was *way* out of bounds. We said to each other: 'Wow, we just caught a huge break.'" Gregg Garrity agreed. "He was way out," he said. "His front foot was out of bounds, and he dragged the other one. The referee was watching him drag [his foot], then looked up to make sure Mike caught it. There were other bad calls that game. It evens out."

I never understood why this play was considered so controversial. Mike made a nice catch and did his best to drag his back foot. There was no instant replay review, and the officials got no help from the hordes of people now hugging the sideline, so they just marked the ball near the 3-yard line. Nebraska made no attempt to stop the game to question the call and—much like us—were too busy sending in their goal-line personnel for the game's final nine seconds.

Incredibly, the following play would upstage McCloskey's catch.

Prior to 1982 very few people outside of his hometown of Mechanicsburg, Pennsylvania, had ever heard of Kirk Bowman. Joe Paterno moved Kirk around to several different positions, a fairly common occurrence that happened to a lot of players. After shifting Heller from tight end to offensive tackle in the preseason, Joe moved Bowman from defensive end to tight end to back up McCloskey. "Joe approaches me at lunch on the second or third day of preseason camp and said, 'I understand you played tight end in high school. Can you catch the ball?'" Bowman said. "I said yes and switched positions that afternoon. When I was 10 years old, I had some fingers caught between two trucks and ended up having half my index finger amputated. It was a major adjustment going from our tight ends coach Pete Giunta lobbing balls to me in warm-ups to Blackledge throwing bullets at me during live team drills. Suffice it to say, I dropped my first few passes. Todd threw me a pass in the Rutgers game, and I dropped that, too. After watching it on film, Kenny Jackson nicknamed me 'Stone Hands,' and it stuck."

That unfortunate nickname didn't stop him from carving out a permanent place in Penn State football lore. In a truly chaotic end to a wild, back-and-forth, edge-of-your-seat game, Kirk made a sliding, diving touchdown catch of a slightly underthrown Blackledge pass with four seconds left on the clock. Bowman's shoestring grab capped a drive for the ages and a dramatic 27–24 comeback victory under the lights. I thought it was a fairly amazing acrobatic catch since Kirk had only played the position for a few weeks. His clutch catch in the back of the end zone was just his second reception of the season. "In practice I ran that crossing pattern too deep near the goal line and went through the back of the end zone so I had to remember to stay inbounds," he said. "During the game I freelanced a bit to get off the line of scrimmage. I took a little jab step and head fake to the outside, then broke inside. All I remember is Blackledge throwing it, the Nebraska linebacker stretching to try and deflect it, and saying to myself, *Go ball go.* I got my arms underneath it and cradled the ball. It was absolutely a clean catch."

Blackledge acknowledged he could have thrown a better ball to Bowman. "I kind of rushed the pass when I really didn't have to," he said. "I threw it as soon as I saw him break open. The second I let it go, I thought I pulled the string and didn't get enough on it."

Delirious Beaver Stadium fans stormed the field after the final gun sounded. They tore down the south end zone goalpost before hauling it across campus and depositing it on the Old Main lawn. Patrick Allen, Pete's older brother and a freshman at Penn State, was among the students who felled the post. "A bunch of us just ran onto the field," he said. "Once the goalpost was down, we transported it out to Curtain Road across University Drive, passing the Shields Building on the left. We crossed over Bigler Road, then made a left onto Shortlidge, chanting the entire time. I am at a complete loss to explain why no security ever bothered to stop us. To my knowledge it was the first time any goalposts were torn down in Beaver Stadium."

Defensive-end-turned-dentist Dr. Al Harris can account for where some of the metal currently resides. "I still have a piece of that goalpost," he said. "Someone in the public works department cut it up, and a girl that was dating my future business partner got a small section and gave it to me. I have a piece of it on my desk in my office."

Harris had transferred to Penn State after Villanova abruptly terminated its football program in the spring of 1981. "I got invited to visit Penn State the day after Villanova canceled football," Harris said. "What got me was the drive up there. As we approached campus, the stadium looked like this giant battleship. It was right in the middle of spring practice so I just toured the locker room, then was told to wait for Joe in the coach's locker room. I was impressed but also a little intimidated. Joe walks in and begins talking to me like he knew me forever, which I found amazing because this was two full years after I graduated high school. He knew my family, my high school coach, my interest in dentistry. He took his glasses off, just looked like and acted like a regular guy. From that point on, he treated me like I was part of the Penn State family."

That exchange between Paterno and Harris may have seemed familiar, but Blackledge's journey back to the locker room was anything but routine. "It was complete chaos and also a little scary," he said. "As I was trying to get off the field, some kid grabbed my arm. To break free from his grasp, I kind of slung him. He fell right into some photographer, and the guy's camera broke. I felt bad, but it was just a mob scene. A few weeks later, the local media was doing an article on Curt, and a writer came to our apartment accompanied by a photographer. He ends up interviewing both of us, and we are re-telling stories about the Nebraska game. I explain the difficulty in leaving the field, and it turned out the same photographer who was in our apartment was *that* guy. The photographer says, 'Yep that was me. That was my camera.'"

The dramatic win enabled our strength coach, Chet Fuhrman, to cash in on a friendly wager. "Boyd Epley was Nebraska's strength coach," Chet said, "a pretty flamboyant, recognizable guy at the time. Boyd was affiliated with some strength training company and would always talk to the other coaches because he was trying to sell you equipment. He comes over to our house Friday night to go out to dinner and gives me a five-foot poster with this panoramic view of the Nebraska weight room. Over dinner he says, 'If you guys win, you can have any piece of weight equipment from this company.' Then he says, 'Don't worry, you don't have to give me anything in return,' as if he was almost guaranteeing that we wouldn't win. I found him after the game, shook his hand, and told him I would call him on Monday. After the game several players came back to my house, and we tore that poster into 500 little pieces. The next week I called Boyd and asked him to send me a tricep extension bench from his company. I was very proud of it. We called it the Nebraska Tricep Exercise."

Both teams combined for over 975 yards of offense, an absolute dream come true for CBS. Many fans who witnessed the game in person still claim the game was the most exciting contest ever played in Beaver Stadium. Blackledge's performance landed him on the cover of *Sports Illustrated*. Little did we know the supposed *SI* cover jinx foreshadowed bad things for us two weeks later.

October 9, 1982
No. 3 Penn State (4-0) at No. 4 Alabama (4-0)

The come-from-behind win against Nebraska boosted our national credibility. It also may have fooled us into believing we were better than we were. With a full week off to prepare for Alabama, we were relatively healthy, had practiced well, and were confident this was finally the year we'd bag the Bear.

Boy, were we wrong.

Teams that find consistent success on the road against ranked teams play opportunistic defense, well on special teams, and error-free offensive football. Unfortunately, we didn't come close on any of those. The game was moved from Tuscaloosa to Legion Field in Birmingham to accommodate the larger crowd. It was the second straight year both teams entered the contest ranked in the AP top 10. We had jumped up to No. 3 in the polls while the Crimson Tide were right behind us in the fourth spot.

I had never been to Birmingham prior to this trip. As I peered out the window on the bus ride to the stadium, I couldn't help but think how it reminded me of the decaying western Pennsylvania towns that had fallen on hard times due to the collapse of the steel industry.

The weather certainly did us no favors. The temperature at kickoff was a stifling 81 degrees, and the humidity was an oppressive 69 percent. The polyturf playing surface easily exceeded triple digits and it felt like walking across hot coals while wearing 20 pounds of equipment. I recall our sideline having only two electric fans with blades that didn't seem to spin very much. They offered little relief from the stifling heat. It would not have surprised me at all had a French Guiana penal colony from *Papillon* (Dustin Hoffman's first starring role opposite Steve McQueen) assembled for roll call during pregame warm-ups. It was *that* hot in Birmingham.

It was downright suffocating on the field. The only thing I can compare it to was the year Jim Mora decided to hold his 1987 Saints' training camp in Hammond, Louisiana, which is 90 minutes northwest of New Orleans. Hammond's practice fields were lined with tall firs and pine trees that seized any cool breeze that tried to provide relief to the players suffering through Mora's full-pad, two-a-days. It boggles my mind how construction workers or asphalt pavers perform their jobs on the Gulf Coast from May through October. If you have spent any extended time in the Deep South during those months, you know exactly what I mean.

We dug ourselves a hole by having our first punt blocked after a three-and-out, setting Alabama up on our 9-yard line, and the Tide scored an easy touchdown a few plays after that. Midway through the first quarter, Todd Blackledge correctly read blitz and hit Curt Warner on a quick slant. Curt proceeded to outrun the entire Alabama secondary untouched for a 70-yard touchdown to pull us even.

Hands down, Warner was the most gifted back I ever had the privilege to block for. Joe Paterno would routinely compare him with the great Lenny Moore. Despite averaging less than 50 rushing yards over the first four games of his senior season, Curt was the third player selected in the 1983 NFL draft behind John Elway and Eric Dickerson. He would go on to outrush the likes of Walter Payton, Tony Dorsett, and Earl Campbell in leading the Seattle Seahawks to their first ever playoff appearance. The Seahawks advanced to the 1983 AFC Championship Game while Curt walked off with AFC Rookie of the Year honors.

Curt's quickness may have been a factor in him tearing up his knee while making a cut on the Seattle Kingdome's spongy Astroturf in the first week of the 1984 season. The ugly play unfolded right before my eyes as I stood on the opposite sideline that day in my Cleveland Browns uniform. The entire stadium went completely silent as the Seahawks medical staff helped Curt limp off the field. His season was suddenly over. Game films later confirmed that not one Browns defender touched Curt on the play. That was no great surprise as the Browns defense didn't touch many other

Seattle players in an ugly 33–0 loss.

I would also suffer torn knee ligaments, and an injury very similar to Curt's, three months later against the Steelers in my hometown of Pittsburgh. It reminded me in a macabre sense of the strange similarities I share with him. Curt and I were part of the same recruiting class, and we lined up right next to each other in the Penn State huddle for two straight years. That both of us fell victim to the same career-threatening injury to the same knee less than 20 months removed from the 1983 Sugar Bowl were pretty long odds indeed. To this day Curt and I remain good friends. I joke often that had Curt been blessed with a better offensive line his senior season he would have been Penn State's second Heisman Trophy winner after John Cappelletti.

Largely overlooked on Warner's long touchdown was the fact that I completely whiffed while trying to block Jackie Cline, Alabama's monstrous defensive lineman. Cline executed a flawless swim move on me and then proceeded to hammer Blackledge a split second after he got rid of the ball. Had Todd taken a full seven-step drop, Cline would have steamrolled him, and I would have looked like an even bigger idiot.

It's funny (or sad, really) how you remember plays like that as if they happened yesterday. The occasional nightmare I still have is in living color right down to the bright crimson shade of Cline's No. 98 jersey. I think most offensive linemen can describe in painfully vivid detail those plays where they completely missed a block that ended up getting their quarterback or running back killed. And if you forget, your teammates sometimes come to your aid to help you.

My ex-Browns teammate, Doug Dieken, politely brings up the name of Rulon Jones pretty much every time I see him (thankfully not often). Dieken is kind enough to remind me of a devastatingly quick spin move the former Denver Broncos defensive end executed on me during a preseason game my rookie year that nearly got Brian Sipe decapitated. I respond in kind by giving Dieken a lot of grief whenever I can but also a fair amount of credit. I don't know too many people who were able to play offensive tackle in over 200 straight NFL games, a remarkable feat in terms of durability yet largely forgotten because the Browns never reached the Super Bowl.

Anyway, when you screw up like I did in Alabama, the thing offensive linemen (or any player for that matter) dread most isn't the earful you get from your position coach on the sideline. Rather it's the sheer agony of waiting until you watch the play being replayed over and over again during the film session the following day. Usually, you are among a jury of your closest peers (in my case, fellow offensive linemen), several of whom secretly want your job and hope your stupid play continues in practice the following week. I always considered letting teammates down in any team sport a fate worse than death.

Despite our two-week layoff, we played lousy against Alabama in all facets. The offense looked out of sync as Blackledge was under siege during the game's first 30 minutes. All told, we turned the ball over six times, had two punts blocked, and missed a long field goal. You simply can't do that when playing against a defense that featured guys like Cline, Mike Pitts, Eddie Lowe, and Jeremiah Castille and expect to win.

By halftime the temperature had climbed to 85 degrees while the humidity had increased to 71 percent. Despite our worst half of football in recent memory (the Alabama game the previous November to be exact), we caught a huge break when one of our co-captains, Walker Lee Ashley, scooped up an errant option pitch by Tide quarterback Walter Lewis early in the third quarter to set us up inside Alabama's 30-yard line. Three plays later Blackledge hit tight end Mike McCloskey at the Alabama 10-yard line, where he had the ball stripped away for our third turnover. More critical mistakes would follow.

Despite the heat, humidity, and quality of opponent, we fought back to get within six points at 27–21 and had driven the ball past midfield with a little less than six minutes remaining in the game. On a crucial third and short from Alabama's 45-yard-line, Dick Anderson dialed up "40 Pitch," a play in which Warner would attempt to run a sweep to our strongside behind McCloskey and me. It was a bad call, as Alabama would slant their line toward the play. Mike and I both blocked poorly, and Curt was knocked back for a three-yard loss. After that play and my earlier whiff in the first quarter that nearly got Todd killed, I wanted to crawl into the nearest hole.

Like most of us that day, McCloskey didn't have a very good game. To his credit he came back strong and worked harder than ever to get better, especially on his blocking at the point of attack. If you want proof, go watch a replay of Curt's second touchdown run in the Sugar Bowl. You will see Mike pancake Georgia All-American strong safety Terry Hoage, who ended up playing a long time in the NFL.

A fourth-quarter mistake continues to live in infamy with Penn State fans, but there is much more to it than most people realize. Mike Suter, who had been a standout for Gerry Faust at Moeller High School in Cincinnati, played the entire second half at Alabama after our All-American safety Mark Robinson hurt his ankle. Mark was also the personal protector on the punt team. The personal protector typically lines up about three yards behind the line of scrimmage to ensure that anyone who breaks through the line is accounted for so the kick isn't blocked. That day in Birmingham, Suter became the only player I have ever seen in over 45 years of either watching or playing football to block his own team's punt.

Having never been the personal protector (or played any position on any punt team), I have no clue what coaching Mike may have received, but backing directly into senior Ralph Giacomarro's foot the very moment the ball was kicked was likely not part of that instruction. In his defense Suter had rarely practiced his assignment as backups on special teams rarely got any reps in practice. Mike's untimely miscue caused the ball to travel 35 or so yards backward, giving Alabama great field position and completely changing the complexion of the game. Had the Internet been around, the play would have gone viral before the final gun sounded. Instead of Ralph pinning Alabama deep in its own territory, we handed both the game and our undefeated season to a gravel-voiced coaching icon donning his famed Houndstooth hat on a damn red and white platter.

Most people only remember the colossal mistake. What folks forget is that Suter had a career-high six tackles and picked off a pass that day to help us climb back into a game we had no right being in. Other than the trombone player who got steamrolled at the end of the 1982 Cal-Stanford game, perhaps no one has ever had to endure their own ignominious replay more often than Mike Suter. "The first thing I felt was this thud on my back and thought, *Why the hell is someone hitting me from behind?*" Suter said. "I turn around and see the ball bouncing 10 yards behind me in the wrong direction, so I hustle and actually recover the ball. After the play I had to stay out there with the defense. Alabama scored a few plays later, so when I finally came to the sideline, Joe doesn't say a thing but gives me this what-the-hell-just-happened look. Before that play I am thinking to myself, *This is a dream. This is why I came to Penn State, to showcase my talents on a national stage.* Our defense found a different gear in the second half, and we held Alabama to six points up until the final six minutes. We crossed into their territory and on third and short ran a sweep, but their defense guesses correctly and slanted toward the play. We lost a few yards, and I remember thinking, *I wonder if Joe is gonna go for it.* We didn't, so the punt protection unit goes out onto the field. We had a punt blocked earlier, so I vowed that nobody was going to break through to do it again."

That mind-set may have played a kay factor in Suter backing into Giacomarro at the worst possible time. "I remember the play like it was yesterday," Suter said. "I have lived with that for over 30 years and run that play over in my mind constantly. All the great plays I made that day were instantly forgotten."

After the gun sounded, all of our team captains made sure they had Suter's back. One used a pretty blunt tactic to demonstrate his leadership. "I recall a lot of reporters' microphones being in my face in the locker room afterward," Suter said. "At one point Ken Kelley walks by and says, 'Hey look, why don't you leave the guy alone?'"

Unfortunately for Suter his *own* family wouldn't leave him alone. "So we get back home to State College, and I get a phone call from my brother," Mike said. "He says, 'Dude, did you watch ESPN tonight? They are now calling you the loneliest man in college football.' We all go out later, so I tell everyone this. Carmen [Masciantonio] turns to me, and in his best *Animal House* impression, says 'My advice to you is to start drinking heavily.' We all had a good laugh, but it was like, what can you do? Joe would always preach that the outcome of games aren't decided by just one play, it's four or five of them."

Greg Gattuso also never hesitated to bust Mike's chops about the incident. "I ruined Suter's life for two years after that," Gattuso said. "Whenever I would see him talking to the female persuasion at a party, I would walk over and casually remind him that he was the guy who backed up into Ralph Giacomarro."

The Next Generation

On August 19, 2016, the Milwaukee Brewers called up a lanky, 6'5" pitcher from the minor leagues. Brent Suter, 26 at the time, had climbed the ranks in the Brewers farm system after a standout Ivy League career. "*Harvard Magazine* does an article on my son, and the reporter calls me and knows all about that play," Mike Suter said. "I got to embrace it all over again. It is what it is. You wouldn't wish what happened on your worst enemy. I have come to terms with it a long time ago. In the team meeting the following day, Joe to his credit never ever singled me out [and] instead said the entire team made a number of boneheaded plays."

It remains to be seen what Brent may do to top his father's unfortunate and infamous gaffe. In many respects Mike handled that situation very similar to how another of my former Browns teammates, Earnest Byner, handled his goal-line fumble against Denver in the 1987 AFC Championship Game—with a ton of class and dignity.

The Crimson Tide scored two plays after our second blocked punt and then made good on a two-point conversion to go up 35–21. On our next offensive snap, Blackledge threw his fourth interception of the day, which was promptly returned for a touchdown. That made the final score 42–21, a misleading result considering we held a decided advantage in total yards 429 to 334. The five interceptions our quarterbacks tossed were the most in Joe's 17 seasons as head coach. I was probably not the only player scratching my sweaty head wondering what the outcome might have been had we converted that third-and-one play near midfield with six minutes left in the game.

Understandably, we were all very down in the locker room after the game, knowing full well we had beaten ourselves. What happened afterward has been well-documented but remains one of the most inspirational and motivational talks I have ever witnessed. Still in his uniform, fullback Joel Coles, one of our fifth-year seniors, proceeded to stand up on the stool in front of his locker and start talking in a very purposeful tone that got louder and more emotional the longer he spoke: "Hey! Get your heads up! This thing isn't over! Monday is the start of a new season and WE ARE NOT LOSING ANY MORE GAMES!"

The words themselves were inspirational but even more so because of who spoke them. Joel had been one of the most sought-after running backs in the country during his senior year at Penn Hills High School in the eastern suburbs of Pittsburgh. He generated over 250 yards of total offense as a freshman tailback while also playing special teams on the '78 Penn State team. The following season Coles started seven games at cornerback and rushed for more than 150 yards in a win against N.C. State. He suffered a severely dislocated ankle against Temple in the third game of the 1981 season and took a medical redshirt.

The presence of both Warner and Jon Williams in 1982 didn't leave much room at tailback, so Joel moved to fullback for his final season. In addition to being an absolutely ferocious blocker, he also became a very effective inside runner and pass catcher out of the backfield. Although not recognized as one of our most outspoken leaders, Joel nonetheless commanded the respect of everyone on the team for battling back from a serious injury. "When I got up on the stool, I saw guys sitting in the lockers with their heads down, some crying, demoralized, just general disappointment. I didn't really plan to do that; it just kind of happened," Coles said. "My goal was to lift folks' spirits and say, 'Hey, this isn't over.' I'm a competitor. That's just who I am. Anytime we don't play as well as we are capable of, I am gonna let guys know. You have to understand the team I played on in high school, Penn Hills, went 39–1–1 when I was there. I just wanted to encourage everyone and remind them this thing wasn't over. I recognized that the talent on the 1982 team was right up there with the 1978 team. Our schedule was so loaded I realized we had a good chance to get back into it."

Had Joel told us we were going to go back out to run 100-yard wind sprints in that Birmingham hot house, every single one of us would have followed him onto the field. At least that's what I still believe to this day. His words were *that* impactful, *that* emotional, *that* inspirational. "We listened to Joel because we all knew the heavy price he paid to get back on the field," Warner said.

We showered quickly then made the long trip back to State College. We were quietly determined to hold each other accountable, to work as hard as we possibly could for the rest of the season so we would never have to taste defeat like that again. Witnessing an entire team draw inspiration from a direct challenge issued by one of our senior leaders remains one of my fondest Penn State memories to this day.

CHAPTER 8

Getting Up off the Mat

October 16, 1982
Syracuse (1-4) at No. 9 Penn State (4-1)

We returned home to face a Syracuse team with something to prove. The Orange arrived in Happy Valley with a revamped defense that featured three future NFL draft picks in Mike Charles, Blaise Winter, and Tim Green up front. This was an aggressive bunch seeking to avenge Curt Warner running wild on them a year earlier in the Carrier Dome.

Joe Paterno felt we needed better balance on offense as well as radical improvement on defense. He challenged the offensive line to establish a more consistent running game, reminding us all week that we couldn't keep relying on Todd Blackledge and the passing game. Running the ball effectively would enable us to eat clock and keep the ball away from the opposing offenses. Doing so would also keep Blackledge healthy and get Warner more involved.

He wasted little time communicating his expectations with us. "Joe was pretty pissed off at the team meeting on that Sunday after the Alabama game," junior Steve Sefter said. "He told us, 'We're gonna start making changes around here. Guys like Sefter have been busting his hump and practicing hard. He's gonna get a shot.' My jaw dropped when I heard that. I show up the next day, and sure enough, there is a dark blue jersey in my locker. That's when the nerves kicked in. I start at defensive end and I don't even know the position! I was more scared than anything else. Hell, I didn't even get *into* the Alabama game."

Paterno's message was clear. Our level of play during the season's first five weeks needed to become more consistent in all phases. There could be no more excuses. Our margin for error was minimal. Senior co-captain Pete Speros interpreted Joe's comments this way: "There's a lot of competition here," Speros said. "Guys can't really take being a [starter] for granted. I think Joe just wanted to get that point across to everybody and I think he really did. He emphasized that we have to go out there and perform every game. If you're a first-teamer, you've got to go out there and play every game and there are no excuses."

Weather for the 1:30 PM kickoff in Beaver Stadium was fairly mild with the sun shining. That soon changed as a storm front brought in nasty, stinging precipitation and turned the field into a slick surface. That made our task of running the ball much more difficult against the aggressive Syracuse defense. The inclement conditions coupled with Joe's renewed emphasis on the running game translated into Blackledge attempting just 15 passes all day, a dramatic change from the previous five games.

The offense started slowly but kept plugging away, and we put together two long touchdown drives in the first half with most of the yards coming on the ground. Warner carried the ball more than 20 times for the first time all year and responded with his best performance of the season. He finished the day with 148 rushing yards, including 34 on a vintage sweep around left end for a touchdown that put the game away in the fourth quarter.

Our defense also responded to Joe's challenge by playing inspired, opportunistic football and forcing seven Syracuse turnovers. Dave Paffenroth, who had found a home at starting inside linebacker, picked off two passes in the first quarter alone and narrowly missed a third. Paffenroth hailed from East Stroudsburg in the northeast corner of Pennsylvania and was tagged "The

Mad Paff" for his rather aggressive mannerisms both on and off the field. Dave was talented enough to play as a true freshman, logging 10 carries for 48 yards as a backup fullback to Matt Suhey.

Injuries gave younger players opportunities to step up and perform. Mike Suter started his first game for still-injured Mark Robinson while former walk-on Brian McCann garnered extended playing time and contributed two tackles for losses. True freshman Mike Zordich replaced Harry Hamilton, who had injured his knee, and led us with seven solo tackles. Joe's decision to move his personnel around paid early and handsome dividends.

"I was pretty jacked about my very first start in Beaver Stadium," Suter said. "Here I am replacing an All-American and contributing to an important win. We really started playing like a Penn State defense, and it couldn't have come at a better time."

The team effort sent our homecoming crowd home happy with a 28–7 win that got us back on track. As we approached the halfway point in the season it was very encouraging to play the more traditional style of football Penn State was known for and to get Curt going again.

Not everyone came away impressed with our effort. *Daily Collegian* beat writer Ron Gardner wrote an article that included an eye-popping quote from Syracuse defensive tackle Mike Charles. "There's no way [No. 8 Penn State] should be ranked that high," Charles said. "We basically shut them down. They didn't impress me at all."

Basically shut us down? What game was Mike Charles referring to? After reading that I wanted to say, "Hey, Mike, here's a newsflash: we scored all four of our touchdowns *on the freaking ground*." That quote struck a nerve with me since I felt we ran the ball effectively despite the extreme weather conditions.

Although this was a different year, it was pretty much the same result against our New York neighbors. Curt ran for nearly 150 yards—we gained over 225 on the ground—but more importantly our offense achieved much better overall balance. We dusted off a more trademark, more recognizable running attack. It was encouraging not only to get back into the win column but to return to playing our more traditional brand of Penn State football.

Warner's breakout game eased some of the angst and anxiety he dealt with through the first month of the season. "It was a difficult period for me since I wasn't getting the ball that much," he said. "To be honest, I wasn't real happy with the old man on the change in strategy, but in the grand scheme of things, it was a key to us winning the championship. I just wished he would have let me in on the plan. I would have been okay with that versus not knowing. It took a lot of patience on my part not to go to the media about it. Nowadays they almost demand that some official reason to be given. Joe pulled me aside after the Alabama loss and said we're gonna get back to what we used to do. Bottom line was that when Joe said to turn the switch on we got back to running the football."

Curt handled an awkward situation with class and maturity. In doing so he helped keep a team unified that briefly teetered on the brink of fracture. Rather than pack it in or sulk and create a big distraction, he dealt with what had to have been a wide range of different emotions privately. I felt it was an unsung personal sacrifice that kept us squarely focused and on point.

October 23, 1982
No. 9 Penn State (5-1) at No. 13 West Virginia (5-1)

Our second road test of the year had us once again facing another ranked opponent. West Virginia had not beaten us since 1955, but this was a much-improved Mountaineers team thanks to a stingy defense and a talented quarterback who had transferred there two years ago from, of all places, Penn State.

Jeff Hostetler had been part of the Nittany Lions' 1979 recruiting class that included Warner, Blackledge, and Mike McCloskey, among others. An exceptional all-around athlete and fierce competitor, Jeff actually started a few games for us early in the 1980 season but was eventually replaced by Blackledge. The following spring Joe Paterno faced a difficult decision on his starting quarterback and called Hostetler into his office for a meeting. Since Jeff's older brothers, Ron and Doug, had been solid linebackers at Penn State, Joe suggested he consider switching to defense. Jeff disagreed and felt

GETTING UP OFF THE MAT

quarterback was his natural position. Shortly afterward Jeff requested a transfer that Paterno granted.

It did not surprise many of us to see Jeff have success in leading West Virginia to back-to-back bowl wins for the first time in school history and finishing seventh in the 1983 Heisman Trophy voting. He later played 12 NFL seasons and quarterbacked the New York Giants to an upset win against the Buffalo Bills in the 1990 Super Bowl.

After sitting out the 1981 season per transfer rules, Hostetler wasted no time getting his new team off to a fast start. In his Mountaineers debut, Jeff threw four touchdown passes in leading his school to an attention-getting upset 41–27 win at ninth-ranked Oklahoma. It was the most points a Sooners team had surrendered in Norman since 1928 and Barry Switzer's first ever opening game loss. Led by seniors Daryl Talley and Todd Campbell, the West Virginia defense was no slouch either as it would limit high-octane offenses led by Dan Marino, Boomer Esiason, and Doug Flutie to under 20 points.

In 1980 our trip to Morgantown had been a grind. Curt Warner's 88-yard kickoff return in the final quarter proved to be the difference in beating an unranked Mountaineers team by five points in a cold, sleeting rain. Their fans' version of giving us a warm reception two years later was to dangle a Paterno dummy in effigy from the upper deck of their newly opened stadium and then lighting the damn thing on fire as we walked onto the field prior to the opening kickoff. That wasn't the only reminder we were far from the friendly confines of Beaver Stadium. "That locker room was the worst," said wide receiver Gregg Garrity. "There was no hot water, and some sort of drainage issue caused water and mud to pool in a few corners. On top of that, it was freezing. We had all underdressed. From midget league through the NFL, that was the coldest game I ever played in."

Our close call in Morgantown in 1980 also signaled an unofficial and unceremonious end to what could be considered the "fancy footwear era" at Penn State. The story goes that Joe had concerns about the spongy playing surface in the Louisiana Superdome prior to the 1979 Sugar Bowl. He left it up to his players to decide what type of shoes to wear. Most chose white ones with sneaker bottoms. Penn State's 14–7 loss meant that the idea of wearing trendy footwear during games would be shelved indefinitely—as if shoe color was a reason for the demoralizing loss.

Todd's Take

The equipment room had no black high-top Astroturf shoes, and we had away games upcoming. They issued these high-top white Nike turf shoes with a cool blue swoosh logo to any player with ankle problems. The following week, a lot more guys developed mysterious mild ankle sprains in order to get their hands on the fashionable footwear. A lot of guys wore them for the game down at West Virginia, which turned out to be a real dogfight.

The narrow victory meant someone or something had to be culpable. Paterno announced in the next team meeting that no Penn State player would wear the fancy footwear again. Tim Bream recalled Joe saying, "You guys wearing the white shoes, you're just a bunch of haaat daaags."

The following day any player who had these precious white turf shoes in their possession arrived at their lockers to find them painted jet black with no logo appearing on them. Oddly, the number of players donning high-top white turf shoes declined significantly. "A lot of guys' ankle injuries healed up pretty quick after that West Virginia game," Blackledge said.

West Virginia entered the 1981 game with a 5–1 record and ranked 13th in the country. Its lone loss was a nail-biting 16–13 defeat at No. 1 Pitt where the Mountaineers blew a 13–0 fourth-quarter lead and then missed a game-tying field goal in the final seconds. This was a dangerous football team playing in front of the largest crowd in West Virginia history, a rowdy audience convinced their Mountaineers would knock us off for the first time in almost three decades. "We came out for warm-up, and their fans threw pennies at us," Brian McCann said. "The coins would hit your helmet and cause a ringing in your ears. It was an intimidating place, not because of the team we were playing but the behavior of their fans. I never understood why their stadium security allowed that stuff to happen."

Ron Heller found out later that coins weren't the only items Mountaineer fans chose to hurl at us. "The following week I walked into our O-line meeting room a few minutes early, and Dick Anderson was playing a film clip back and forth, back and forth," Heller said. "After a few minutes I asked him what he was looking for and he replied, 'I am just wondering why Curt made this particular cut. He should have run the ball outside, but he saw a whiskey bottle bounce near him on the field and so he cut it up inside to avoid getting hit with it.'"

Referees made sure to keep the game close as penalties were pretty much a one-sided affair. By the end of the third quarter, we had been penalized 11 times for 82 yards while the home team had been flagged just twice for 10 yards. It got so bad at one point that we were called for unsportsman-like conduct after Blackledge was tackled well out of bounds...on our *own* sideline.

Heading into the final period we clung to a precarious 10–0 lead thanks to our rapidly improving defense that would post Penn State's first road shutout since 1978. Led by co-captains Ken Kelley and Walker Lee Ashley, this crew had morphed into a bend-but-don't-break takeaway machine, including the one that salted the game away.

In a script similar to the 1981 Notre Dame game, another underclassman emerged as an unlikely hero when junior linebacker Scott Radecic picked off a Hostetler pass and ran it back 85 yards for a fourth-quarter touchdown. "They were driving to make the score 10–7. We were playing man coverage on that play or else I would have dropped into a zone," Radecic said. "Jeff got pressured, throws this little dump pass, and I step right in front of it. Everyone was behind me. All I saw was goal line, but it was a *long* way away. I had no idea what yard line I was on. I just knew it was the fourth quarter and I was tired. At that point all you're thinking is get to the sideline and run as fast as you can. As I am running, I see Walker Lee out of the corner of my eye providing this personal escort. The way I tell the story, he came up beside me on three different occasions to block somebody. How does a guy have that much time to do that? It was the first time I ever scored a touchdown. I was both elated and exhausted, but then I had to go right back out on the field. I thought to myself, *How am I gonna go out and play another series?*"

Radecic's game-clinching effort was the third longest interception return in school history and longest ever by any Penn State linebacker. The win against a ranked opponent on the road was pivotal because it proved we could play disciplined, error-free football in front of a hostile crowd, something we obviously failed to do against Alabama. We also kept our eyes on our upcoming opponents, particularly our in-state, No. 1-ranked neighbors to the west. The fact that the Mountaineers had played Pitt so tough on the road only reinforced that the Panthers were entirely beatable.

Convincing wins against West Virginia and Syracuse helped immensely in terms of getting our swagger and confidence back. Our practices the following week were focused, crisp, and efficient. A refuse-to-lose, backs-against-the-wall mentality had become the new norm.

October 30, 1982
No. 8 Penn State (6-1) at Boston College (5-1-1)

Fresh off two impressive wins, we ventured onto the road for a second straight week to play in front of another raucous crowd and face another eastern rival off to a surprisingly strong start. Boston College came into this contest at 5–1–1, having tied Clemson while losing only to West Virginia by seven points in Morgantown. This was the most competitive B.C. team in decades thanks to a wide-open offense led by sensational sophomore (and future Heisman Trophy winner) quarterback Doug Flutie. Another attendance record, this time at Alumni Stadium in Massachusetts, would be broken.

The similarities between Boston College and West Virginia were striking. Both programs were surprisingly ranked in the AP top 20 and had high-scoring, pro-style offenses run by future NFL quarterbacks. Both considered their matchups with us as statement games. Taking down a top 10 program in front of their home fans would deliver instant credibility. Both teams realized they needed to score a lot of points to have a chance to beat us, and each moved the ball effectively between the 20s. In the end both West Virginia and Boston College followed the same script we had authored in Birmingham where turnovers at inopportune times led to a discouraging defeat.

Despite Flutie's record-setting passing performance—he threw for an unconscious 520 yards—we turned what was expected to be a back-and-forth shootout into a rout by halftime. Scott Radecic and Dave Paffenroth each picked off errant Flutie passes to set us up with great field position while Walker Lee Ashley led a pass rush that sacked the B.C. signal-caller four times.

Our offense, meanwhile, demonstrated devastating efficiency. Senior Ralph Giacomarro did not have to punt until midway through the third quarter as Todd Blackledge launched his own aerial assault, much to the chagrin of the overflow crowd in Chestnut Hill. Todd found Gregg Garrity and Kenny Jackson for first-half touchdowns while Curt Warner darted in, out, and around a tentative B.C. defense, shredding it for 183 yards and three touchdowns. It turned out to be our finest offensive performance in recent memory as we piled up 309 yards passing and matched that total on the ground. "All we kept hearing was: 'This is gonna be the year B.C. will beat us' and 'Flutie really has his offense clicking, running on all cylinders,'" Radecic said. "I remember him throwing the ball all over the field and being unsure as to why we didn't play more man coverage. Unlike the previous week where Jeff stayed in the pocket, Doug almost never did. He was one of the first true scramblers we played against and could create an open receiver by moving around."

Undecided as to if they should defend the run or the pass, Boston College's defensive players struggled the entire day. They ended up doing neither. Their linemen stood straight up after the ball was snapped and then tried to read and react rather than penetrate. Their giant defensive tackle, Junior Poles, all 6'6", 275 pounds of him, played as though he was content to watch the game unfold around him. Their only player who showed up wanting to make a difference was linebacker Steve DeOssie, who later carved out a nice NFL career with the New York Giants.

In less than a month, our offense had transformed itself from a mistake-prone outfit in Birmingham to a deadly efficient one in Boston. Our defense, which surrendered 83 points in our first four games, had given up a total of 24 in the past three. Three straight impressive wins helped us climb again in both polls. And it was starting to look like Joel Coles was getting exactly what he had demanded in that Birmingham locker room. "That stretch turned out to be a real test of our maturity and it brought us closer together," Mike McCloskey said. "The challenge was: can you come back to work? We were 21 years old, we weren't perfect. Joe made it difficult on us over the next few weeks, but we got right back up off the mat."

Others noticed how well we rebounded from the Alabama loss. John Fidler, author of *The Ultimate Boston College Football Game (Old Guy Edition) 1970–1999*, wrote: "Penn State and Joe Paterno were the standard bearers for eastern football. In 1982 [an upset] looked possible, but an outstanding Penn State team, as a matter of fact, the greatest team I have ever seen come to Chestnut Hill, withstood a 520-yard passing performance from Doug Flutie to roll to a 52–17 win."

Warner reached a milestone against B.C. on his first carry of the third quarter, surpassing Lydell Mitchell as Penn State's all-time leading rusher despite having missed two full games his junior season. Curt and Todd were easily the two catalysts of our offense. Warner was lightning quick and especially dangerous on Astroturf. Some of his best games occurred on synthetic surfaces at Nebraska, Syracuse, and Boston College. He could cut on a dime and hand you a nickel in change (along with your jockstrap) as he ran by you.

The clearest example of what Curt meant to our success was the fact that we never lost when he ran for more than 100 yards. By the time he left campus, Curt would own nearly every major Penn State rushing record, including career rushing yardage (3,398), 100-yard rushing games (18), all-purpose yards in a game (341), and career rushing attempts (649). His career all-purpose yardage record stood for 20 years until it was broken by Larry

Johnson in 2002. Warner was a two-time, first team All-American and the third overall selection in the 1983 NFL Draft. Without question he was *the* best player on some of the best teams in Penn State's illustrious history.

Blackledge possessed a rifle for an arm, the aptitude to read complex coverages, the poise to stand in the pocket, and a toughness underappreciated by most. He was the recipient of the prestigious Davey O'Brien Award as the nation's top quarterback, following the 1982 season. What most people overlooked, though, was Todd's toughness. Few recall that he was actually our lead blocker on two misdirection plays near the goal line that resulted in rushing touchdowns. Watch film against both West Virginia and Alabama and you see Todd throw himself into the oncoming defender in what were violent, physical collisions. Most other quarterbacks would make the pitch to the ballcarrier and then mysteriously peel away from the point of attack. Not Blackledge. We had a guy who, given the chance to be a lead escort, fully intended on bloodying somebody's nose.

"Blackledge was no prima donna," Garrity said. "He was willing to get his uniform dirty and block."

November 6, 1982
N.C. State (5-3) at No. 7 Penn State (7-1)

We returned home to face N.C. State, a team that always gave us trouble. One year earlier—and the week following our upset loss in the rain at Miami—we needed a fake punt that Harry Hamilton ran in for a touchdown to escape with a seven-point win in Raleigh. Back in 1977 future Minnesota Vikings running back Ted Brown rang up an incredible 251 yards rushing against an 11-1 Penn State team with a defense that included Bruce Clark, Matt Millen, and Lance Mehl.

N.C. State entered this game with a deceiving 5-3 record because all three of its losses were to opponents that would eventually be ranked. This time around, though, the Wolfpack never had a chance. Our defense picked up right where it left off, continuing to force turnovers. Scott Radecic picked off a pass for the third straight game and turned it into his second

Pick-6 of the season. "Penn State linebackers were taught things that just weren't coached at other schools," Radecic said. "We were taught to pattern read-route combinations like '604' or '408.' That meant if you ran to a particular spot, there will be a '6' route being run by the receiver right behind you. We were also playing combination packages. For example 'silver' was a strong-side zone, backside man rather than straight zone. On my pick against N.C. State, we were pattern reading, and their quarterback threw it toward our sideline. I had a tight end run right at me and I knew he would either break in or break out just like we practiced. Compared to the play in the West Virginia game, I liked that I only had to run 30 to 35 yards rather than 80 to 90 yards."

John Bove felt the type of players Joe Paterno recruited—like the cerebral Radecic—gave Penn State a decided edge. "Our kids being good students was a big advantage for us," Bove said. "We could teach complex schemes or coverages, and they could learn them. We could put stuff in the opponent hadn't seen before."

That concept crystallized for Radecic after he left the program and played for the Kansas City Chiefs at the next level. "I didn't realize until I got to the NFL that we were a lot more advanced as far as what we were asked to do at Penn State," he said. "When I went to Kansas City, I found out most of the other linebackers didn't even know about pass route combinations or pattern reading. Until that point I just assumed every college team did what we did. It was a huge advantage for me at the next level."

Scott may have been Joe's first player to successfully navigate Penn State's extremely difficult architectural engineering program. This course of study required students to complete five full years' worth of credits to secure an undergraduate degree. Despite earning academic All-American honors in 1982, Scott needed to return to graduate with honors in an incredibly challenging field, following his first two seasons with the Chiefs. "I took one full semester of classes [21 credits[after my rookie season, then a semester of classes [22 credits] after my second NFL season and still had to take a final elective via correspondence," Radecic said.

Without question Scott, along with Dr. Al Harris (dentistry) and the late

Dr. Stuart McMunn (orthopedics), were the three sharpest tools in the shed we had on the defensive side of the ball.

Our offense picked up where it left off against Boston College, racking up close to 500 yards against N.C. State. Curt Warner gained over 100 on the ground for the third time in four weeks against a defense that seemed at a total loss as far as how to defend us. In a year in which players like John Elway (Stanford), Eric Dickerson (SMU), Irving Fryar, Mike Rozier, and Roger Craig (Nebraska), Bo Jackson (Auburn), Marcus Dupree (Oklahoma), Steve Young (BYU), and Herschel Walker (Georgia) were all making head-lines, our offense boasted the most talented skill-position personnel in the country.

The score stood at 47–0 after three quarters, and Paterno pulled the start-ers early for the second consecutive game. Shortly thereafter, somebody in the first row right behind the bench leaned over the railing to say, "Hey, did you hear the news? Notre Dame just knocked off Pitt!" We all knew what that meant. Suddenly, we found ourselves right back in the hunt for the national title.

After the game reporters asked Joe his thoughts on Pitt's loss to Notre Dame, and he referred to our final three games as a "playoff" for the national championship. I felt that was pretty uncharacteristic of a coach who usually erred on the side of caution when publicly commenting on his team. Joe also began making bold, confident assessments to the media much to the effect of "We think we're awfully good" and "It will take a great team to beat us." Joe had always advocated a college football playoff and now began casually tossing the word around to the media. We interpreted that as a "Hey, I really believe in you guys" message from the top.

Joe's statements were in stark contrast to his usual cautious approach of never providing bulletin board material to our opponents. I felt invigorated to hear him speak in this animated and confident manner in public. His endorsement had a lot of us really believing we really were on the verge of becoming one of the better teams in Penn State's proud history. "It was *very* uncharacteristic of Joe to talk about his own team," linebacker Al Harris said. "I thought to myself, *Was he just throwing it out there for the media?*

Would him doing that help us move up in the polls? Was he trying to draw attention to a team that had just rung up 50-plus points in the past two weeks against pretty solid football teams or was he truly that impressed with how well we were playing?"

CHAPTER 9

The "Playoff" Stretch

November 13, 1982
No. 5 Penn State (8-1) at No. 13 Notre Dame (6-1-1)

The Monday following our win over the Wolfpack, *Philadelphia Daily News* sports columnist Ray Didinger published the first of a week-long series of articles titled "The Real Joe Paterno." Didinger presented another side of Paterno by interviewing players who, for a variety of reasons (poor play, team rules violations, lack of playing time, etc.), did not share the general public's idyllic view of the iconic Penn State coach. Though it was a negative depiction, Didinger oddly contradicted himself by writing: "92 percent of Penn State's football players graduate...What's more is that 90 percent finish right on schedule." Didinger also cited "37 former PSU players [were] in the NFL in 1982 and that all but two have their degrees. Impressive particularly when you consider only 29 percent of all NFL players have their college degrees."

The timing of the articles did not deter our laser focus. Joe's "playoff" began with us facing our third ranked, one-loss opponent on the road. Penn State's first ever trip to South Bend coincided with Notre Dame returning home as conquering heroes after knocking off top-ranked Pitt in Pitt Stadium.

We arrived in South Bend late Friday afternoon, and the local media wasted little time cornering Joe, peppering him with questions about his team's chances against the vaunted Fighting Irish. He reiterated what he had said following the N.C. State blowout. "I think we have a great football team," Joe told reporters. "I don't know if we're the best in the country, but it would take an excellent team to beat us." In truth, Joe found a lot of the questions unflattering and, while he handled them with his typical diplomacy, he was incensed. Later that evening he gave us an unusually impassioned pep talk during the team snack. "Joe was quite candid with us, saying, 'What I wanted to tell [those reporters] was: what does it feel like to have a top-ranked team come to South Bend? You know we have a bit of a tradition at Penn State too!'" Mike Suter said. "I just thought it was *sooo* cool that he told us that. It really pumped us up and reinforced an us-against-the-world mind-set. He reminded us to just play our game despite what would be written in the paper. His comments reaffirmed his contention that his team was prepared to play well the following day."

Fighting Irish fans believed that Gerry Faust's second year at the helm was going to be the year their storied program returned to prominence. Their confidence would grow after Notre Dame came out of their tunnel sky high and promptly took the opening kickoff 80 yards for a touchdown. Golden Domers sensed a second consecutive upset of a top five team from the Keystone state.

Todd Blackledge had other ideas.

Todd quieted the boisterous crowd by finding Kenny Jackson on a deep crossing route for 30 yards on our first offensive play. He connected with Jackson a second time before the drive fizzled and sophomore kicker Nick Gancitano missed a field goal. It was evident the Irish secondary feared Jackson's deep threat potential and gave him a nice cushion. Kenny exploited the soft coverage by catching three more passes in the game's first 19 minutes.

Jackson's 23-yard catch on a post route early in the second quarter set us up with a first and goal at the Irish 2-yard line. Blackledge snuck the ball over the goal line three plays later to knot the score at seven. Our defense found traction and began corralling a suddenly inept Irish offense. Gancitano redeemed himself by nailing a long field goal to give us a lead before disaster nearly struck.

We had been exceptionally fortunate to get this far into the season with no major injuries on offense other than Curt Warner's occasional leg cramps. Despite being hit hard several times in Alabama, Blackledge had survived the season largely unscathed as the revitalized running game lessened his workload as well as the number of hits he endured.

That all changed with 8:30 left before halftime. Blackledge dropped back to pass from the Irish 20-yard line, and Notre Dame gambled with a corner blitz. The line picked up the inside rushers, but with no backs in the backfield, defensive end Kevin Griffith had an unobstructed path to our quarterback. As Todd released the ball, Griffith's helmet caught him directly under his chin, a hit that would draw a 15-yard penalty and possible ejection in today's game. This time around our otherwise durable quarterback didn't get up.

Todd's Take

 I was knocked out for a few seconds. I wasn't out long and by the time any of the trainers got out there I was conscious again. I only missed one play, but I would forget some stuff in the huddle. I remember Curt having to occasionally remind me what play I called or what the cadence was. As the game went along, I gradually felt better. I remember being in the locker room after the game being able to recall the key plays but had no recollection at all of the first half. I felt like I was in a tunnel. It was a bizarre feeling. Had it happened today, I don't think there is any way I would have been allowed to go

back in the game and would maybe even miss the next week. It's a different world today, a safer world. I was lucky that I suffered no major aftereffects. I may have had a headache the following day.

Concussion protocol in the early 1980s was radically different than it is today. "Back then if you played hurt or saw stars, it was a red badge of courage," trainer Tim Bream said. "The protocol was that if you observed someone coming off the field looking disoriented, the training staff would have the player repeat some numbers backward, ask them if they were dizzy or if they had a headache. Doc Whiteside would have the player repeat three words in order something like 'Blue, Kentucky, Wildcat.' We would also check nerve status, their balance, then go back a few minutes later to check on them again and have the tests. It was very rare for a guy to be removed from the game back then. These days you immediately take the player off the field and inside for evaluation. Blackledge would have absolutely been taken into the locker room."

After the training staff escorted our thoroughly dazed and confused signal-caller to the sideline, backup Doug Strang handed off to Jon Williams to get us in position for another Gancitano field goal, which increased our lead to 13–7.

With just 1:46 left in the half, Joe decided to kick the ball to dangerous freshman Allen Pinkett, who had burned Pitt the previous week by taking a draw play 76 yards for the touchdown that put the finishing touches on Notre Dame's 31–16 upset win. Against us, Pinkett caught the ball in the middle of the field and then angled toward the right sideline. For some reason every official managed to miss a Notre Dame blocker openly tackling our special teams demon Brian McCann. "It was a blatant hold," McCann said. "I got up and yelled to the ref, 'Hey! You gotta call that,' but it fell on deaf ears. What a homer call that was."

Pinkett raced untouched 93 yards for a score that woke up the docile crowd and gave Notre Dame a 14–13 halftime advantage. Joe would later admit it was a mistake to kick it to Pinkett. His decision to do otherwise in the fourth quarter would prove to be a major factor in determining the game's final outcome.

Just like a year earlier in Pitt Stadium, we had taken the home team's best shot and were in position to come out in the second half and earn another hard-fought victory over a ranked team steeped in tradition. Having gone on the road and beaten two eastern rivals who were having arguably their best seasons in decades, we were well past the point of letting any team or situation intimidate us. "There was absolutely no panic in there at halftime," Gregg Garrity said. "There rarely ever was."

The teams traded blows during a scoreless third quarter, and Notre Dame was 15 minutes removed from ruining Joe's self-declared three-game playoff. At the start of the final period, we took possession on our own 20 in a game that had evolved into a field-position battle. Todd found Kenny for 28 yards on a deep corner route and then hit Curt on a quick slant against a blitz, the exact same play we scored on in Alabama. Warner flew by safety Dave Duerson and raced 48 yards to register the six points that gave us back the lead. The three-play drive took less than two minutes.

Our try for two points failed, and Massimo Manca booted the ensuing kickoff deep but away from Pinkett. Their other returner, Pat Ballage, misjudged the ball's flight and caught it awkwardly while simultaneously touching his right knee to the turf on the 2-yard line.

The next play call bordered on the bizarre. Notre Dame attempted to run a sweep directly at our senior co-captain Walker Lee Ashley with precious little space to do so. Anticipating the snap perfectly, Ashley knifed inside an attempted block by tight end Tony Hunter, knocked off the pulling guard, and then tackled Pinkett a full seven yards deep in the Irish end zone. It was a spectacular individual effort from our best defensive player in one of the most critical moments of the game. The two points meant the Irish had to score a touchdown if they were to beat us.

They never did. Warner erased any remaining doubt by sprinting 44 yards down the sideline to set up a Gancitano field goal. Warner ended up torment-ing a Notre Dame defense that was ranked third in the country in rushing defense (yielding only 64.9 yards per game) for 140 hard-earned yards.

The 24–14 win marked our second fourth-quarter comeback against a ranked opponent. We were becoming a resilient group that understood what it took to come from behind in tough games. The Fighting Irish had gone the length of the field following the opening kickoff, but our defense kept them out of the end zone after that and held them to 268 yards of total offense. We became only the fourth team to beat Notre Dame on its first ever visit to South Bend.

As was the case the previous week, Paterno did not mince words with the media when asked how he felt about his team. "We are playing the best football that any Penn State team ever has played," Joe said. "We're a very good football team, and I know it's going to take an outstanding team to beat us." These reflections came from someone who had coached three undefeated teams and had seen his share of elite football teams over the years. Joe's comments reinforced a growing sentiment in the locker room that we *were* as good or better than anybody in the country.

Our upcoming game with Pitt was slated for the day after Thanksgiving, which meant we had the following Saturday off. Most of us watched undefeated SMU come from behind before settling for a 17–17 tie against Arkansas in Dallas. That stalemate would vault us over the Mustangs to No. 2 in both polls, right behind undefeated Georgia.

Steve Sefter and Scott Radecic recall watching the game while chomping on pizza. "I couldn't believe SMU played for a tie," Sefter said. "I almost choked on a piece of crust. That tie made our decision on which bowl game we would play in pretty easy."

His Other Sport

Steve Sefter earned All-American honors as a heavyweight wrestler after both his freshman and senior year. He also co-captained the Penn State wrestling squad in 1984. Not bad for a guy who did not rank grappling at the top of his list of favorite activities. "Wrestling was my better sport," Sefter said, "but I liked football more."

Sefter was one of the smallest wrestlers in the heavyweight class, frequently entering matches against opponents with weight advantages ranging from 20 to 150 pounds. "In my sophomore year, I wrestled Gary Albright from Nebraska who weighed around 380," Sefter said. "I was around 225 for that match. Albright went on to wrestle Tab Thacker in the 1984 finals. At the time Thacker weighed in at 447 pounds."

Sefter posted a sixth-place finish in the NCAAs his freshman year and then advanced all the way to the NCAA semifinals before finishing fourth in 1985. He dropped a narrow 5–4 decision to eventual champion Bill Hyman despite entering the tournament as a 10-seed and usually weighing significantly less than most of his opponents.

Sefter also shared a rather odd similarity with fellow classmate Kirk Bowman. "Part of my finger almost got cut off my sophomore year trying to tackle Jon Williams in practice," Sefter said. "My right ring finger got caught between two helmets and I was taken to the hospital. It was bleeding like crazy. Hoch brought along the tip of my finger to the hospital.

A year later I almost blocked a punt against Notre Dame with my right hand by leaping over their personal protector. We won the game, so we're all feeling pretty good and, as we watched the film, one of the coaches commended me by saying, 'This is a great effort, Steve.' Without any hesitation Greg Gattuso chirps up from the back of the room and says, 'Yeah, and if you had the tip of that finger, you would have blocked it.' Most of us laughed out loud, but it also made me feel like I finally really belonged."

November 26, 1982
No. 5 Pitt (9-1) at No. 2 Penn State (9-1)

Six days prior to the Pitt game, we received invitations from several major bowl games, including the Sugar Bowl. Joe Paterno held a team meeting before practice, allowing us to choose where we wanted to spend New Year's Day. Since we always voted to play the highest-ranked team possible, the decision was easy. We wanted a shot at the title and unanimously agreed to play Georgia and Herschel Walker, the Bulldogs' talented junior tailback. Walker would become the fourth Heisman Trophy winner (Marcus Allen, Mike Rozier, and Doug Flutie being the others) our defense would face during this 15-game odyssey.

I am not sure how the schedulers pulled this off, but we hosted Pitt at Beaver Stadium for the third time in four years. That's pretty rare for an in-state rivalry. Pitt brought its 9–1 record to Happy Valley fully intent on spoiling our championship hopes and returning the very same favor that resulted from the previous year's 48–14 debacle. Doing so would give them their own shot at winning the title since they had committed to playing SMU in the Cotton Bowl. They would need to beat us, hope Georgia lost in the Sugar Bowl, and hope that Nebraska fell to LSU in the Orange Bowl.

Some things had changed since our previous meeting. Shortly after Pitt beat Georgia in the 1982 Sugar Bowl, Jackie Sherrill accepted a lucrative offer from Texas A&M. Pitt promoted longtime defensive coordinator Foge Fazio to head coach. Fazio had recruited western Pennsylvania for years, so those of us who grew up in that area were well-acquainted with his competitive drive and extensive football knowledge. We were all keenly aware that he coached a talented and motivated team. If we were to get our chance to play for the national title in New Orleans, we sure had one hell of an opponent to go through to get there. Pitt teams in the late '70s and early '80s were tough, hard-nosed bad boys and won a fair number of games on sheer intimidation. The stakes for this contest were once again incredibly high and carried the obvious national implications.

A lot of players on both sidelines knew each other well by virtue of being high school teammates. Our nose tackle, Greg Gattuso, would line up directly across from his former Seton LaSalle Catholic High School teammate and Pitt center Jim Sweeney. Kenny Jackson would run pass routes against Pitt cornerback Troy Hill. (They both attended South River High School in New Jersey.) Dan Biondi and Joel Coles would be playing their final home games at Beaver Stadium against Pitt All-American candidates Tom Flynn and Bill Fralic. All four players hailed from Penn Hills High School. Penn State's Rocky Washington and the Pitt's Dwight Collins had each been multi-sport athletes at Beaver Falls High School.

Pitt's defense returned virtually all of its starters from the previous season, including Bill Maas, Chris Doleman, Dave Puzzuoli, Rick Kraynak, Flynn, and Tim Lewis. All would go on to play in the NFL. Their offense, however, was an enigma. Despite featuring future NFL All-Pros like Dan Marino, Jimbo Covert, and Fralic, Pitt had trouble scoring points. The Panthers had managed just seven points against North Carolina, 14 (plus a safety) against West Virginia, 14 at Syracuse, and 16 in their lone loss of the season to Notre Dame. Still, this was a very dangerous and well-coached team coming to town.

Making things even more interesting was that both teams were ranked in the top five, a rarity for a rivalry game this late in the year. As was the case the previous year, we felt we had an advantage in regard to the schedule in that Pitt had played WVU and Notre Dame at home while we had beaten both those teams on the road.

In the 1982 version, Pitt moved the ball well during the first 30 minutes while we did ourselves no favors by turning the ball over twice. Both factors enabled the Panthers to take a 7–3 lead into the locker room at halftime. Just like the week before in South Bend, we had to come from behind in the second half to keep our national championship hopes alive.

Paterno elected to have the wind at our back for the third quarter, and that turned out to be a critical factor in the game's outcome. The increasingly unpredictable wind gusts Marino faced at the start of the second half really hampered his ability to move his team through the air while our defense clamped down on Pitt's ground game. Their kicking game faltered twice when their normally reliable punter, Tony Recchia, shanked one ball to set us up inside the Pitt 40-yard line and then mishandled another snap and tried but failed to run for a first down.

We took advantage of great field position throughout the third quarter and scored the next 13 points. Our lone touchdown came after Todd Blackledge read an all-out blitz and found Jackson on a crossing route. Jackson proceeded to outrace Hill, his high school teammate, to the end zone to give us the lead for good.

Todd's Take

All I remember was the wind. As a quarterback I would rather play in snow, rain, sleet, or hail rather than wind. Nothing affects throwing or kicking the ball like a strong wind. Nothing affects the mind of the person throwing and even more so the person kicking a ball like gusting winds either. This game was a bruising battle between two very physical football teams that completely swung in our favor in the third quarter—when we had the wind at our backs.

Pitt didn't go down without a fight. Trailing 16–7 but with the wind now at his back, Marino drove Pitt inside our 5-yard line early in the fourth quarter. Pitt couldn't punch the ball into the end zone, and Fazio went the conservative route, opting for a field goal that cut the lead to six points. We went three-and-out on our next series, but Ralph Giacomarro saved the day with a booming 51-yard punt into the wind. Pitt came right back and had a first down on our 37-yard line with six minutes left in the game. Our resilient defense held, and Pitt missed a long field goal.

Our final possession started on our own 30-yard line. This drive needed to be a run-oriented, time-consuming effort. Pitt knew it. We knew it. Everybody in the stadium knew it. We had to eat clock while going into the wind against a defense ranked second in the nation in rushing defense, surrendering a stingy 82 yards per game.

We would not be denied.

Curt Warner, Jon Williams, and Joel Coles all ripped off huge gains behind the very same offensive line that had been labeled a huge question mark at the beginning of the year. We eventually drove the ball inside Pitt's 15-yard line, and with less than a minute remaining, Nick Gancitano put the game on ice with a chip-shot field goal to make it 19–10.

For the second time in two months, delirious fans stormed the field to tear down the goalpost in the south end zone. Exiting the field with your uniform intact proved to be difficult (somewhere, someone has my elbow pads), but it was a nice problem to have, especially since the win solidified our hold on the No. 2 spot in both major polls.

Our defense ended up limiting Pitt to one offensive touchdown. It was only the second time in Marino's final three seasons that his offense scored fewer than 14 points. On paper these Panthers may have possessed more raw talent, but our second-straight comeback win over our bitter, in-state rivals reinforced the old adage that our sum was indeed greater than Pitt's individual parts.

## CHAPTER 10

The Sugar Bowl Timeline

January 1, 1983
No. 1 Georgia (11-0) vs. No. 2 Penn State (11-1)

For the second time in five years, the Sugar Bowl would match the nation's two top-ranked teams. It would also mark only the sixth time in NCAA history that the No. 1 team would meet the No. 2 team in a bowl game to determine the national championship. Despite being the lower-ranked team, we would enter the contest as three-point favorites. Oddly, it would be the third consecutive season the No. 1-ranked team entered their bowl game as the underdog. The attendance of 78,124 would set a record for the largest crowd to ever witness an indoor football game. Media coverage would also be at an all-time high.

Vincent Joseph Dooley would square off against Joseph Vincent Paterno, the former returning to the Big Easy for the third straight year while the latter was trying to win his first Sugar Bowl after failing on three previous occasions. Joe's lack of success in New Orleans was the only scar on his otherwise stellar 9–4–1 record in bowl games. This would be the very first meeting between the two prominent programs.

Just as he had done in the preseason, Joe held several spirited, up-tempo, physical practices in the weeks leading up to the Sugar Bowl. Across the parking lot from the locker room and adjacent to the campus ice rink, which served as our indoor practice facility, he installed huge speakers in the airplane hangar. He played crowd noise at full volume to acclimate us to what was expected to be a raucous Superdome crowd. When those practices ended, Todd Blackledge headed straight to the training room, hoarse from straining his vocal cords. The rest of us walked across the asphalt in the dark mostly in silence because we were temporarily deaf.

As we prepared to face the Bulldogs, junior safety Mark Robinson found the motivation to get in a little upper body strength training. "One of the coaches gave me a great compliment while we were watching film," he said. "He said, 'Herschel is one of the great ones,' then stopped the film and in front of all my peers says, 'We are gonna string him out, and Robby, you are gonna clean him up.' I was so fired up to meet that challenge I went back to my dorm room afterward and started doing one-handed push-ups while saying: gonna...clean...up...Herschel...Walker."

12:55 PM EST Sunday, December 26th

Our charter flight left Harrisburg, Pennsylvania, the morning after Christmas. We touched down in New Orleans shortly after noon central time and headed straight to Tulane University. Joe Paterno opened with a surprisingly physical session in full pads designed to get our full attention after the three-day Christmas break.

Our first practice in the bayou got off to an ominous start as right guard Dick Maginnis partially tore his hamstring. Publicly, Joe dismissed the injury with levity, saying, "Whoever heard of a big fat guard missing a game with a hamstring? They don't have to run that far." Privately, I have to believe he was very disappointed that the redshirt junior, who grew up in State College, might miss the biggest game of his life.

Maginnis had quietly been playing great football for us in his first year as co-starter with Dave Laube at long side guard. Ron Heller believed he had his own home remedy for what ailed his close friend and teammate. "We were gonna enjoy the night life a little regardless," Heller said, "So we went out a few times, drank some beers, and threw darts."

Head trainer Jim Hochberg had no problem with this rather unorthodox rehabilitation regimen. "Hoch knew Maginnis and Heller intended to spend a few evenings in the French Quarter throwing darts," Tim Bream said. "Later that week when Dick returned to practice quicker than expected, I remember Hoch telling Joe he thought part of the reason Maginnis' hamstring got better so quickly was not only proper fluid intake, but also because the stance he used throwing darts may have actually helped break up the adhesions quicker than normal to heal the injury. Maginnis was still all black and blue behind the knee, but he played in the game. I don't think people realized how tough he was."

9:00 AM EST Monday, December 27th

Six FIGI fraternity brothers wedged their way into a cramped station wagon and departed State College hell-bent on making it to the Big Easy in time to ring in the New Year with nothing more than game tickets in hand. The group included North Allegheny High School graduate Mike Bellaman, who, along with fellow NAHS alum Gregg Garrity, had been part of the same FIGI pledge class the previous spring. "To get our game tickets, we had to sleep outside overnight in a line that extended down from Rec Hall and past our fraternity house," Bellaman said. "Tickets were only available to students on a first-come, first-serve basis, so we had to camp out in the bitter cold. Luckily, our house was close by so we could rotate people in and out. This was a huge deal for us. We gotta get down there to see our FIGI brothers [Gregg, Kevin Baugh, Jeff Brunie, and John Gurski] play for all the marbles. It was a very athletic house—football players, lacrosse players, baseball players, you name it. We drove straight through [to New Orleans]. It took us a total of 22 hours, and there was never a time when someone wasn't sleeping in the back. I think I took along a backpack or a duffel bag with nothing in it other than the standard FIGI outfit—blue jeans and gray T-shirts. It was a freaking *adventure*."

No place to stay? No advance hotel reservation? No problem. "We just didn't worry about that at the time," Bellaman said. "We were playing for the *national* championship. We just figured it was what college kids did. Once we got in the south, all we heard on the radio was 'Herschel this and Herschel that.' The talk shows all made it sound like we were 10-point underdogs. Every single station we listened to seemed to have some overconfident Bulldog fan calling in, convinced Georgia would beat us. At some point we decided that the very first bar we landed at would be our meeting point. The plan was that in case any of us got lost, we were to meet back at that bar four hours or so after the game, then drive back to campus. We did that because there was no social media, no cell phones, no way to keep in touch if we split up or got lost."

The six-pack of sleep-deprived FIGIans arrived in The French Quarter mid-morning on December 28. "Once we hit town, we drove straight to Bourbon Street, then randomly chose one the bars to designate it as our rallying point," Bellaman said. "It was around then that we started weighing our options as far as sleeping arrangements. We all ended up finding places to stay by either meeting people who were [from New Orleans], running into friends, fellow Penn State students, or alumni. We just asked if we could just crash on their floor. I ended up sleeping in a different hotel room every night. It was all clean fun and it worked out fabulously."

10:00 AM EST Tuesday, December 28th

Back at Tulane Greg Gattuso had different practice issues to deal with—namely, a surly head coach who looked for a reason to get his players' attention. "I was benched for half a practice down at the Sugar Bowl for slouching," Gattuso said. "That's right, *slouching*. I was in the meeting room early for a change but was a little slouched over in my seat with my foot up on another one. Paterno walks by in the hallway, stops, then starts yelling at me to sit up straight. 'Hey! Gattuso! Don't slouch in ya chay-ah.' Like an idiot I shot back with 'What? C'mon, there's no one even in here!' Joe hits the roof. 'That's it! You are *not* gonna start this game!' Then he throws me out of the meeting before it even started. And I'm not even doing anything!"

It didn't end there. "Sure enough, when I get to my locker later that afternoon, they changed my practice jersey color," Gattuso said. "I went outside before practice literally in tears and began pleading with the coaches. All I could think of was embarrassing my father, or that he was probably gonna kill me. I went out there and was cheap shottin' everyone I could, just really getting after it. Near the end of practice, I get put back with the first group."

A decade later Gattuso was told why he had been made an example of that day. "They were looking for someone to set the right tone at practice, and Joe did that by scaring the hell out of me," he said. "Could you imagine being in that situation? It was unbelievable. He understood that you gotta call out your best players from time to time. You had to have a certain edge to play there."

Gattuso eventually found his own coaching success at both the high school and college level. At Duquesne University in Pittsburgh, Greg has become the school's all-time winningest coach by posting a .752 winning percentage, amassing 97 victories, and collecting multiple conference championships over 12 seasons. He is currently the head coach at the University of Albany. He now applies a similar approach with some of his players. "Guys like me, those with a somewhat independent or rebellious nature, I can now see that in a few of my players," Gattuso said. "A lot of successful people aren't straight-line guys, so you gotta find a way to mold and motivate those types of people. I always felt Joe's real genius wasn't in the schematics but rather his ability to motivate people to get the most out of them. Sometimes it is shocking, but that's the beauty of it. Calling someone out was done with a specific purpose—not personal—but to get everyone's attention by singling out a few individuals. Joe's ability to motivate was done on Tuesdays and Wednesdays not some emotional speech right before the game. It's a blueprint I follow, tactics I use in my coaching today. Anything requiring preparation to get people to perform, to do better, or gain confidence in themselves, well, he was a master at that."

3:30 PM EST Thursday, December 30th

Four Penn State players, including Scott Radecic and Mark Robinson, were scheduled to participate in a press conference at the Hyatt Regency following a late-morning practice. Radecic had a little secret he wasn't about to share. "I sprained my ankle in practice [on Wednesday]," Radecic said. "Knowing I was selected for the press conference the next day, Joe approaches me and says, 'If you limp at all tomorrow, you aren't going to that press conference.' So the next day after practice, I had a trainer tape up my ankle pretty heavily, then pull on [a] mid-calf argyle sock over it. Joe didn't want anyone picking up on the fact I wasn't quite 100 percent. I always felt that was another example of Joe being one step ahead and paying attention to those little things he always preached."

4:15 PM EST Friday, December 31st

The day before the game, the team captains organized a players-only meeting after a short walk-through—our final practice—in the Superdome. The idea for this meeting came from an unlikely source, one of the least-tenured coaches on the staff. "The previous day after practice Scrap Bradley pulls me aside," said co-captain Pete Speros. "Scrap says, 'Hey I think we're ready, but some guys may need to be reminded that this is a once-in-a-lifetime thing, something that's never been done before. It may be a good idea to have a players-only meeting just to remind everyone what it took to get here, all the personal sacrifices, all the hard work we put in to get to this point. That's one thing I wished my class had done prior to the 1979 Sugar Bowl game against Alabama.'"

A Family Affair

The Speros family was no stranger to college football's biggest spotlight. Pete's older brother, Jim, played on Clemson's 1981 national championship team. Another brother, George, played at Temple while their father, Leo, played at Maryland. All three brothers played in bowl games in 1979, and Penn State's ultimate triumph in the 49th annual Sugar Bowl may have marked the first time in college football that two brothers were national champions in consecutive years at different schools. "I made sure to stay in touch with my older brother while he was at Clemson," Pete said. "I would bust his chops and say, 'We would have loved to play you guys and would have beaten you because we had already knocked off Nebraska at their place to boot. [Clemson would defeat Nebraska in the 1982 Orange Bowl to claim the nation's top prize.] At the end of my freshman year, we were all featured in *Sports Illustrated,* something like, 'Three different teams, Three different bowls.' George played in the Garden State Bowl, Jim played in the Peach Bowl, while I went to the Liberty Bowl. That may have been unprecedented—three brothers playing in bowl games in the same year."

After the coaches exited the Superdome floor, we gathered near midfield and sat cross-legged on the red-white-and-blue 49th Annual Sugar Bowl logo. Speros and fellow captains Walker Lee Ashley, Ken Kelley, and Stuart McMunn all reinforced the magnitude of the moment, quietly and confidently stressing the need to "close this thing out," emphasizing how we had earned the right to play in this game. Joel Coles, Dave Opfar, and Mark Battaglia also shared their experiences as true freshmen on the '78 squad that came so agonizingly close against Alabama in the same building four years earlier. "That meeting didn't involve any impassioned pleas or vocal tirades," Battaglia said. "It was more a recap of what it took to get to this point. Guys commented on how far we have come, the hard work we put in during the preseason, how close we are to achieving something no other Penn State team had ever done. We all walked off that field fully aware of what stood in front of us, the task at hand. What we were totally unaware of was how impactful this game would be for the legions of Penn State fans, this blue and white army chomping at the bit to finally celebrate their 'We're No. 1' claim."

Battaglia's status as a fifth-year senior—and the sacrifice he made in returning for a final season—was recognized by some of the younger linemen. "Dick Maginnis and I were best friends," Ron Heller said. "After that meeting he pulls me aside and says, 'Hey it is *so* important we win this game. Batman came back for his fifth year. He literally put off the start of rest of his life to come back and play one more year here. He made a pretty major personal decision here, so we better make sure we do whatever we can to make this happen for him.'"

11:45 PM EST Friday, December 31st

The 24 hours or so before any football game can be agonizing for both players and coaches. Your mind tricks you into thinking you may not have prepared enough, haven't studied enough film, or won't react if the opposition presents some wrinkle you hadn't seen before. Then again our final game was in New Orleans, which presented potential distractions of another kind.

"Maginnis and I were in our room, and we could hear all the people partying in the streets," Ron Heller said. "All we were thinking was, *Here we are in New Orleans on New Year's Eve, and we're stuck in this hotel room. Just think of what we're missing!*"

Down the hall, Walker Lee Ashley set out to do something about that. "They set me, Stu McMunn, Ken Kelley, and Walker Ashley up in this over-sized captains' suite," Pete Speros said. "The bedrooms all had adjoining doors. We already had bed check, so I was watching TV and get a knock on my door. Walker enters and said, 'Hey man, I am all keyed up. It's New Year's Eve, we're in New Orleans, and we don't play until tomorrow night. I'm gonna go out for a couple hours and ring in the New Year.' So the night before the biggest game of our lives, he sneaks out of the hotel! I fell asleep right after that, so don't know if it was 10 minutes or all night, but he was back in his room by the next morning. One can only wonder what Walker ended up doing on Bourbon Street that night. He ended up playing one helluva game despite being out after curfew."

If Walker did sneak out after curfew, he would have been amongst revelers that included the boisterous, carpetbagging FIGIans. "The atmosphere that night was crazy," Mike Bellaman said. "The entire street was packed. We drank Hurricanes at Pat O'Brien's, wore Mardi Gras beads, just soaked in all that culture. There were some Georgia fans wearing T-shirts that said, 'We do it doggie style.' It was really neat to meet new people. No one got hurt, no one did anything stupid or got thrown in jail. We all had a blast that night. By the time the ball dropped in Times Square, we were all busy working every angle to secure a place to stay for the night. After a while it was almost like a competition amongst some of the friendliest people you ever met. *Hey man, stay with us. No, stay with us!* That kind of stuff. People were very, very welcoming."

11:00 AM EST Saturday, January 1st

There is an incredible amount of time spent planning a bowl game itinerary. The goal is to avoid interruptions at any cost. On the afternoon of the most important game of our lives, some players' attendance at the pregame meal was unavoidably delayed. "The elevator I was on got stuck between the fourth and fifth floors for about 20 minutes," trainer Tim Bream said. "There were 15 or 16 of us in there, including some big people. Everybody was sweating. Nothing like a little extra stress before the biggest game of your life, right? At one point the doors open a little, and Joe pokes his head up at us and says, 'Hey, everything is gonna be all right. We're gonna get some people here as soon as we can to get you outta there.' Problem was it was New Year's Day, and no one was working."

"I was wedged in shoulder to shoulder with Maginnis and some other oversized guys," Ron Heller said. "Everybody was cool about the whole ordeal; nobody freaked out. After about five minutes, Maginnis leans over and whispers to me, 'I *told* you we should have snuck out last night.'"

2:00 PM EST Saturday, January 1st

Consumption of Hurricanes, which helped ring in 1983 eight hours earlier, was once again in full swing down on Rue Bourbon. The whole wash-rinse-repeat cycle was evidently necessary to reclaim the buzz from the previous evening and ensure hydration. "We get back down there, and now it's this giant New Year's Day tailgate," Mike Bellaman said. "Our main concern was that after three days our funds had dwindled rather rapidly. Since none of us had any credit cards, the challenge was to preserve enough of our remaining money for the ride home. We began connecting with any alumni who would buy us a drink or pick up our tab. We also made sure we weren't too plastered to get the game."

By late afternoon a legion of Penn Staters began making their way uptown to the Superdome. The FIGIans decided to join them. An ill-advised stop along the way proved costly.

"We strolled by a street vendor running a shell game [like three-card monte]," Bellaman said. "We had played the game before with no money and won every single time. I even remember watching another person play, and we got it right, and they got it wrong. By that time our judgement was slightly impaired, so I figured, 'Why not try our luck?'"

This absurd, alcohol-induced logic proved penny-wise and pound foolish. "So I dug around in my pocket, pulled out the very first bill I could find, and plunked it down on his little table," Bellaman said. "Now, remember, we all agreed to save up our remaining funds for the ride home, so ponying up $20 was a *lot* of money at the time. In a heartbeat my 20 was gone. My prior winning at this con game was all part of their flawless set-up, and the guy was an absolute pro. I had taken the bait—hook, line, and sinker."

6:50 PM EST Saturday, January 1st

Many athletes follow some type of strange ritual when they dress for games. One trick offensive linemen typically used in the early 1980s was to tape excess cloth tightly around their upper bicep to ensure no defender could grasp onto them to gain an advantage. As he dressed for the biggest game of his life, Mark Battaglia received a surprise addition to his wardrobe from a trusted ally. "Frank Rocco Jr. came in with our recruiting class," Battaglia said. "After exhausting his eligibility, Frank now served as a grad assistant. Evidently, he also fashioned himself an aspiring artist as he added Batman insignias to my elbow pads using a black magic marker. I actually still have one of those, dried sweat and all. It really took the edge off but was also a nice gesture from someone I really respected."

Meanwhile, the six sleep-deprived FIGIans had made their way up Canal Street, hung a left, and shuffled through the Girod Street entrance into the hulking Superdome. "We were fired up because we knew they served alcohol [inside the stadium]," said the now-lighter-in-the-wallet Mike Bellaman. "We got our first round of Hurricanes, then found our way to our seats, which were five or six rows up from the field in the corner of one of the end zones. We were in just absolute awe of our surroundings. It was this massive indoor facility with a huge scoreboard hanging over the center of the field. The teams are warming up, we're sipping on our Hurricanes, checking out Herschel Walker from a distance, just enamored with the whole pomp and circumstance."

7:30 PM EST Saturday, January 1st

We were assigned the hometown Saints' dressing room, which is a good two-to-three minute walk to get to the tunnel that leads to the field. "It was just like the gladiators getting ready to enter the Roman Colosseum," Mark Battaglia said. "Loud music is playing, and the crowd is really vocal even during warm-ups. Penn State fans were shouting their usual 'We Are' while Georgia fans were screaming 'How 'Bout Them Dawgs,' hoping these charlatans in their plain vanilla uniforms would be sent home, tails between their legs, by yet another SEC school."

8:10 PM EST Saturday, January 1st

Our captains met their Georgia counterparts at midfield with a significant number of other people crowding around the coin flip ceremony. Ken Kelley's successful tails call gave us the choice to kick or receive. His emphatic "We'll take the ball" was broadcast over the Superdome loudspeakers, delighting the Nittany Lions fans in attendance. The referee quietly slipped the coin to Ken before the captains retreated to their respective sidelines. "I actually still have that coin in my home office," Kelley said. "I gave it to one of the equipment guys, I think it was the late John 'Hubba' Fee, and he gave it back to me in the locker room after the game."

Kelley had pulled no punches with the media leading up to the game. In an article published in *The New York Times* on December 30th, Kelley had said, "[Herschel Walker] is going to take very big punishment, he's going to have six people tackling him at all times. By the second half, I think he's going to be hurting."

That wasn't bravado by Ken as much as it was a competitor's reaction to the Herschel hype leading up to the Sugar Bowl. "I recall being at the co-captains' press conference before the game and getting tired of having to address all the 'Herschel walks on water' stuff," Kelley said. "Now, I'm not a real vocal guy, but I remember saying, 'Hey our own guy [Curt Warner] is pretty good too, and Walker will go down just like everybody else.' At that point in the season, I figured Joe couldn't yell at me for saying stuff like that."

8:15 PM EST Saturday, January 1st

Already clad in our no-nonsense white road uniforms, Todd Blackledge added his own personal fashion statement by sporting high-top throwback Bobby Layne-style turf shoes, even though our school had ties with Nike. "They were high-top black Adidas tennis shoes with sneaker bottoms," Blackledge said. "Curt ran track in the spring and had struck up a conversation with the Adidas rep. The guy later came over to our apartment and gave us all kinds of gear so we started wearing Adidas stuff. It really pissed [equipment manager Tim] Shope off to the point where he made me tape over the three stripe Adidas logo. Few people noticed that Kenny [Jackson], Curt, and I wore Adidas all year."

8:25 PM EST Saturday, January 1st

Leading up to the game, Georgia coach Vince Dooley told reporters he expected us to exploit his undersized, banged-up defensive line by running the ball. If Joe had a conservative gameplan, it vanished as quickly as Mike Bellaman's $20 had in the shell game. Todd Blackledge drilled tight end Mike McCloskey down the middle for a 33-yard gain, unveiling a gameplan that included stretching the field. Four plays later and with the game less than three minutes old, Curt Warner swept left end untouched for the first of his two rushing touchdowns. *Sports Illustrated's* John Papanek would later describe Dooley as "being shot with a gun he never saw."

That proved to be true in a sense. There was no way Dooley could have predicted Blackledge would complete four straight passes and dissect a defense that came into the game leading the country with 35 interceptions. "Our three-wide-receiver set may have created a coverage problem for them," said Dick Anderson of the tone-setting pass play to McCloskey. "Joe didn't necessarily reach into his bag of tricks as much as doing what all great coaches do—spot, then exploit weaknesses. Sometimes it's a matter of studying film and just copying what another team did to the opponent or creating something similar to exploit it, to do things to take advantage of a team's weaknesses and tendencies."

We could not have scripted a better start. Then again we were used to this as Warner had scored the very first time he touched the ball in each of our previous two bowl games. Given the caliber of competition, Warner's performances in New Year's Day bowl games were particularly outstanding. Publicly and to honor Paterno's unwritten rule to never provide opponents with bulletin board material, Curt would patiently explain to the media what a privilege it was to be on the same field as players like Marcus Allen and Herschel Walker. Privately, he took the challenge very personally. "I was perceived in the media as a bit of an underdog, but I wasn't about to take a back seat to anyone," Warner said. "Deep down I believed I was as good as or better than those guys. I have always been competitive when it comes to playing football in general, so I didn't pay much attention to the hype. I didn't look at it as being the 'other' back—rather that you better be ready for a dogfight because we plan to play some hard-nosed football. Make no mistake, the kid from Pineville came to play."

After Warner's score Ron Heller jogged off the field in awe of what had just happened.

"I was so jacked up looking up at the scoreboard, scarcely believing we were already up 7–0," Heller said. "I knew Penn State normally didn't get off to great starts in Sugar Bowl games and I was impressed with how quick and efficient that drive was."

8:45 PM EST Saturday, January 1st

Mark Robinson had intentions on finding out if Herschel Walker was a man, a myth, or a legend. "We knew he had sore shoulders going into that game," Robinson said. "I think Walker's second carry was an outside pitch, so I made sure I came up like a missile because I wanted to see what he had. I hit him hard, and he went down pretty quick. From that play I felt he wouldn't deliver a big blow. It gave me a whole different perspective." At that point in his college career Walker owned the NCAA record for rushing yards (5,259) and carries (994).

Robinson later intercepted two errant John Lastinger passes. "Probably should have had another one too," he said.

9:20 PM EST Saturday, January 1st

Over the second half of the season, our kicking game, like our defense, made steady improvement. Sophomore Nick Gancitano emerged as a reliable placekicker while Ralph Giacomarro continued to handle our punting chores. Ralph had nailed down the punting job about a week after he set foot on campus in the fall of 1979 and would turn in another consistent performance this night, averaging 45 yards per punt. Gancitano, meanwhile, came through with two long second-quarter field goals.

Our real difference-maker on special teams turned out to be our ultra-elusive punt returner, the late Kevin Baugh. Special teams coach John Rosenberg devised a seldom-used middle return, and with a little over eight minutes left in the half, Baugh electrified the crowd by weaving his way through the Bulldogs' punt coverage unit for 65 yards. Kevin would average a gaudy 21 yards on his five returns this night. "We practiced the middle return a lot while we were in State College preparing for Georgia," said Mike Zordich, who had emerged as a key special teams contributor as a true freshman. "I remember Rosey kept stressing the need to 'stay on your blocks longer.'"

9:40 PM EST Saturday, January Ist

As play continued, attrition became a factor. "During the second quarter, I got a major stinger," Ron Heller said. "As a kid I was a big fan of Muhammad Ali, and when I'd fight with my brother, I would always say, 'Hey, the Champ wouldn't stay down. Get up! Be the Champ!' When I got hurt, the mere thought of leaving this game was unheard of, but I also thought it would be pretty cool that the guy behind me, Stan Short, could tell his family he got to play in the Sugar Bowl."

Short replaced the injured Heller for one play. Meanwhile I had intentions on doing a little stinging of my own. Watching film I noticed their safety, Terry Hoage, would take a running start from five or six yards behind the line of scrimmage during field-goal and extra-point attempts and then try to vault over the center to block kicks. Hoage was quite good at that tactic, having blocked a field goal against Notre Dame in the 1980 Sugar Bowl. My protection responsibility on any placekicks was to secure my inside gap first and then the outside gap. Georgia rarely rushed anyone in either of my gap responsibilities, so I decided to try and time the moment Hoage planned to leap over our long snapper, Mike Stillman, and hammer him in the ribs. Let's just say I discouraged Hoage from jumping over our center.

10:10 PM EST Saturday, January 1st

With less than four minutes left in the first half and leading 10–3, we reached the Georgia 9-yard line thanks to another nice return from Kevin Baugh, a deep sideline route to Gregg Garrity, and a couple of solid inside runs by Jon Williams. On first down Joe Paterno sent in our goal-line personnel (double tight ends and full-house backfield). The Bulldogs countered with six down linemen, and most of their other defenders crowded the line of scrimmage.

The play we called had right guard Dave Laube pulling to kick out the end man on the line of scrimmage while Curt Warner would follow a Joel Coles escort through the tackle/tight end gap. Warner took the handoff and a few quick lateral steps before making a move only a truly elite player can pull off. Curt shuffled then executed a 90-degree stutter step cutback to the inside of the hole opened by Laube, Coles, and Ron Heller, who had pulled from the weak side. Warner sprinted untouched into the Georgia end zone for his second touchdown, increasing our lead to double digits. The Penn State faithful immediately broke into another deafening "Warr-nerr…Warr-nerr" chant that nearly shook the roof off the building.

Decades later (it may have been at our 30-year reunion), I stood alongside Curt in the tunnel where the players run out prior to kickoff at Beaver Stadium, maybe 50 feet from the back of the south end zone. The Blue Band comes out before the team, forcing us to stand with our backs against the side wall to avoid being trampled. There was a slight delay in the band taking the field, and this massive procession of blue and white clad minstrels slowed to a standing halt. A young man with an enormous trombone draped around his neck ended up standing right in front of us. Thirty seconds or so go by, and I caught him looking at Curt and me out of the corner of his eye, likely wondering who these two old graybeards were standing in the tunnel. To break the awkward silence while simultaneously trying to embarrass my former teammate (a skill I have become quite good at over the years), I asked the kid, "Hey, did you ever hear this crowd chant 'Warr-nerr…Warr-nerr?'" Startled at the rather offhanded question, the kid responds back with, "Yes, several times." I tilted my head toward Curt and replied, "Well, the dude standing next to me *is that guy*." The young man's lips parted, and his lower jaw dropped. As the band began moving forward again, the look on his face was absolutely priceless. Curt just smiled.

10:20 pm EST Saturday, January 1st

Nick Gancitano's 45-yard field goal (a Penn State bowl record at the time) upped our lead to 17 points. It looked as if we were turning this much-anticipated, No. 1 versus No. 2 matchup into a rout. Nick's kick, however, must have awakened the sleeping Bulldogs as Georgia took all of 39 seconds to drive the length of the field for the touchdown that closed the gap to 20–10 at halftime.

Our feeling in the locker room was no different than many of the games that had gotten us to this point. Joe Paterno reinforced the need to continue to play hard and play error-free, opportunistic football. He didn't need to blow smoke because of our comfort level in tight games and confidence in ourselves. Plus, the building already had enough smoke without anyone adding to it. "When we came out of the locker room after halftime, I will never forget looking up and seeing this haze, this huge cloud of smoke near the ceiling of the Superdome," Mark Battaglia said. "People were still permitted to smoke indoors in those days, and one look up at that haze, and I said to myself, *This is the fog of war.*"

10:50 pm EST Saturday, January 1st

Georgia took the opening possession of the second half, marched right down the field, and scored to close the gap to 20–17. Worse, they managed to slow down our offense using tighter pass coverage and run blitzes. The Bulldogs' Freddie Gilbert was a very quick, athletic defensive end for his size.

He ran track in high school and would later go on to play for the Denver Broncos. Put a dude like that indoors on an artificial surface against an offensive tackle beginning to tire a bit (like me), and that could spell trouble. As this game wore on, I struggled a bit to keep Gilbert off Todd Blackledge's back.

Late in the quarter, I let him slip past me on a third-down play, and he sacked Todd for a big loss. After walking off the field embarrassed, I plopped down on our bench and glanced up at the clock. I realized my college playing days would be over in about 30 minutes and that I was really screwing things up for us. Curt Warner sat nearby in his own agony, receiving treatment to alleviate recurring leg cramps.

Curt would occasionally bark out "Alright, let's cut the *crap!*" in the huddle when we needed to get serious or whenever things weren't going particularly well for us. I told myself, *Contz had better cut the crap and start blocking better, or else we're gonna choke away the national championship.*

11:25 PM EST Saturday, January 1st

By this time the intensity in the stands was off the charts. "Imagine the final minute of the Nebraska game; it was like that...but for the *entire game,*" Mike Bellaman said. "I don't think we ever sat down not even at halftime. Everybody was just *sooo* into it."

Five straight running plays to start the fourth quarter set us up with a first down on Georgia's 47-yard line.

With Georgia's defense likely expecting more of the same, Todd Blackledge called "6-43," a play-action pass. Todd took the snap from Mark Battaglia, faked a handoff to Curt Warner, and dropped back. He launched an absolute rocket into the Superdome stratosphere that eventually came down in Gregg Garrity's outstretched arms as he dove across the goal line. The place went absolutely nuts. You could sense this play sucked a lot of the life out of Georgia.

The second the ball was snapped, the FIGIans knew where Blackledge would go with the ball. "We all knew where Gregg lined up because we had been watching him the entire game," Bellaman said. "I mean you had to. He was someone you knew and hung out with all the time."

The play seemed to happen in slow motion. "Blackledge dropped back, and this play just unfolds right in front of us," Bellaman said. "Todd unleashed this bomb. We all follow the flight of the ball, look down, and see Gregg tearing down the sideline running *right at us*! We start yelling, 'Gregg! Gregg! Gregg!' When he caught the ball in the end zone, it just became pure pandemonium."

Fans seated near the delirious FIGIans immediately understood the significance of the play and responded in kind. "By then the people in the seats around us already knew who we were," Bellaman said, "so we became these instant celebrities, high-fiving everyone in sight. People from other sections were coming over to high-five us! I mean this was *our* frat brother who just happened to score what ended up being the clinching touchdown in the game that won us the national championship! We're all screaming, yelling, just going nuts. From a fan's perspective, it was one of the most unbelievable moments ever."

To the FIGIans, Garrity was just another fraternity brother, just one of the guys. "Gregg was never the rock star on the team," Bellaman said. "He was just a dependable receiver, always making key catches. For him to be *the* big play guy in this game was unreal. He was always just this regular guy to us and he ends up on the cover of *SI*. We were so happy for him because he was so humble. We all knew him and loved him."

Garrity beat Georgia cornerback Tony Flack, a talented freshman, on the play. "If memory serves, Flack talked a lot of trash, something to the effect that no one in Georgia history ever started as a true freshman," Garrity said. "I don't think he thought I was as fast as I was. We all ran seam routes, just four guys all running nine [also called fly] routes. Up until this game, Todd usually threw it to Curt, Joel, or JW because they had linebackers covering them."

When asked if he left his feet on purpose, Garrity said, "I think I could have caught it in stride, but I just wanted to catch it. I knew it was gonna be long but didn't know it was gonna be in the end zone. I just kept telling myself, *Don't drop it, don't drop it* while the ball was in the air. Most of the time they were not in press coverage because the [defensive backs] could hit you anywhere and at any time. The guy we were concerned about as far as their secondary was their strong safety, Terry Hoage. On film he was notorious for trying to take your head off when you ran routes. What's funny is that Hoage and I ended up as teammates along with Kenny [Jackson] on the Philadelphia Eagles, and we never really talked about this play or that game. He was a really good guy, one of my best friends."

On the play Georgia was in three-deep zone coverage with Hoage, who led the country in 1982 with 12 interceptions, among those providing a last line of defense. "You shouldn't get beat deep when you're in a coverage like that," Bulldogs defensive coordinator Bill Lewis said. "It was a great throw and a great catch."

Todd's Take

We ran the ball five times in a row, so it was a good bet the safeties may be getting a little nosey. Gregg was the receiver to the short side and had single coverage. We executed the play-action fake, and I saw right away that Georgia cornerback Tony Flack had no help. Gregg got up on him quick and then literally ran right by him. I knew what I had—a dependable senior receiver who caught everything I threw at him going against a true freshman. I never really even looked at the other receivers. When I first let it go, I thought maybe I overthrew it, but Gregg was sneaky fast. He caught up to it and made a great catch."

Garrity's touchdown gave us some much-needed breathing room, and we now held a 10-point cushion with a little more than 12 minutes left to play. Two series later Walker Lee Ashley notched a huge third-down sack of Bulldogs quarterback John Lastinger. This was the third straight game in which Ashley wreaked havoc in the opponent's backfield and had a profound impact on the game. He had tackled Allen Pinkett in the Notre Dame end zone for a crucial safety and temporarily knocked Dan Marino out of the Pitt game with a vicious blindside hit. It was becoming apparent that our Walker was outplaying their Walker.

Ashley's sack, which came with under eight minutes remaining, should have put Georgia away. However, we committed our biggest mistake of the night when Kevin Baugh fumbled away the punt, giving the Bulldogs new life in our territory. Georgia eventually found its way to the end zone with what looked like a gadget play. Lastinger hit tight end Clarence Kay on a cross-field pass a split second before Ken Kelley lowered the boom on him. Trailing by four with four minutes left, Georgia decided to go for two points. If successful on the conversion, the Bulldogs could potentially deploy their own long-range weapon, All-SEC kicker Kevin Butler, to win the game with a field goal.

Everyone in the building, along with the estimated 40 million watching the game on TV, knew Herschel Walker would get the ball. Sure enough, Lastinger pitched the ball to him on a student body sweep to the right. He had no chance. Ashley, Steve Sefter, Joe Hines, and Mark Robinson all anticipated the play. They beat their blocks and swarmed Walker for no gain. It was a huge defensive stand because Georgia now had to score another touchdown to beat us.

Our defense did a phenomenal job on Walker, backing up Kelley's pregame prediction. They bottled up Walker for most of the night, limiting him to just 28 rushing yards in the second half. Walker needed 28 carries to rush for 103 yards. It would be the *only* game in his collegiate career that he did not break a run of longer than 12 yards. And for the second straight year, a Penn State defense throttled a Heisman Trophy winner in a New Year's Day bowl game.

Even with the stop of Walker, our once comfortable 17-point lead had dwindled to a precarious four points. We anticipated an onside kick, but Georgia kicked the ball over the head of Baugh, who managed to bring the ball back to the 14-yard line. Nearly four agonizing minutes (3:54 to be exact) remained on the clock, and it seemed like an eternity. Here is where playing a ridiculously tough schedule worked to our advantage.

11:25 PM EST Saturday, January 1st

Our offense found itself in the same situation we had faced against Notre Dame and Pitt. We had to protect both the ball and a lead late in the fourth quarter while also trying to burn clock. The rebuilt offensive line—the single biggest question mark early in the season—now had one last chance to demonstrate how far it had come.

We gutted out a crucial first down after Curt Warner carried twice for nine tough yards before Todd Blackledge snuck for another one on third and inches. We made things more difficult for ourselves by getting flagged for an illegal formation. When you are inside your own 25-yard line trying to grind out time-consuming first downs, giving the defense five extra yards to work with isn't exactly textbook football. Regardless, we needed to find some way to gain 15 yards in order to move the sticks again. Two running plays netted 11 yards, and we faced a third and 4 from around our 40-yard line.

11:35 PM EST Saturday, January 1st

With 1:37 left on the clock, Joe Paterno called timeout to talk things over with Todd Blackledge, Fran Ganter, and Dick Anderson. A conservative play call could mean punting the ball back to the Bulldogs. That Georgia drove 66 yards in 44 seconds for six points right before halftime may have carried considerable clout with this decision.

While the coaches contemplated what play to call, an unlikely conversation ensued. Blackledge turned to trainer Tim Bream and casually asked, "Hey, what do my pants look like?" A startled Bream said, "What do you mean?" Todd said, "Well, I had to go to the bathroom so bad and knew I couldn't leave the field, so I just went in my game pants. You can't see any type of stain, can you?" With the game, season, and Penn State's first national title hanging in the balance, Blackledge inquired if anyone could tell whether or not he had peed his pants. "I remember that like it was yesterday," Bream said. "Joe had to yell at Todd to get his attention, and Todd just turns back to Joe and says, 'Hey I got it,' indicating everything was under control."

Todd's Take

To this day I have a small bladder and have to use the restroom a lot. I had been drinking my share of fluids before and during that game. I knew I went to the bathroom at halftime, but I was miserable and my stomach hurt. I was afraid of getting hit in the stomach, figured I had already completely sweated through my uniform, and that my urine had to be clear at some point so I just stood there on the sideline near the end of the third quarter while the defense was on the field and just peed my pants. I felt a whole lot better after that.

The coaches were unanimous. They all wanted to run the ball and punt if we didn't make it. I suggest a run/pass option, and if the coverage was soft, then let me go ahead and throw it. I was in my third year as a starter, and the coaches trusted me that if the coverage tightened up, that I would just throw it away, toss it up in the stands. I had learned a tough lesson from the 1980 Pitt game. We were driving very late in the game, and instead of throwing the ball away, I tried to force a ball on a quick out route. The interception allowed a pretty talented Pitt to escape with a narrow 14–9 win."

We needed just one first down to close out the game. "In those situations Joe is always gonna make the final decisions on the play calling," Anderson said, "but in that particular instance he deferred to Todd."

When play resumed Blackledge calmly took the snap and a three-step drop. He then rifled a pass to Gregg Garrity, who ran a quick out route against surprisingly soft coverage. Game. Set. Match.

In postgame interviews Vince Dooley said we should have been called for a false start or illegal procedure on the play. Replays confirmed this, but the officials threw no flag. No matter. The kid who had arrived on campus as a 155-pound walk-on after receiving exactly zero scholarship offers from Division I schools had snagged his second of two of the biggest fourth-quarter catches in Penn State history to salt the game away. "It took a national champion and a perfect throw by one of the game's best throwers [Dan Marino] to keep us from chalking up three consecutive Sugar Bowl victories, which would have been quite a feat," Dooley said. During that three-year span, the Bulldogs compiled a 33–3–0 record, largely behind the running of Herschel Walker—with two of those defeats coming at the hands of opponents that finished No. 1. Eighteen points separated Georgia from three full seasons without a loss.

11:47 PM EST Saturday, January 1st

At social functions I occasionally offer up a trivia question to Penn State fans: "Who was the last offensive player to touch the ball in the Sugar Bowl?" The answer is center Mark Battaglia. Our final offensive play of the Sugar Bowl was the sweetest of them all (no pun intended), and one player may have relished it the most. Our victory formation meant we would approach the line of scrimmage, get down in our stances, and then...do absolutely nothing.

Todd Blackledge barked out meaningless signals as precious final seconds ticked off the clock before officials finally stepped in to flag us for a delay of game. The offense exited the field stage left, and several players pointed skyward with their index fingers. The final punt of Ralph Giacomarro's outstanding college career nearly hit the gondola hanging above the stadium floor. Gravity did not pull the ball back to Earth until the Superdome clock read all zeroes.

Camera bulb flashes began exploding throughout the stadium while a throng of media jockeyed for position to snap photos of players hoisting Joe Paterno onto their shoulders. In the chaos they managed to drop Joe, who damaged his glasses, before lifting him up again. Fans chanted, "We Are… Penn State" at the top of their lungs while others relished a truly unprecedented event in school history.

11:53 PM EST Saturday, January 1st

The very same unlikely source that pulled Pete Speros aside a day earlier ended up with the game ball. "So Ralph punts the ball with six seconds left, and Georgia puts no one back to return it," Scrap Bradley said. "I remember thinking, *Why didn't we just let Todd run around then throw the ball as far as he could?* An official finally retrieves the ball and hands it to me amidst all of the chaos. So now I'm thinking, *Hey, this is a pretty nice thing to have but it probably belongs to Joe.* So I took it with me back to the locker room, then to the Hilton with the intent to personally give it to him. I knew Joe invited a bunch of people back to his hotel suite after the game. I was the youngest member of his staff at the time and kind of knew my place. I figured it would probably get me in that hotel room with all the well-wishers, players, and their parents."

11:58 PM EST Saturday, January 1st

In the belly of the Superdome, cigars were passed out in our dressing room along with congratulatory hugs and handshakes. "I met and briefly chatted with David Hartman," said Mike Suter, who caused a Bulldog fumble a few hours earlier. Hartman, the host of ABC's *Good Morning America*, had received permission from Joe Paterno to watch the game from our sideline and would invite Joe, Curt Warner, and Todd Blackledge to appear on the show in New York a few days later.

Mark Robinson recalls watching everyone around him celebrate. "I just sat in front of my locker spent, exhausted, so tired. Joe was standing close by, getting blistered with reporters' questions. He says, 'Look I'm done answering your questions. You need to talk to the players.' Then he looks over, points his finger at me, and says, 'They were the ones that made the plays and won the game.' As tired as I was, that made me feel good."

He had reason to feel that way. Robinson capped his junior season in which he earned All-American honors with nine tackles and two interceptions against Georgia.

Amidst all of the joyous chaos, Ron Heller literally lost his shirt. "There was this Sugar Bowl representative, who I became friends with while down there, and he had introduced me to his 12-year-old daughter," Heller said. "I'm not sure how, but the guy came into the locker room after the game, and he says, 'Hey! Great game! My daughter asked if she could have your jersey,' and I gave it to him! I always regretted that. It was so emotional that I just gave away my jersey without even thinking about it."

Back in in the stands, the FIGIans had no intentions of going anywhere. "After the game ended, it seemed like none of the Penn State fans wanted to leave," Mike Bellaman said. "I can't remember how long that was, but when we finally exited the building, we joined up with this huge throng of Penn State people and walked back down to Bourbon Street. Everybody talked non-stop about the game, all the great plays. We knew a lot of the players personally, and to us these were just our buddies who had finished playing on this world stage performing incredibly well under a lot of pressure. It was an experience I'll never forget."

Todd's Take

Curt, Gregg, and I are all doing interviews in the press room after Joe gets done. After we finish we're all just savoring the moment, a truly unbelievable feeling. We were the last ones to get our uniforms off. We grabbed a shower then went outside only to find that all the buses are gone! I have this MVP trophy, and we have no ride back to the hotel so we all just start walking. After a few minutes this van with two guys and two kids in it pulls up. They asked us if we needed a ride, so we just jumped in. Turned out they were just college football fans that came in from out of town to go to the game. I think they knew who we were, but I wasn't exactly sure. They do get us back to the hotel now jammed with Penn State fans all having the time of their lives…So fast forward to late 1998, and I remember this because it was the very first year of the BCS playoff with Tennessee playing Florida State in Tempe and I am working for ABC. About two weeks before the game, I get this message delivered to me which said, 'You may not remember me, but back in 1983, my son and I gave you a ride back to the hotel after the Sugar Bowl. We are die-hard Tennessee fans. Is there any way you can get us tickets to the game?' I was eventually able to get them four tickets to that national championship game and actually met them right before the broadcast."

12:45 am EST Sunday, January 2nd

Joe and Sue Paterno entertained players, their family members, and other well-wishers on the polished hardwood floors of suite 2737 of the New Orleans Hilton. Downstairs the celebration was in full swing. "There was a huge reception in a big ballroom just off the lobby in the hotel," Ken Kelley said. "I actually walked in holding the championship trophy. My parents were there, my little brothers, my whole family. It was packed. Later, we went back up to our suite to find beer and champagne on ice, and no one to help drink it. We had to scramble to invite people back to our rooms to drink that stuff. We were trying to round up people after the game to 'hydrate.'"

The three stars, who had to do all the interviews after the game, arrived to find it difficult to even get to the festivities. "We actually couldn't get into the hotel," Gregg Garrity said. "We saw some hotel employee with a walkie-talkie, and said, 'Hey, can you help us get upstairs?' We went up the service elevator to get up to the party. I finally found my dad and he says, 'Where the hell have you been?'"

Having had to hitchhike to the hotel with Gregg, Todd Blackledge was in the same predicament. But it was worth the wait. "I remember going to the party in the giant ballroom. It was really cool—food, wine, beer, a giant No. 1 ice sculpture on the main table," he said. "My junior high school coach Harry Johnson was there. He was beaming like it was the greatest moment of his life."

Mark Robinson recalls walking into the ballroom with Joe Hines and Dave Paffenroth. "There were so many people that wanted to congratulate us," Mark said. "You couldn't quite grasp what had happened. They had bottles of champagne stacked up in a pyramid. Paff took one look at that and said, 'Whoa, this could get ugly.'"

Back in the French Quarter, the FIGIans found the overflow crowd to be anything but bipartisan. "Bourbon Street was absolutely jammed," Mike Bellaman said, "but not one red shirt...anywhere. There were Georgia fans all over the place before the game but nowhere to be found afterward. It was bizarre—almost as if their fans went home right after the game ended. It was pretty tough to even get inside a bar to get a drink. Penn Staters were everywhere, like we had taken over the town."

1:30 PM EST Sunday, January 2nd

Pete Speros was packing up his belongings in a suite littered with half-empty bottles when he heard a commotion in the adjacent room. "I turn the corner, and Dave Paffenroth is in the process of placing a large suitcase on a nearby sofa and begins to open it," Speros said. "It's empty so I say, 'Hey, Paff, what are you up to?' Without missing a beat, Mad Paff responds, 'I'm filling up this bad boy with as much booze as I can haul back to State College.' I just shook my head and laughed."

Adult beverages were also the subject of a small wager between Dave

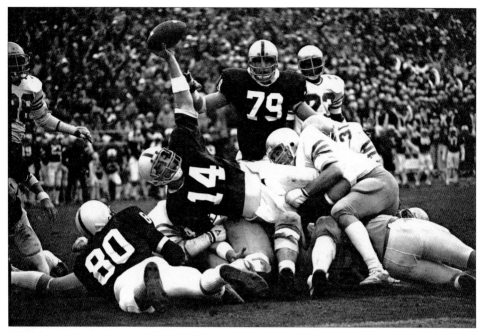

With less than three minutes left in the game, quarterback Todd Blackledge scores from a yard out for the game-winning touchdown against Notre Dame on November 21, 1981. Tight end Ron Heller (80) enjoys a close-up view of the play. (AP Images)

Curt Warner rushes through the Pitt defense during our 1981 upset against our in-state rival, which was ranked No. 1 in the county. (USA TODAY Sports Images)

After catching a touchdown pass from Todd Blackledge during the second quarter of our Fiesta Bowl victory against USC, wide receiver Gregg Garrity (19) jumps into the arms of Mike Meade. Garrity had a great game despite his mechanical bull mishap at a bar earlier in the week. (AP Images)

Our leader, quarterback Todd Blackledge, guided us on the field and was the Big Man on Campus off of it. (USA TODAY Sports Images)

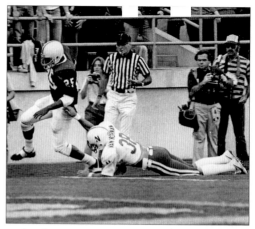

Nebraska's Kris Van Norman tries to bring down Penn State back Curt Warner, who steps out of bounds just before crossing the goal line in the first half. He would go on to score on the next play. (AP Images)

Penn State linebacker Dave "Mad Paff" Paffenroth levels star Nebraska running back Mike Rozier during our win against the No. 2 team in the nation on September 25, 1982. (AP Images)

Todd Blackledge was under seige all day during our 42–21 road loss to Alabama. It was our lone blemish of the season. (USA TODAY Sports)

Part of a stout defensive effort that limited the explosive Pitt offense to one touchdown, Penn State linebacker Ken Kelley hits quarterback Dan Marino in the second half of our pivotal November 26, 1982, victory with Greg Gattuso in close pursuit. (AP Images)

Penn State coach Joseph Vincent Paterno jokingly offers some shrimp to Georgia coach Vincent Joseph Dooley prior to our epic bowl matchup in the Bayou. (AP Images)

Georgia running back Herschel Walker, who received most of the national attention, parties at a Mardi Gras celebration attended by both teams before the Sugar Bowl. (AP Images)

Our terrific defense bottled up Heisman Trophy-winning back Herschel Walker, limiting him to just 28 rushing yards in the second half of the Sugar Bowl. (USA TODAY Sports Images)

Joe Paterno, Dick Anderson, and Fran Ganter discuss options with Todd Blackledge during our final timeout in the Sugar Bowl. (USA TODAY Sports Images)

Georgia defensive back Terry Hoage tries to chase down Curt Warner, who rushed for 117 yards and two touchdowns, in the Sugar Bowl. (AP Images)

Gregg Garrity records "the Catch," a 47-yard touchdown reception in the fourth quarter of the Sugar Bowl to put the game out of reach. (AP Images)

Todd Blackledge, Mark Battaglia, me, and Kirk Bowman celebrate our 27–23 victory against Georgia, which would earn us the No. 1 ranking. (USA TODAY Sports Images)

Opfar and Greg Gattuso. "Oaf and I were tied with the number of tackles going into the Georgia game, and we had a little wager going as far as who would finish the season with more," Gattuso said. "I won the bet, so the next morning, he shows up at my hotel room with a case of beer, which I have to believe he 'borrowed' from the captains' suites. I took it back home on the plane with me. By the time we got to the locker room around midnight, I think there was three bottles left. Can you imagine taking a case of beer with you on a plane these days?"

Seven hours earlier the massive postgame party on Bourbon had finally wound down, and the FIGIans reassembled at the designated bar to begin their long trek north. "We all managed to meet back at the rallying point, then piled into our rented station wagon," Mike Bellaman said. "We rotated drivers every two and three hours pretty much the whole way back to campus. We almost made it but got pulled over for speeding outside State College around five in the morning. Can you imagine? We drive for over 43-plus hours and get stopped less than an hour from our final destination. Go figure."

8:45 PM EST Sunday, January 2nd

There is no way to quantify the number of Penn State fans who braved a raw, cold night to greet us after we touched down in Harrisburg, Pennsylvania, and during the journey our multi-bus entourage made up Route 322 to State College. It is a safe bet that more than a few were adjusting to the reality that well-paying jobs in the declining steel industry were gone and their futures were very much up in the air. This night afforded them one more chance to celebrate an especially sweet and long-overdue moment, to savor a victory that left little doubt as to who would be voted No. 1 the following day. The celebration reaffirmed a togetherness and a communal connection with the university.

It seemed that people from every small town along the highway from the Harrisburg airport to State College turned out just to wave at our buses as they went trundling by. "I sat right next to Dick Maginnis, and we were both just amazed as there were people everywhere, leaning out of their cars, honking their horns," Ron Heller said. "At one point Dick leans over and says, 'You know, Ron, we will never forget this for the rest of our lives. Look what this meant to all of these people. This just isn't about us. There were a lot of people who really aligned with and believed in Paterno's Grand Experiment.' And he was right."

Pete Speros also sensed how special the experience was. "I had a window seat, and it was one of the most incredible scenes that I will never forget," he said. "I get chills even thinking about it. You weren't human if that didn't have an impact on you. The bus I was on was very quiet and it seemed like the guys were just taking it all in. These people have been waiting for this for so long. I tied it back to what we spoke about during that players-only meeting on the Superdome floor. We really had no idea how many people truly wanted to be a part of this."

Tim Bream enjoyed the parade from a different vantage point. "Kirk Bowman had parked his 1975 lime green Vega at the airport. When we landed we drove it back to State College between the sixth and seventh buses," he said. "One advantage we had versus the guys riding in the buses was that we could roll our windows down and wave at people as we drove past them. There was literally no gap the whole way from Harrisburg—just a non-stop gauntlet of well-wishers."

Chet Fuhrman is a Pennsylvania native and summed up the prevailing mind-set of the people who stood outside to cheer on the passing motorcade. "Being from [Harrisburg] that loss to Alabama in '79 was still on a lot of people's minds. The win over Georgia made a very bitter pill a lot easier to swallow."

11:45 PM EST Sunday, January 2nd

Given the time of day, I was also pretty blown away at the number of people who braved bitterly cold weather to greet us in State College. Prior to arriving at our final destination (the Indoor Sports Complex near our locker room), we stopped at the Hills Plaza out on Route 322 to an overflow parking lot full of well-wishers. I remember this vividly because my future brother-in-law, who had graduated the prior year and was interning with the local police department, emerged from the crowd and banged on the window I was peering out of and shouted, "We're No. 1!" It scared the hell out of me, to be honest. To this day I don't know how he managed to spot the bus I was on and barge his way through the giant crowd to pound on my window.

We finally got back to the Indoor Sports Complex around midnight and were greeted by another overflow crowd (including several standing on the roof of the locker room) that had patiently awaited our arrival in the freezing temperatures.

6:00 AM EST Monday, January 3rd

A private jet transported Joe Paterno, Todd Blackledge, and Curt Warner to New York for an appearance on ABC's *Good Morning America* with David Hartman. "It was a whole different feel to Joe that day," Blackledge told Frank Fitzpatrick in *Pride of the Lions*. "It was more personal, friendly, and relaxed. I think Curt and I both got to see a side of him we had never seen before." The traveling party had returned to campus by mid-afternoon.

4:00 PM EST Monday, January 3rd

Winter semester had resumed, and, as a senior whose eligibility had expired, I can tell you that classroom attendance that week wasn't a real high priority. Governor Dick Thornburgh had declared it "Penn State National Championship Week" in Pennsylvania, which I loosely interpreted as "classes optional."

More than 15,000 students and townspeople, a fair number waving oversized Styrofoam index fingers, jammed onto Old Main lawn for a raucous pep rally. Earlier in the day, we had officially been voted national champions. With an enormous "We Are Number 1" white banner hanging between two giant pillars behind him, Fran Fisher served as the event's emcee as Joe

Paterno, athletic director Jim Tarman, and school president Dr. John Oswald spoke as well as various players.

Mark Robinson likened it to a game-day atmosphere. "I recall walking to the pep rally and when I arrived there were so many people it was literally like a football game," he said. "It was pretty hard to navigate your way up to the podium because so many people were stopping you to say 'great game' or shake your hand."

During his turn at the podium, Gregg Garrity extended an invitation to all in attendance to come celebrate at his Phi Gamma Delta (FIGI) fraternity. "We get back there, and FIGI's house president Dan Haffner asks, 'What the hell did you say at that pep rally? I just got a call from the owner of W.R. Hickey who said he heard on the radio we were having a party and asked if we wanted to place your usual 20 keg order?'" Garrity said. "There was a long-ass line out the door. We typically had social gatherings on Wednesdays, Fridays, and Saturdays, so a gig on a Monday was a bit unusual."

Kegs were emptied almost as fast as they were tapped. The impromptu Monday afternoon gathering lasted long into the night.

1:30 PM EST Saturday, January 15th

Folks in Centre County awakened to find a foot of snow that had fallen overnight. Nonetheless, more than 4,000 fans lined a freshly plowed College Avenue for a celebration that was part of Love Ya Lions Day. Joe and Sue Paterno led the procession in an open convertible followed by players standing on a slow moving flatbed. "Anheuser-Busch Clydesdales led a parade that started down by University Drive and up College Avenue," Gregg Garrity said. "It was a lot of fun but very cold. They gave us mini-footballs to toss to the crowd. We did so, and then the well-wishers on the street and students on the sidewalks began pelting us with snowballs. We couldn't go anywhere! It was like shooting fish in a barrel."

"It was still snowing a little from the night before, and people thought we were throwing snowballs," Mark Robinson said. "In hindsight, someone should have given us different colored footballs. We were open targets on a flatbed, just getting pelted with snowballs, but we had a lot of fun with it."

CHAPTER 11

The Secrets to Our Success

several factors played crucial roles to our 1982 success. We got incredibly consistent efforts from guys experiencing their first real taste of extended playing time or at new positions.

Mike Battaglia stepped in for the graduated Jim Romano at center and played so well that by the end of the season Joe Paterno was referring to him as "one of the best centers he ever had at Penn State." That is saying something, considering guys like the late Bill Lenkaitis, Tom Rafferty, Chuck Correal, Jim Romano, and others who had previously played the position.

Ron Heller was a reserve tight end prior to finally shifting to tackle in August. Despite playing the short tackle position (a running joke considering Heller was 6'6") for less than a month, he gave up very few sacks, and that is even more impressive because he rarely had a tight end line up next to him.

Ken Kelley commanded enough respect from his teammates to be named co-captain despite only a handful of collegiate starts. Ken helped set the tone for a relatively inexperienced defense that shut out two of our final seven opponents while holding both Notre Dame and Pitt to a single offensive touchdown.

Senior Dan Biondi and junior Greg Gattuso would emerge as full-time defensive starters while Scott Radecic, Dave Paffenroth, Al Harris, and Steve Sefter were all first-year starters at linebacker and defensive end. By November they were playing like seasoned veterans. Joe would later claim his decision to shuffle his defensive personnel by inserting Sefter into the lineup before the Syracuse game was "a hunch that turned out to be one of the best moves I've made in a long time."

Mike Zordich, Todd Moules, and Rogers Alexander were good enough to play as true freshmen enabling Joe to redshirt guys like Shane Conlan and Bob White. Zordich had nine tackles against Syracuse, eight against West Virginia, and six against Boston College.

John Bove summed up the improvement on defense best. "It may have been a case of the new faces in new places finally settling in," he said. "The more you play, the better you get at really learning the position."

Zordich attributes much of his success to the guidance he received from the upperclassmen. "I can't say enough about the leadership from the '82 seniors," he said. "It was a true learning experience for me to see how they handled things. That may have been part of the torch that was passed to the 1985 and 1986 teams. We had great leadership and togetherness in 1982. You couldn't just see it; you could *sense* it. To win a championship, you have to have a bond. We did things together, went to parties together. Team success hinges on leadership more than camaraderie. You go through the ups and downs of a season and you gotta trust that the guy next to you is gonna get his job done."

Al Harris cited a lack of hubris as a key factor. "There really were no egos on the '82 team despite a lot of great players," he said. "Joe stressed we should accept winning graciously, and the coaches all did a great job of keeping us grounded. We approached the Sugar Bowl almost like every other game. No chest pounding or rah-rah stuff, just business as usual. There was so much confidence and such mutual respect in that locker room, the type of respect that was a given. It was an intense, talented group who knew their capabilities. Guys were given flexibility to flourish, to be themselves. They earned that right by being a PSU football player."

Tom Bradley felt past experience was a critical element. "One reason the

'82 team had a great year was the fifth-year seniors understood what playing in a title game was all about since they were freshmen for the '79 Sugar Bowl against Alabama," the coach said. "They knew what to expect, what to prepare for, and how to prepare for it."

Tim Bream recalls a distinct closeness among 1982 team members. "Every Thursday night guys were out together at FIGI, Phi Delta Theta, socializing as a group as opposed to just getting shit-faced drunk," he said. "It was pretty amazing camaraderie coupled with leadership and maturity— all critical factors to that team's success. Just look at what the guys still do for each other. Scott Carraher passed away in 2015, and they hold a memorial golf tournament to raise money for his family. I was amazed at how many guys showed up. The '82 success was all about the relationships between the players. I think we won it because of those relationships from the seniors all the way down to freshmen. A lot of those bonds formed 35 years ago still exist today."

Indeed, being a Penn State football player means something more than wins and losses. Joe Paterno made that poignantly clear in his final team meeting of his last season. Jay Paterno documents some of the comments his father made in his book *Paterno Legacy*. "You know there were a lot of guys who played here before you," Joe told his team. "They always played hard and they always played the way we want Penn State to play. They made sacrifices to make this place something special. But what I want to know is this: you share something with all the guys that played here before you. No matter what happens we will always—all of us—we will always be teammates."

Joe's words hold true to this day. Here is one example: Tom Ricketts is a former All-American offensive lineman at Pitt, a first-round NFL draft pick and a friend of mine. I usually see Tom a few times each year at charity golf outings. I ran into him in May of 2016 at Beaver Valley Golf Club at an annual golf tournament hosted by former New York Jet and Robert Morris head coach Joe Walton. Tom approaches me while I am having a conversation with longtime NFL assistant coach and former Nittany Lions player Dan "Bad Rad" Radakovich. As the three of us talk, Radakovich introduces us to Ralph Baker (PSU Class of '64) and later to Lance Mehl (PSU Class of

'79). I had known Lance for several years but had never met Ralph. However, we all proceed to have an extended conversation with Rad regarding proper linebacking technique, the league, and an assortment of other football topics. Later, as Tom and I walk toward our golf carts, he said, "I can't understand how you Penn State guys all seem to be friends. It's like one giant fraternity. Frankly, it's pretty amazing."

Ricketts' observation regarding this encounter was spot on. Over time, I have found the fraternity of former Penn State players is cross-generational. My relationships with John Skorupan (PSU Class of '73) and Brian Gelzheiser (PSU Class of '95) are two more examples. Both hail from western Pennsylvania, played the exact same position, and captained unbeaten Penn State teams 20 years apart. Whenever I speak with them about their college experiences, I find it fascinating to hear how similar they are.

The common bond most former Nittany Lion players share is Joe's Grand Experiment, which meant competing at the highest level without compromising your principles and winning with players who would work hard, graduate on time, respect tradition, and would not embarrass the university. I have to believe the same life lessons Joe preached to Mike Reid and Jack Ham were also stressed to LaVar Arrington, Sean Lee and Paul Posluszny. My personal experiences in getting to know players from different eras reaffirms the notion that most chose to go to Penn State because of how former players conducted themselves both on and off the field while respecting what it was they represented. "That fraternity thing is very real," said Dick Anderson, who played at Penn State for Rip Engle and coached under Joe in five different decades. "It is unique and exists because of the tenure of the coaches and the stability of the staff. The longevity of the coaches creates an atmosphere where once players leave they feel very comfortable returning because they know the coaches. Players from different generations get to know and relate to one another because they were pretty much all coached the same way. They transcend one another. It is a very precious thing Penn State has."

There were other keys to our success in 1982. We had great offensive balance. The offense scored 43 touchdowns to establish a new single season record; 21 came on the ground, and 22 came through the air. Though we were the first team in college football to win a national championship with more yards passing than rushing, re-establishing a Penn State-style running game after the Alabama loss was essential to attaining true balance on offense. "We were a very difficult offense to defend by the time we played the Sugar Bowl," Todd Blackledge said. "Defenses had to respect our ability to run the ball because Curt was as good as anyone in the country. We had speed on the outside, a big tight end who could catch and could run. You had to pick your poison."

To go along with a dynamic offense, our defense really improved. Challenged with replacing six starters, that unit found ways to slow down several high-octane offenses in the second half of the season. It held opponents to 10 points per game during our final seven contests despite playing three ranked opponents (West Virginia, Notre Dame, and Georgia) away from Beaver Stadium. We were one of only three teams to hold Nebraska under 25 points, pitching a shutout until 1:15 remained in the first half of the 27–24 contest. Nebraska ended up leading the country in scoring, averaging 39.5 points a game. After the Alabama loss, our revitalized defense allowed only three rushing touchdowns over the final six regular season games while tossing two shutouts. Three of these six games were against opponents ranked in the AP top 15.

Our special teams was solid, too, after enduring some initial struggles. Joe began the season with true freshman Massimo Manca handling all placekicking duties. When Manca missed three field goals and an extra point against Nebraska, he turned to sophomore Nick Gancitano, who converted 11-of-14 field goals, including two in the Sugar Bowl. Nick was a perfect 23-for-23 on extra points. Ralph Giacomarro continued to be an extremely reliable punter and left campus owning several records. He went on to punt for the Atlanta Falcons from 1983 to 1985.

Perhaps most important and fortunate was our overall health. No starter suffered a major injury causing them to miss extended playing time or multiple games. Curt Warner (hamstring), Mark Robinson (ankle), Harry Hamilton (knee), and Dick Maginnis (hamstring) were all dinged up, but the lineup Joe elected to start the season against Temple was virtually the same that battled Georgia. The health of the team helped develop cohesion on the offensive line and enable a relatively young defense to mature.

Finally, the schedule, in particular the first four games of the season, was a bigger factor than most people realize. With several first-year starters and new faces in new places, the weakest part of what was a brutal schedule enabled a fairly young group to gain valuable experience. We had the luxury of spending the first month of the season at home, playing three unranked opponents prior to the gauntlet of a schedule that started with Nebraska.

As a result, one year removed from scoring touchdowns against Southern Cal, Gregg Garrity and Warner would deliver encore performances against Georgia. Curt rushed for two touchdowns against the Bulldogs while Gregg hauled in another long scoring pass ("the Catch") from Blackledge. That victory against Georgia marked the first time a Paterno-coached team won in New Orleans, having lost in all three previous attempts.

Though Penn State has not appeared in the Sugar Bowl since its win over the Bulldogs, our Sugar Bowl win paved the way for the future. Several freshmen who arrived on campus in 1982 were on the field for Penn State's win over Miami in the 1987 Fiesta Bowl, which resulted in the school's second officially recognized national championship. Fifteen players were part of *three* different Penn State teams that competed in national championship games (against Georgia in 1983, against Oklahoma in 1986, and against Miami in 1987) and own *two* national championship rings. The players are: the late John Bruno, Drew Bycoskie, David Clark, Duffy Cobbs, Chris Collins, Darrell Giles, Don Graham, Eric Hamilton, Sid Lewis, Dan Morgan, Keith Radecic, Brian Siverling, Steve Smith, Bob White, Conlan, and Manca.

Walk-Ons Who Walked Off With a Ring

Gregg Garrity's unlikely path from walk-on to cult hero has been previously chronicled. Two other former walk-ons, Dan Biondi and Brian McCann, made it abundantly clear how special it was for them to be part of the team. Both seemed to recall things even more vividly than the other former teammates I interviewed—as if their experiences meant just a little bit more to them because of the how they came to be part of this unique cast of characters.

Joe Paterno had been around long enough to recognize athletic ability when he saw it, so he would invite players to join his squad as walk-ons under the premise they would be offered scholarships if they were able to make an impact on the team.

Unlike some of the more recognizable, big-name recruits like Curt Warner, Todd Blackledge, and Mike McCloskey, Biondi arrived on campus without much fanfare. Despite starting at tailback on Penn Hills' WPIAL championship football teams in both his junior and senior seasons, Biondi flew under the national recruiting radar. He received very few scholarship offers as most college scouts from Division I schools considered him under-sized despite impressive scholastic credentials in multiple sports. "I started as a sophomore and junior at Penn Hills but hurt my ankle early my senior year," Biondi said. "I played through it, but it did bother me. When you are a smaller person, you have to rely on my speed and quickness so an injury like that is a little more noticeable."

Biondi received scholarship offers from William & Mary and Idaho, while also considering Dartmouth. The success his older brother, Lou, experienced in his first season at South Carolina, despite being dubbed as too small, convinced Dan he shouldn't settle for less when it came to the next level. "One day my brother called the Penn State coaches' office and asks to speak directly to Joe," Dan said. "To our surprise the secretary put the call right through. Lou proceeded to explain to Joe, 'Hey, my younger brother plays at Penn Hills. He's a good player, and you ought to take a close look at him.' Joe responded by saying, 'We are aware of him, but we don't have any scholarships. We are only gonna take two walk-ons, but we'll be down to talk to him.'"

The news on available scholarships didn't discourage Biondi, who concluded that if he was to play football at the next level, it would be at a place where he would get to enjoy the experience. "I was looking for a great education and to play great football," Biondi said. "Penn State was the only place where I would have wanted to walk on. I dreamed of going there since I was

12 years old. I watched them on TV and read about them in the newspapers. It was an opportunity to realize a dream. It meant a lot to me for Joe Paterno to pick up my brother's random phone call."

After walking on at Penn State, an early message Paterno delivered to the incoming freshmen about priorities resonated with Biondi. "We came in a few days before the upperclassmen showed up, and I remember one of the very first talks Joe gave us," Biondi said. "Joe explained that, 'Less than 2 percent of you will go on to play at the next level. You are not here to get a shot to play pro ball. You are here to get a good education. Your priorities should be God, family, education, and football in that order. If something gets in the way of that, I am gonna have a problem with you.'"

The same freshman who made an impression on fellow walk-on Garrity also played a role in determining Biondi's ultimate fate on the football field. "During the very first practice with the other freshmen, they asked what position I played," Biondi said. "I told them, 'Running back on offense and cornerback on defense.' Shortly after that the very first guy I see is Curt Warner and [I] quickly realized I was never gonna play running back here. I got moved to defensive back in the second practice and stayed there for the rest of my four years. I realized I could play there right away and within a few weeks I was the fifth [defensive back]. We were a little thin in the secondary so I kept getting looks. I actually did okay. I played quite a bit against West Virginia my freshman year. When guys found out I was a walk-on, they were a little surprised given how well I was doing. I was treated the same as everyone else."

Input from his older sibling proved to be a key factor in the smoother-than-expected transition. "Lou gave me a lot of great insight helping me understand what to expect in college," Biondi said. "We worked out very hard together in the summer. I always felt very prepared physically, but the mental discipline was really the key. As a walk-on you have to recognize that you may only get one chance and that you will be tested. You also have to realize that making mental mistakes will really limit your chances at playing. You have to expect to get moved up and down the depth chart, too. You may think you are doing well, and they will move you. You gotta keep your head."

Pound for pound, Biondi was arguably the toughest kid in that 1979 recruiting class. He ended up with the rare distinction of becoming one of few walk-ons to earn four letters over a four-year span in Penn State's rich football history.

In contrast to the path Garrity and Biondi followed to Penn State, McCann was already two years removed from his high school graduation. Having just finished his second season playing wide receiver at West Chester University, he arrived at a rather blunt conclusion:

"I realized I was going nowhere fast," he said. "Growing up I had always loved watching those black and white Penn State re-runs on Sunday mornings where I grew up outside Philly in Delaware County, so I decided to transfer to Penn State in February of 1981."

His motives transferring to Penn State weren't exactly football-related. "Truth be told, I chased a girl who was taking classes there," McCann confessed. "I told all my West Chester teammates I planned to try out for this team and was gonna make it. They all said I was out of my mind."

Shortly after McCann arrived on campus, he asked around the football office and found out that John Bove was the recruiting coordinator. "Coach Bove had an office in Rec Hall," McCann said. "I went over there and sat down with him to ask about walking on and he responded with, 'What makes you qualified?' I told him, 'Well I was a high school All-American,' and he fires back with, 'Brian, we have a roster full of high school All-Americans.'"

McCann was determined to prove what he could do. "I was one of seven kids in my family, the third youngest and the first to go to college," McCann said. "My goal was to get a scholarship because it would help with some of the bills. My folks didn't have the money for me to go to college, so it was pretty much a, 'Hey, you're on your own' situation."

His official invitation to join the team didn't happen without being attentive and some prodding. "That year both Coach Bove and Scrap Bradley were charged with evaluating the walk-ons. A lot of kids tried out, about 80 candidates or so," McCann said. "They were going through final cuts after a winter workout, and I was tossing the ball around with [backup quarterback Dan] Lonergan. I said, 'Hold on, I didn't hear my name called,' so I went up to Scrap and said, 'Hey, I didn't hear you call my name.' He says, 'What's your name again?' Which wasn't exactly the vote of confidence I was hoping to hear. I said, 'McCann,' and he replies, 'Oh, yeah, you made it.' Had I not asked why my name wasn't called, I don't think I would have played on the team. It's a life lesson I teach my kids to this day. If you really believe in something, if you really feel like you belong, then you have at least earned the right to ask the question."

McCann's first few weeks in uniform proved both painful and productive. "I had an awesome spring. I enjoyed playing on the scout team, but I got the crap beat out of me. Walk-ons are granted no favors; you can't get up after a play and argue with somebody, you gotta keep your head. It's a different kind of discipline, a different kind of pressure, but it helped me better understand the Penn State Way in that you can't make mistakes, and you have to maintain your poise. I knew if I did well on the scout team I could raise a few eyebrows. Some guys on the scout team would pass up their turns in drills. I was just the opposite. I would always take as many reps as possible. After a few weeks there, I convinced myself, *Hey, I can do this at this level.*"

Notification of a position change soon came directly from the program's highest ranking officer. "One day we were walking over to the stadium for one of those marathon scrimmages, and Paterno comes up from behind me and grabs me by the shoulder pads. I thought it was Lonergan. Joe had never talked to me before and he says, 'Brian, I have good news and bad news. You've done a bang-up job on the scout team; we think you can do a better job on defense. The bad news is you're never gonna play receiver here. The good news is we're gonna move you to Hero. Do you wanna do that?' The following fall, I was running off and on with the [second-team] defense. I had heard guys on both the first and second-teams on the depth chart got scholarships, so one day at practice I pulled Joe aside and asked, 'Hey, Coach, is there any scholarship money available?' He says, 'I'll check into it.'"

A phone call home on the eve of the season opener would include surprisingly exciting news. "A few weeks later at the hotel at Milesburg, I am on the pay phone in the lobby right before curfew talking to my mom Friday night before the Temple game telling her, 'Hey, I may play a little this season.' Paterno walks up to me and asks, 'Who are you on the phone with?' I said, 'Sorry, Coach, it's my parents. I'll be done in a minute.' He says, 'Well, tell your folks I said hello and that you got a scholarship.' Just like that. He walks away, and I'm crying, my mom is crying, my dad is crying, we're all crying— just all so excited about that. Walking out onto Beaver Stadium before that Temple game the following day as a scholarship player was *the* coolest feeling in the world. Some guys may have had butterflies, but I was rarin' to go. It was just an incredible feeling. There was no way I could ever imagine I would be playing for the national title four months later."

Game action along with an epiphany of exactly where he was soon followed. "I made my first tackle a few games later against Rutgers. Another walk-on Rocky Washington and I got to the ballcarrier at the same time, slammed him to the ground, got up, and hugged each other. Later on Harry Hamilton got hurt, and I played a little defense. Let 'em tell you, it is a big difference being in the defensive huddle versus just being on the field for a single special teams play. I was really nervous and remember saying to myself, *Wait a minute here, I'm on the field now. This is Penn State. This is the real deal.* Just absolutely awesome."

A few weeks later a fifth-year senior also made a lasting impression on McCann. "Joel Coles' post-Alabama speech was amazing. I was really taken back with how emotional he got, how badly he wanted it. The energy he generated was literally going through you. [During his] 'We can still do this' message, that room was dead silent. Everyone was listening."

McCann's attempt to similarly inspire the troops during the Sugar Bowl almost backfired. "So we go into the Superdome locker room at halftime and we're up by 10 points. It's my senior year, I never spoke up at any game, so I figured, What the heck? I'm gonna try and get everybody fired up so I yell out, 'Hey, guys, we got this, we can see the light at the end of the tunnel.' No sooner I said that, and Joe goes, 'Who said that? There's no light at the end of the tunnel! We gotta work hard in the second half to win this thing!' I just looked around and acted like it wasn't me. I look over at Lonergan, and he was just shaking his head, smiling. I call it 'my Sugar Bowl halftime blunder.' I'm the only one scarred by it, and it haunts me to this day. I did help carry Joe off the field though."

Transportation options to these big games were a step up in class, though he nearly missed the trip to that Sugar Bowl. "I recall thinking two years earlier I am riding on a bus to go play Army and now here I am flying on planes to go play up at Boston College and out to South Bend to play Notre Dame. It was like night and day. All the hard work I put in to get to that point—that alone made it worth it. Just a tremendous feeling to be there, to be part of all of it.

"I almost didn't make it to the Sugar Bowl. The morning after Christmas, my dad was gonna drive me to the Harrisburg airport. Halfway there we got a flat tire. There were no cell phones at the time, so there was no way I could call and tell anyone. I was pretty sure I was the last guy on the plane, and as I tried to sneak by Joe, he says, 'Ya gotta be on time.'"

Despite intermittent playing time at the Hero positon behind Hamilton in 1982, McCann finished tied for third on the team in interceptions and 15th on the team in tackles and ahead of guys like Joe Hines and our special teams captain, the late Dr. Stuart McMunn.

The unlikeliest walk-on who was part of the '82 team never even played high school football. According to strength coach Chet Fuhrman, one of the most amazing walk-on stories ever was that of Robert "Rocky" Washington. "The story goes that Rocky was watching the 1981 Pitt-Penn State game at his sister's house in Los Angeles and boasted, 'I am gonna walk on at whichever team wins this game.' Penn State prevails 48–14, and a few weeks later, Rocky shows up into the coaches' office and asks to meet coach Paterno," Fuhrman said. "The secretary explains to Rocky that Joe is out of town but then asks why he wants to see coach Paterno. Rocky responds, 'Because I want to walk on here.'"

It's understandable Rocky didn't play high school sports, considering he was 5'4" when he graduated from Beaver Falls High School in 1978. A growth spurt later that summer prior to enrolling at Penn State's satellite campus in

Beaver helped land him a spot on the basketball team there as a 6'0" freshman. The following spring he led the baseball team in home runs, RBIs, and stolen bases. He attracted the attention of the Cincinnati Reds, who signed him to their Class A affiliate in 1981. He later became roommates with future two-time National League All-Star outfielder Eric Davis. "I never actually believed he knew Davis until later on when I was the Steelers strength coach," Fuhrman said. "The Reds were in town playing the Pirates, and Rocky meets up with him in the Steeler weight room."

Gary Petercuskie was in charge of evaluating walk-ons in the spring of 1982. "Gary asked Rocky to run a 40-yard dash for us," Fuhrman said. "Rocky agreed so I help stretch him out and warm him up. Rocky runs a few striders and, when it comes to the point where I get ready to time him, he gets down into this sideways crouch at the starting line like he is getting ready to steal a base. I yelled, 'Hey, what kind of stance is that?' He says, 'Well, I was simulating stealing a base. I never played football, so nobody ever asked me to run a 40-yard dash.' So I work with him, demonstrating how to get in a sprinter's stance, and he runs a legit 4.4 [in the] 40. The problem was he comes out that spring weighing 165 pounds soaking wet. He later bulks up to 190 pounds of pure muscle. He was an amazing athlete. For a guy who never played football before, he worked very hard to become an outstanding special teams coverage guy."

Fast forward to one year after making the prophetic prediction to his sister. A Nick Gancitano field goal increased Penn State's lead to 13–7 with a little more than three minutes left in the third quarter. Keeping Dan Marino and his Pitt offense deep in their own end of the field while we had the wind was a key factor in three scoring drives during the period. On the ensuing kickoff, Rocky sprints down to cover the kick like a man possessed—five full yards clear of any other Penn State special teamer and he nails their returner with an unassisted tackle at the Pitt 10-yard line. *And this was a guy who never played football until he got to Penn State?* The crowd just absolutely exploded, and momentum was now clearly on our side. I always felt it was one of the turning points of the game. Two plays later and on third down, Foge Fazio pulled his offense off the field and sent his punting unit to quick kick the ball right back to us, which set up another field goal.

Unfortunately, he blew out his knee prior to the 1983 season. Rocky, though, later received his MBA and built a very successful career in medical sales. He was inducted into the Beaver County Hall of Fame in 2008 despite never having played any sport at the scholastic level.

CHAPTER 12

Rebuttals

Penn State won the 1982 national title despite facing an extremely difficult schedule. Consider five of our opponents.

Maryland went 8–4 with all four of their losses to ranked opponents by a total of 12 points. The Terrapins finished 20th in the AP poll. Nebraska recovered from the last-second loss in Beaver Stadium to win all of its remaining games and the Big Eight. The Cornhuskers squeaked by LSU 21–20 in the Orange Bowl to finish third in the final AP poll. West Virginia went 9–3, which included an upset 41–27 win at Oklahoma. All of its losses were to ranked opponents, including a narrow 16–13 loss at then No. 1 Pitt. It was the first time in school history the Mountaineers had won nine games in consecutive seasons. Boston College made its first bowl appearance in 40 years and finished 8–3–1. All non-wins were to Top 20 foes, including a tie against defending national champ Clemson. Pitt finished 9–3 with a narrow loss to SMU in the Cotton Bowl.

SMU and Nebraska fans still argue, some rather vehemently, that their teams were more deserving of the 1982 national title. To each fanbase I respectfully offer the following rebuttals.

SMU supporters must acknowledge that a ridiculously soft schedule coupled with an NCAA investigation looming over the program were two pivotal reasons why their Mustangs ended up a distant second in the polls after the 1982 season.

Although SMU did go undefeated, their schedule that year was pedestrian—at best. Three-point wins against mediocre Baylor and TCU squads coupled with wins against UTEP, Tulane, and North Texas did little to impress pollsters. Additionally, close calls in their final two conference games were cause for concern. A last-minute win in Lubbock against a 4–7 Texas Tech squad raised eyebrows as the winning points came on a lateraled kickoff return 17 seconds before the final gun sounded.

The following week against Arkansas in Texas Stadium, SMU trailed 17–10 late in the fourth quarter. A very questionable, 40-yard pass interference penalty (the on-air reaction from ABC's Keith Jackson is particularly telling) helped extend a drive the Mustangs eventually converted into the game-tying touchdown. The decision to kick the extra point instead of going for the outright win caused the game to end in a 17–17 stalemate.

The Mustangs accepted a bid to play in the 1983 Cotton Bowl at Fair Park Stadium in Dallas. Talk about a home game! SMU didn't even leave its home city, let alone the state. Furthermore, SMU called that stadium home from 1932 to 1978. Despite the home-field advantage, the Mustangs managed a meager seven points, just enough to beat a disinterested No. 6 Pitt team that twice lost the ball on turnovers at the SMU 10-yard line.

To an extent I can sympathize with SMU players and fans who argue their team got a raw deal and deserved a shot at the national title. They can get in line behind all the players from Joe Paterno's undefeated teams in 1968, 1969, 1973, and 1994. If SMU had produced more convincing wins against ranked opponents, this might be a different story, and it remains one extremely valid reason why not *one* single poll voted the Mustangs as the 1982 national champion.

Had we agreed to play SMU rather than Georgia, I ask all Mustang fans to consider these two questions. 1) Given that we found ways to shut down Marcus Allen in Tempe, Arizona, and hold Herschel Walker to one of the lowest rushing totals in his career in New Orleans, would it not stand to reason that we would have devised some scheme to slow down SMU's one-dimensional attack? 2) Even if the Pony Express generated sufficient yardage on the ground, could the SMU defense have found a way to slow down a Penn State offense that scored three touchdowns in both the '82 Fiesta Bowl and '83 Sugar Bowl?

Two Nittany Lions occasionally cross paths with Eric Dickerson and Craig James, the two most famous Mustangs from that SMU team. The topic of discussion is almost always the same. "I used to see Craig all the time when he was doing the TV side," said Mark Robinson, now the color analyst for South Florida football games. "He played in the USFL with my brother. Every time he sees me, he'd say, 'Hey, lemme see my national championship ring!' It was a running joke between us for the longest time."

When Curt Warner sees Dickerson, the conversation is always the same. "Eric still can't get over the fact that we won the title," Warner said. "He still thinks they could beat us. We've had several conversations over the years, and all have been friendly, but they always start with, 'There is no way you should have been the national champions.' It is the very first thing that he brings up when we see each other. It's been close to 35 years, and he still can't get over the fact that he doesn't have a ring! I tell Eric, 'Hey, we were the ones that held all the cards. We were an independent while you guys had to play in the Cotton Bowl. We had the choice as far as who we were gonna play and we were always gonna play the highest ranked team. We made sure people knew we were not about to back down from anybody.'"

SMU wasn't the only program to make a misguided argument. The general consensus among die-hard Nebraskans is that their program's patriarch, the distinguished Tom Osborne, was jobbed out of his first national title in 1982. Husker Nation continues to bemoan Mike McCloskey's controversial sideline catch in the final minute of our 1982 contest, citing homer officiating as the prime culprit. These detractors somehow forget that we generated 505 yards of total offense that day, had two touchdowns called back on penalties, missed three field goals as well as an extra point. In contrast, the vaunted Husker offense was shut out for all but the final minute of the first half.

Although the call on the McCloskey catch may have worked in our favor, the game should have never come down to the final drive. Nonetheless, the events that took place during that final drive have continued to impact some of the key participants. In some respects, they have taken on a life of their own. "Years later I am asked to attend a fundraiser for Father Flanagan's Boys Town, which is just west of Omaha," McCloskey said. "They invited me because Turner Gill was going to be the featured speaker. Right before the event, someone suggests to me, 'Hey, when you are up there with Turner, say something like, 'You know, after all these years, I just can't take it anymore. I gotta come clean. Here's my ring.' I do exactly that while they're showing the play on a projection screen to the whole audience. It was all in fun, and we had a good time with it. Later a reporter took our exchange completely the wrong way and wrote a 'McCloskey Admits Guilt' article. It became the headline in one of the local newspapers the next day. After that a bunch of wire services picked up on it, and I started getting phone calls from radio stations all asking me to comment on me finally admitting I was out of bounds. I said, 'Come on, we were just having fun. What difference does it make what I believe? The refs ruled me inbounds.' It's not like I blatantly cheated. There are close calls in every game, and all you ever hope for is that you get some of them to go your way. The only time I got upset was when someone implied that we cheated. We didn't cheat; we just played. We had nothing to do with the decision the ref made. If I was ruled out of bounds, we would have just run another play. It is remarkable how this one play has literally taken on a life of its own."

Three decades after McCloskey's banquet incident, Dick Anderson had a similar experience. "I traveled to Nebraska with current Arizona Cardinals center A.Q. Shipley, who had won the Rimington Award as the nation's best center. They hold the dinner in Lincoln, and during the presentation, I am asked to introduce him," Anderson said. "Now, I have always known Nebraska to have absolutely tremendous fans. They never ever boo and always show great respect for the opponent. I remember us being given a standing ovation coming off the field after that '81 game. So at the dinner, I said, 'At Penn State, we are meticulous in how we manicure our field, and there's this little out patch down near the 5-yard line...' I pause, don't finish the sentence, and people at the banquet immediately get up and started booing! We all laughed. I do give Nebraska fans their due. They are very comparable to our fans, very respectful."

Todd's Take

I caught a lot of grief while I was with the Kansas City Chiefs, then also years later during my first year back at ESPN, the network decided to pair me with Mike Patrick to work Saturday night games and flew me out to Omaha to meet with Mike since he was working the College World Series. We all went to some big tailgate at a local restaurant. I told my producer, "I am just gonna tell you this in advance—the first person that recognizes me or my name will bring up that Penn State-Nebraska game and McCloskey being out of bounds. Trust me. It's been happening to me my whole life." The producer said, "You're crazy. There's no way." Sure enough, one of the people in the very first group we meet is the mayor of Omaha. He introduces himself, shakes my hand, and the first thing he says is, "You know that guy was out of bounds on that play." Great fans for sure, but they don't forget *anything*.

Penn State graduate Pete Allen, now an executive vice president at Vizient medical sales company, found a unique way to re-enact the Kirk Bowman catch against Nebraska, something he witnessed firsthand at Beaver Stadium while selling Cokes there as a high school student.

Allen's company hosts a national industry conference every year, and as the emcee, he incorporates a sports-related theme into the event, something that has allowed him to play catch with Emmitt Smith, the NFL's all-time leading rusher, and shadow box with Sugar Ray Leonard.

The 2016 conference was held at the Bellagio in Las Vegas and featured Bob Costas. With the legendary broadcaster's blessing, Allen set out to recreate a famous sports scene. "I initially chose the home run Kirk Gibson hit to beat Oakland in the World Series," Allen said. "However, two days before the event, I decide against doing that. Being a die-hard Penn Stater, I suggest a different sports moment involving another Kirk—Kirk Bowman and his last-second catch against Nebraska. I convince others to do this since it's one of the most memorable games ever in Beaver Stadium but also because Bowman happens to work in my field and will actually be in the audience. Our production company scours the Internet and locates the footage, but at this point, very few people, including Bob Costas, knew we were gonna do this."

Costas was more than willing to go along with it—and play the role of the foil. "He watches the clip exactly once in the green room and calmly says, 'Okay, I got it.' Bob then goes onstage, captivates the audience with a 45-minute speech, then asks me to join him. Now this was a really cool moment for me, one of the highlights of my life. We chat for a minute or two, and just as he is about to conclude his comments, he says, 'Oh, wait, Pete, we have one more thing to do, don't we?'"

Did they ever. Costas and Allen proceeded to call one of the greatest finishes in Beaver Stadium history as clips from the game played on video monitors in the cavernous ballroom:

Costas: "It's Joe Paterno against Tom Osborne. Both coaches are seeking their first national titles. Pete had six siblings, all of whom went to Penn State. You've always wanted to be a sportscaster, right? Gill scores from a yard out. The Huskers pull ahead. Your heart sinks, doesn't it?"

Allen: "Just barely broke the plain, Bob. I can't believe it.'

Costas: "Blackledge now back to pass, looking for Mike McCloskey. It appears *both* of his feet are out of bounds."

Allen: "No, no, Bob, both of those were inbounds. There is no doubt, no doubt."

Costas: "An obvious hometown call. There's just nine seconds left."

Allen: "My God, they've just put in Kirk Bowman. I can't believe it! 'Stone Hands' Bowman has only one catch in his entire career. He's a converted defensive lineman!"

Costas: "Blackledge takes the snap, play-action, looks to the back of the end zone and hits...who?"

Allen: "Kirk Bowman! It's a touchdown! Penn State wins!"

Costas: "Shockingly, with his eight career collegiate receptions, he was not drafted in the NFL and had to find another career."

Allen: "He ended up working at Smith's Medical, which is almost as exciting as the NFL."

Costas: "Bowman's catch won one of the most dramatic games in Penn State history. So Pete tell me, what is the relevance of this footage other than it brings you great personal joy?"

Allen: "Not only did Penn State go on to win its first national championship later that year, but 'Stone Hands' Kirk Bowman, the hero of that game...is *in* the audience."

Indeed, he was. "I'm just sitting in the audience enjoying his presentation when Pete Allen joins Costas onstage," Bowman said. "My ears perk up when Costas says, 'Hey, Pete, let's have some fun and talk about the 1982 Nebraska game.' The next thing I know is Costas asking if I can join them onstage. So I get up there, and Pete asks Costas, 'Hey, would you like for Kirk to sign a ball for you?' Costas says, 'Yes, but be sure to include Stone Hands in italics.' Pete had two footballs onstage, so as I sign one, Costas grabs the other, and says, 'Now, we'll all see just how stone handed you are,' and tells me to go out into the audience for a pass."

Without hesitating Kirk complied with the directive. Thirty-four years removed from his last-second heroics, he proceeded to make a catch that may have rivaled his grab against Nebraska in terms of pressure and difficulty. "I step down off the stage and run the pass pattern, making sure to include a head fake for effect," Bowman said. "Costas throws me the ball, and I momentarily lost the flight of it in the stage lights but at the last second manage to see and catch it. I returned to the stage and handed him the ball back, and the crowd erupts."

Allen laughed as he remembered the scene. "Afterward a lot of folks told me they really enjoyed the human interest part while others thought it was so cool," he said. "Some came up to me to ask, 'Hey, did Bowman know you were gonna do that?' There were a lot of Penn State people in that audience who told their own stories about that game as well as a few Nebraska people who got in my face saying that not only was McCloskey out of bounds but Bowman trapped the ball. It really became the buzz of the rest of the conference. We held a private reception with Costas afterward and took lots of pictures. Right as he was leaving, Costas pauses, stops his entourage, and says, 'Wait a minute, I forgot my Bowman football. I have to go back to get it.' Really a magical little exchange we had a lot of fun with."

It's always fun to relive that triumphant 1982 season, which was about redemption, unfinished business, and closure. It enabled a resilient group to provide a marvelous encore to a highly successful 1981 campaign. A stirring comeback against Notre Dame and decisive wins over Pitt and USC to close the previous season helped fuel an underlying sense of unfinished business among the players who returned for what would prove to be a very special 1982 season. It involved people who went about their business with a quiet urgency to reach heights few thought attainable.

The season showcased a talented team that performed magnificently in high pressure situations and determined to live up to standards established by previous standout Penn State teams. That helped set the tone for continued success. Stars checked their ego at the door while veteran upperclassmen embraced a freshman class that would lead the Nittany Lions back to two more national championship games in 1985 and 1986. Players shared both a mutual respect for each other and the storied program they were part of.

That year turned out to be not as much about rebuilding as it was about reloading. Lesser experienced but still talented personnel proved remarkably resolute despite facing bowl-caliber opposition on a near-weekly basis. True believers were conditioned to stare right back at the abyss, accept challenges head on, and stand tall in the face of long odds. In some respects the run to the 1982 national championship began right after

Chet Parlavecchio's attempt to annihilate a Pitt wide receiver in the '81 Pitt game. It sent a subtle but direct message that there was a new breed of cat in Happy Valley. Despite spotting the Panthers 14 points on their home field, we systematically dismantled the No. 2 team in the country in that game's final 30 minutes and never looked back.

## CHAPTER 13

One of the Greatest

S
o Penn State played a few ranked opponents on the way to winning its first national title. What's the big deal? Didn't *every* national champion play a tough schedule? Well in general, yes; however, some traveled a more difficult path than others, and Penn State navigated a brutal schedule in 1982.

A discussion involving a comparison between great teams from past and present often results in a fierce debate. How would the 2016 champion, Clemson, match up to Nebraska's 1971 juggernaut or Miami's insanely talented 2001 squad? In addition there are few, if any, proven methods to compare teams bearing the same school colors but from different eras. For example, how would the Alabama squad that outdueled Clemson 45–40 in January 2015 match up against, say, Bear Bryant's undefeated 1979 squad or Gene Stallings' 1992 crew? With no universally accepted way to adequately address this issue, the inevitable "my team was great while your team sucks" argument will rage on indefinitely in sports bars or at tailgates across America.

Since winning the national championship represents college football's ultimate crown jewel, it should serve as the basis for identifying teams that seem to be a cut above others. In other words a team should, at the very least, have the necessary hardware in their trophy case to be included in this argument. Let's next agree that simply comparing these teams' won-loss records won't suffice since every national champion finished their season either undefeated or with one loss. Since the Internet affords us access to an almost unlimited amount of data on this topic, we likely have the resources necessary to perform the number-crunching needed for this exercise. A thorough review of a team's opponents and their ranking at the time the games were played (as well as where and when) are all practical things to consider when comparing teams from past and present.

With respect to the many great teams that have captured college football's coveted national title, we will limit our analysis to only those who won national titles since 1970. The year of 1970 is a solid starting point for several reasons. Pollsters finally began waiting until after the season was over to cast their final ballots, the sport's popularity increased dramatically around this time, and athletes started benefiting from more refined training and conditioning regimens as schools began expanding their athletic budgets.

Until the late 1960s, pollsters couldn't consistently make up their minds regarding *when* to vote, let alone for *whom* to vote. According to Bob Kirlin, a college football historian and the editor of the *College Football Researchers Association*, the Associated Press rankings began in 1936 and consisted of a poll of sportswriters and broadcasters nationwide. A coaches' poll, featuring voting from head coaches across the country, began in 1950. Both produced different champions. The coaches' poll did not recognize teams on probation while the AP did permit their inclusion. United Press International (UPI) poll began voting on college teams in 1950 but stopped doing so in 1995.

In 1965 the AP took its final poll after the bowl games for the first time and then dropped the practice for two years before resuming after the 1968 campaign. The first year in which the United Press International took its final poll after the bowl games was 1974. The coaches' poll that UPI had been publishing became the *USA TODAY*/CNN poll in 1991. And then in 1997, the coaches' poll became the *USA TODAY*/ESPN poll.

Another reason 1970 will be our starting point is the sport's popularity began to surge around this time. At the pro level, teams from the fledgling American Football League provided fans a more entertaining, wide-open brand of football in an era before cable TV or personal computers found their way into consumers' homes. This more exciting version combined with the violent and unpredictable nature of the sport meant it was only a matter of time before football would eventually overtake baseball as our national pastime.

A likely tipping point was the New York Jets' upset win against the heavily favored Baltimore Colts in Super Bowl III, a game broadcast to a nationwide audience in late January of 1969. This single sporting event ushered in a radical changing of the guard by delivering a brand new technicolor hero for the younger generation.

The NFL's poster child for 1950s assembly line efficiency was the aging, emotionless Johnny Unitas with his trademark crew-cut and black high-tops. "Johnny U'" and his superbly talented Colts typified the traditional old guard while the upstart Jets from the rogue AFL represented the new world order. Despite being 18-point favorites, the Colts were upstaged in prime time by a team quarterbacked by a brash, outspoken, white-shoe-wearing signal-caller from Beaver Falls, Pennsylvania, named Joe Namath.

This unlikeliest of outcomes gave the fledgling league instant credibility and helped pave the way for an eventual merger with the parent NFL. The game rekindled Americans' love affair with their underdogs. It also introduced them to a new breed of sports icon in the flamboyant Namath, who boldly predicted a Jets upset victory. This event also helped create a huge increase in female viewership due primarily to Namath's sex appeal, charm, and charisma.

The game's increased popularity prompted ABC to launch *Monday Night Football* in the fall of 1971, which helped pro football penetrate the work week. The network paired the controversial Howard Cosell with the likes of Frank Gifford, "Dandy" Don Meredith, O. J. Simpson, and Alex Karras to describe the play on the field. The ploy dispelled the myth that former jocks couldn't complete meaningful sentences.

Eight days after "Broadway Joe" orchestrated one of the biggest upsets in professional sports, Richard Milhous Nixon was inaugurated as our 37th president. Nixon, as it turned out, was a huge college football fan and regularly attended a number of games. His fellow Americans followed their commander-in-chief's lead, and attendance at college games climbed steadily.

The viewing public had grown increasingly weary of the networks' decision to air graphic footage of the battlefield carnage from Southeast Asia. College football provided an escape from the Vietnam War. Pageantry, clean-cut All-Americans, and amateur athleticism were more wholesome alternatives to the horrific military theater. It soon became must-see TV on Saturday afternoons.

The increased interest in college football prompted the expansion of both campus stadiums and athletic department budgets. Competition among the upper-tier schools for top talent became more fierce, and significantly more resources were needed to fill the seats. This increased investment in human capital began producing vastly superior, better-conditioned athletes who began devoting much more of their free time to mastering their craft.

Metrics

The Dunkel index, *USA TODAY's College Football Encyclopedia*, and the NCAA's Toughest Schedule Ratings each employ a slightly different method to quantify a team's schedule strength. Sports-reference.com is an invaluable resource. The website calculates a metric called Strength of Schedule or **SoS** for every college football team known to man. Doug Drinen defined the **SoS** metric back in 2006 as follows: "Strength of Schedule evaluates the opponents a particular team played without factoring in any point differential."

I like this metric primarily because it does not factor in any margin of victory values, which tend to favor offensive-minded teams playing modestly challenging (i.e. cupcake) schedules. Doug's colleague at sports-reference.com, Mike Lynch, provides clarity by explaining **SoS** like this: "if a team has an **SoS** of 10, it means that on average their opposition was 10 points per game better than an average opponent."

From 1970 through 2016, a total of 56 teams were either voted a share of or won the national championship outright. Nearly half of those teams (29) finished with perfect seasons while co-champions were crowned eight different times (1970, 1973, 1974, 1978, 1990, 1991, 1997, and 2003). Narrowing down this list of champions isn't easy. The following two parameters demonstrate minimal bias toward any individual team or school while placing significant emphasis on schedule strength.

- A team had to play at least *three* teams that finished in the final AP top 10 poll. To be the best, you have to beat the best. This helps identify some worthy champions that played relatively soft schedules, which included their fair share of teams considered to be inferior opponents. Through this criteria we pared our list of 56 teams down to 47.

- A team had to play a schedule rated at least the *fourth* toughest in the country, according to sports-reference.com, in the year they won their title. This criteria helps us to further pare down our list from 30 teams down to nine semifinalists.

PAM is a simple acronym for **P**erformance **A**gainst the **M**inefield that further emphasizes schedule strength. The "Minefield" is the final six opponents, including the bowl game, and the **PAM** is the winning percentage of the sum total of the six opponent's records at the time the games were played. It is intended to try and quantify a team's stretch run to their title. For example, using data from sports-reference.com, I created two tables, which compare the seasons and **PAM**s of 1990 Colorado and 2009 Alabama:

Schedule Strength 3 / 107		**1990 Colorado (11-1-1)**			
		Team (AP Rank)	Final Rec	PAM Data	
	31	**Tennesee (8)** neutral	9-2-2		31
Opp W/L % 0.587 88-58-4	21	**Stanford**	5-6-0		17
	22	**at Illinois**	8-4-0		23
	29	**at Texas**	10-2-0		22
	20	**Washington (12)**	10-2-0		14
SoS 9.06	33	**at Missouri**	4-7-0		31
	28	**Iowa State**	4-6-1		12
	41	**at Kansas**	3-7-1	1-4-1	10
POTAB = 53.8%	32	**Oklahoma**	8-3-0	5-2-0	23
	27	**at Nebraska (3)**	9-3-0	8-0-0	12
	41	**Oklahoma State**	4-7-0	3-6-0	22
BPP = 36.8%	64	**Kansas State**	5-6-0	5-5-0	3
		1991 Orange Bowl			
CO Nat'l Champ	10	Notre Dame (5)	9-3-0	9-2-0	9
	399				229
Avg / game	30.7				17.6

PAM = combined record of Final 6 opponent's records: **31-19-1 = 60.78%**

Schedule Strength 2 / 120		**2009 Alabama (14-0-0)**			
		Team (AP Rank)	Final Rec	PAM Data	
	34	**Va. Tech (7)** neutral	10-3-0		24
Opp W/L % 0.598 107-72-0	40	**Florida Int'l**	3-9-0		14
	53	**North Texas**	2-10-0		7
	35	**Arkansas**	8-5-0		7
	38	**at Kentucky**	7-6-0		20
SoS 6.62	22	**at Mississippi**	9-4-0		3
	20	**South Carolina**	7-6-0		6
	12	**Tennessee**	7-6-0		10
POTAB = 64.3%	24	**LSU (9)**	9-4-0	7-1-0	15
	31	**at Mississippi State**	5-7-0	4-5-0	3
	45	**Chattanooga** nonmajor	6-5-0	6-4-0	0
BPP = 26.5%	26	**at Auburn**	8-5-0	7-4-0	21
	32	**Florida (1)** neutral	13-1-0	12-0-0	13
		BCS Champ Game - Pasadena, CA			
	37	Texas (2)	13-1-0	13-0-0	21
	449				164
Avg / game	32.1				11.7

PAM = combined record of Final 6 opponent's records: **47-14-0 = 77.05%**

180

PAM quantifies the difficulty a championship team faced as it headed down its home stretch and addresses prior concerns over relying just on a team's won-loss record. In some respects **PAM** is similar to how an Olympic diving event is judged where additional points are awarded for attempting a more difficult, complex dive. More importantly, **PAM** exposes some critical information that is otherwise not reflected in a national champion's won-loss record. "Most people who rank college football teams—possibly all of them—emphasize the second half of a season over the first half and put the greatest emphasis on the bowl game results," said James Vautravers at *TipTop25.com.* "It makes sense to give more weight to a bowl game than to a regular season game because with the extra time to prepare teams theoretically show up at their best: healthier and with sharper game plans. And if two teams are comparable overall, but one was markedly better in the second half of the season than it was in the first half, it makes sense to rate the improved team higher."

The 10 teams below distinguished themselves from the other champs in the modern era because they are the *only* title holders to play at least three teams ranked in the final AP top 10 while also facing one of the four toughest schedules in the country during the year they were crowned national champions. There is no specific relevance to the order in which these teams are listed in this table. If two teams had the same schedule strength, they are listed according to the total number of teams ranked the year they were crowned champion. The mix of both past and present is intriguing. There is at least one team from each of the five decades in our modern era. For a complete and sortable list of this data, please visit billcontzpsu.com.

Year	Team	Record	SoS	Schedule Strength	Opp. W/L Record	Opp. W/L %	PAM W/L Record	PAM W/L %
2015	Alabama	14-1-0	7.46	1 / 128	135-63-0	.682%	58-11-0	84.06%
1988	Notre Dame	12-0-0	7.68	2 / 105	73-61-4	.529%	34-18-0	65.38%
1990	Colorado	11-1-1	9.06	2 / 107	88-58-4	.587%	31-19-1	60.78%
2009	Alabama	14-0-0	6.62	2 / 120	107-72-0	.598%	47-14-0	77.05%
1978	USC	12-1-0	13.20	2 / 138	94-53-2	.638%	43-15-0	74.14%
1982	Penn State	11-1-0	10.27	3 / 113	88-50-2	.629%	41-7-2	82.00%
1975	Oklahoma	11-1-0	11.32	3 / 137	77-58-2	.562%	37-12-2	72.55%
2006	Florida	13-1-0	6.95	4 / 119	110-70-0	.611%	39-23-0	62.90%
2016	Clemson	14-1-0	6.54	4 / 128	125-70-0	.641%	51-17-0	75.00%
1977	Notre Dame	11-1-0	9.93	4 / 145	76-56-4	.559%	32-21-2	58.18%

Of these 10 champions, only five of them have an opponent win/loss percentage greater than .600. As such, 2016 Clemson, 2015 Alabama, 2006 Florida, 1982 Penn State, and 1978 USC are our five finalists.

2016 Clemson—Dynamic DeShaun Watson spearheaded Dabo Swinney's up-tempo offense that ran off an astounding 99 offensive plays and scored 21 fourth-quarter points to dethrone defending champion Alabama 35–31 in an epic national title game played in Tampa, Florida.

2015 Alabama—Nick Saban's Crimson Tide used a 24-point fourth quarter to vanquish unbeaten Clemson in the second ever college football playoff one week after dismantling Michigan State 38–0. According to sports-reference.com data, this is the only team in college football history to win the title while playing the nation's No. 1 rated schedule in terms of difficulty. First-round NFL draft picks from this squad include center Ryan Kelly, Jonathan Allen, Reuben Foster, O.J. Howard, and Marlon Humphrey.

2006 Florida—In just his second year at the helm, Urban Meyer's Gators shook off a midseason loss at Auburn to win their final seven games and bury top-ranked Ohio State in the BCS Championship Game. Future first-round NFL draft picks included Percy Harvin, Derrick Harvey, Jarvis Moss, Reggie Nelson, and Tim Tebow.

1982 Penn State—A misleading 42–21 loss at No. 4 Alabama denied Joe Paterno his fourth perfect season in 14 years, but the Lions rallied to beat their seven remaining opponents, four of whom were ranked in the top 15 and included fifth-ranked Pitt and No. 1 Georgia. Players selected in the first-round draft included Curt Warner, Todd Blackledge, Kenny Jackson, and Shane Conlan.

1978 USC—The Trojans used a 14-point fourth quarter to break open a tight contest at Legion Field against then-No. 1 Alabama on their way to a share of the national title with the Crimson Tide. Southern Cal's opponent won/loss percentage (.638) is highest among the finalists from the pre-playoff era. Former standouts who later became first-round NFL draft picks included Anthony Munoz, Brad Budde, Keith Van Horne, Ronnie Lott, Dennis Smith, Charles White, Marcus Allen, Roy Foster, and Chip Banks. White would go on to win the 1979 Heisman while Allen would win the award two years later.

Let's compare the combined win/loss records for these five teams' opponents, the number of ranked teams they played as well as their **SoS**. Doing so offers revealing information. The quality of opponents these finalists faced during their championship seasons, specifically the number of ranked teams they played as well as their final six opponents' records (i.e. **PAM** values), help distinguish 2015 Alabama and 1982 Penn State from the others.

	2016 Clemson	2015 Alabama	2006 Florida	1982 Penn State	1978 USC
National Championship Season	14-1-0	14-1-0	13-1-0	11-1-0	12-1-0
Opponent Win / Loss Record	125-70-0	135-63-0	110-70-0	88-50-2	94-53-2
Opponent Win / Loss %	.641%	.682%	.611%	.629%	.631%
Strength of Schedule (SoS)	6.54	7.46	6.95	10.27	13.20
# of opponents ranked in Top 15	4	6	5	6	5
# of opponents ranked in Top 10	4	5	3	4	3
# of opponents ranked in Top 5	2	3	1	4	2
PAM (Final 6) Opponent W/L records	51-17-0	58-11-0	39-23-0	41-7-2	43-15-0
PAM (Final 6) Opponent W/L %	75.00%	84.00%	62.90%	82.00%	74.14%

One key difference is the number of Penn State's opponents because it played fewer games than any of the other teams. Additionally, if you include bowl opponents, then five of Penn State's final six foes had no more than one loss at the time they played them, and the Nittany Lions faced four of those five one-loss opponents away from Beaver Stadium.

Another important criteria is the number of opponents that appeared in bowl game. Teams obviously had no way to predict how many of their opponents would end up in a postseason bowl at the time the games were scheduled. Still, receiving a bowl invitation usually meant that a team had a pretty successful season and was generally considered a quality foe.

Until the mid-1980s, the only teams appearing in bowl games were either conference champions or teams that won at least 67 percent of their games (i.e. an 8–4–0 record). That said, some pretty decent teams chose to voluntarily opt out of playing in postseason contests.

Bo Schembechler's Michigan Wolverines finished with an 11–1 record in 1972, a 10–0–1 record in 1973, and a 10–1 record in 1974 yet chose to stay home after each of those seasons. In 1982 and fresh off their upset of top-ranked Pitt (at Pitt Stadium no less), Notre Dame owned a 6–1–1 record and were ranked 13th in the AP poll at the time the Fighting Irish hosted Penn State. They dropped that game as well as their final two contests and decided not to go to a bowl game.

Two more metrics, **POTAB** and **BPP**, help account for a team's bowl-bound opponents. **POTAB** stands for the **P**ercentage of **O**pponents **T**hat **A**ppeared in **B**owls. It is simply the ratio between the number of a team's opponents that went to bowl games to the total number of games the champion played the year they won their national title. **BPP** is an acronym for **B**owl **P**articipation **P**ercentage. It is the correlation between the number of a champion's opponents that appeared in bowl games to the total number of bowl games played in the year a team won its national title.

Using one of our semi-finalists, the great 1975 Oklahoma team, as an example to better understand these metrics, Barry Switzer's Sooners squad finished 11–1–0 despite facing six opponents who appeared in one of the 11 bowl games played that year. That gives them a **POTAB** value of 50 percent. Even more astounding is OU's **BPP**, which is an incredible 54.6 percent, the highest **BPP** among all 56 national champions in the modern era. This means that over half of all bowl games played in 1975 involved a team Oklahoma faced on its way to the national title.

It is important to note it became much easier to generate a **POTAB** above 50 percent after 1999 because by then the number of bowl games (23) were more than double what they were in 1970 (11). In other words, the greater the number of bowl games, the better chance that a team's schedule included more bowl participants and thus a higher potential **POTAB** value. The college football playoff adopted in 2014 now ensures that every national champion crowned under this format will likely have a **POTAB** value of at least 70 percent in part because these champions essentially play in two bowl games.

To put these two new metrics in perspective, imagine you set your Mr. Coffee machine each night by adding four scoops of Mrs. Folgers to the filter prior to pouring in the necessary amount of water for your usual robust morning brew. Now imagine that, after nodding off in your Laz-E-Boy, your wife flips open Mr. Coffee's lid and inadvertently adds more water. The next morning you're sipping on what is essentially a mug of hot water with a brown crayon dipped in it. That's what the NCAA has done to the bowl season. Virtually 90 percent of the games are basically watered down and tasteless. Think of a stout **POTAB** or **BPP** values as the equivalent of sucking down a triple espresso. Weak numbers here indicate that a national champion played a fairly weak schedule relative to other titlists.

One of our illustrious finalists posted both impressive **POTAB** and **BPP** values.

Penn State's 1982 **POTAB** value is 58.3 percent in 1982. That is second highest among all national champions between 1970 and 2004. (1998 Tennessee sets the pace with a **POTAB** of 61.5 percent.) This date range is significant because beginning in 2005 no less than seven different teams would eclipse Tennessee's impressive mark as **POTAB** values began to routinely exceed 60 percent due to the number of bowl games played.

With regard to Penn State's **BPP** value, seven of the 12 opponents on its 1982 schedule appeared in one of the 16 bowl games played that year. This gives the Nittany Lions a **BPP** of 43.8 percent, which is third highest in the modern era behind only 1975 Oklahoma (54.6 percent) and 1973 Alabama (54.5 percent).

Now recall the earlier point about 1982 Notre Dame deciding against going to a bowl despite a 6–4–1 record that included an upset of top-ranked Pitt. Had the Fighting Irish elected to go to a bowl, then Penn State's **POTAB** would jump to 66.7 percent, which would be the highest of any national champion before the current playoff system was implemented. In addition, Notre Dame's bowl game participation would have elevated 1982 Penn State's **BPP** to 50 percent and enabled Penn State to join 1975 Oklahoma as the *only* two teams in NCAA history to win a national championship in the modern era while playing a schedule where at least half their opponents participated in bowl games.

One final point to illustrate how oversaturated the bowl system has become. The 2014 Ohio State Buckeyes faced 12 opponents who accepted bowl bids. Four of those bowl participants finished their regular season with at least six losses. By contrast none of the opponents that 1982 Penn State faced that appeared in bowl games lost more than four games. Even though teams are now playing more games, the overall quality of the champions' schedules are getting diminished.

The current college football playoff format means the eventual national champion now plays more games than ever. The past three champions, for example, 2014 Ohio State, 2015 Alabama, and 2016 Clemson all played 15 games in seasons that began in late August and ended in the second week of January. To address this disparity in games played and establish some common ground between all 56 champions, let's look at extended, 15-game seasons for any national champion in the post-1970 era who failed to play the same number of games as our two most recent titleholders did. Despite the obvious year-over-year roster turnover, coaching changes, and other factors, doing this does provide us with one way to compare the past with the present at least in terms of the number of games played.

Each team's extended season includes the necessary number of contests from their previous campaign. For example, if a team only played 13 games in the year they claimed their national title, then we included that team's final two games from the prior season to create their extended 15-game season for that team.

For the 1982 Penn State team, its expanded, 15-game season includes the final three games from 1981, a year when it won 10 games and finished No. 3 in the AP poll despite facing what was widely recognized as the toughest schedule in the country. After scrutinizing 15-game data for all national champions since 1970, we find:

- The 15-game Nittany Lions are one of only three teams to ever beat two top-ranked opponents away from home before the advent of the current playoff system. The 2012 Alabama and 1985 Oklahoma teams also accomplished this rather noteworthy feat. Those Sooners, led by the outspoken Brian Bosworth, beat Penn State in the Orange Bowl to win the title.

- The 15-game Nittany Lions are one of only three title holders to ever face eight teams ranked 15th or higher. (The other two are 1993 Florida State and 1997 Michigan.)

- The 15-game Nittany Lions are one of only two champs, along with 2009 Alabama, to face six teams ranked in the top 10.

- The 15-game Nittany Lions are one of only two national championship teams to face five opponents ranked in the final AP top 5 poll. (The other is 1985 Oklahoma.)

Including 15-game data, the analysis of category leaders in the grid below shows two teams have distanced themselves from the others, one each from both the pre-playoff and post-playoff era. Our goal of a fair and unbiased comparison between teams from both the past and present may not be as far off as previously thought.

	2016 Clemson	2015 Alabama	2006 Florida	1982 Penn State	1978 USC
National Championship Season	14-1-0	14-1-0	13-1-0	11-1-0	12-1-0
Opponent Win / Loss Record	125-70-0	135-63-0	110-70-0	88-50-2	94-53-2
Opponent Win / Loss %	.641%	.682%	.611%	.629%	.638%
Strength of Schedule (SoS)	6.54	7.46	6.95	10.27	13.20
# of opponents ranked in Top 15	4	6	5	6	5
# of opponents ranked in Top 10	4	5	3	4	3
# of opponents ranked in Top 5	2	3	1	4	2
PAM (Final 6) Opponent W/L records	51-17-0	58-11-0	39-23-0	41-7-2	43-15-0
PAM (Final 6) Opponent W/L %	75.00%	84.06%	62.90%	82.00%	74.14%
# of opponents who went to bowls	13	12	9	7	6
# of bowl games	41	41	32	16	15
POTAB (% Opp. That Appeared in Bowls)	86.67%	80.00%	64.29%	58.33%	46.15%
BPP (Bowl Participation Percentage)	31.71%	29.27%	28.13%	43.75%	40.00%
Extended 15 Game Season					
# of opponents ranked in Top 15	4	6	5	8	4
# of opponents ranked in Top 10	4	5	3	6	3
# of opponents ranked in Top 5	2	3	2	5	2

In addition to this added information to the table, consider that 2015 Alabama and 1982 Penn State are the only two national champions in college football history that played four opponents ranked in the top 15 on the road during the year in which they won their title. The catch here is that Alabama played three more games, and the two playoff contests were at neutral sites.

Interestingly enough, the '82 Nittany Lions are the *only* national champion in the modern era to play four opponents ranked in the AP top 5 the year they were voted No. 1. Penn State is one of only two national champions (1997 co-champion being Michigan the other) to play six opponents ranked in the top 15 while playing a 12-game schedule. Four other teams that also accomplished this feat did the same, but those teams all played at least 13 games. The Lions' 82 percent **PAM** value is highest among all title holders in the pre-playoff modern era.

When using schedule strength metrics to rate and rank the top teams in college football's modern era, the 1982 Nittany Lions appear to be as one of the better teams in the college football history, but careful consideration must also be afforded to the 2015 Alabama squad that navigated a grueling schedule that included multiple games against top-ranked opponents very late in the season. The 2015 Crimson Tide faced 12 opponents that appeared in bowl games (a **POTAB** of 80 percent) and an incredible 14 that finished with winning records. This can be attributed to the ridiculous number of bowl games now being played as well as inflated winning percentages, a byproduct of schools scheduling lesser-ranked opponents to ensure their own bowl eligibility. That Alabama team joins 1987 Miami as the only teams since 1970 to play five teams ranked in the AP top 10 the year it won the national title. It should be noted the Canes only played 12 games while Alabama faced 15 opponents. Alabama also posted incredible numbers as far as opponent win/loss percentage (.682) and **PAM** (84.06 percent). Both are the highest of all champions crowned since 1970 and due primarily to the Crimson Tide's final three opponents having a combined record of 36–3–0.

But three of the Alabama's 14 wins in 2015 came against Charleston Southern (an FCS school) and Middle Tennessee State and Louisiana-Monroe (the latter two being from lower-tier FBS conferences). All three schools are generally considered inferior opponents, and playing games against them inflates several of the metrics, including opponent win/loss percentage, **PAM, POTAB,** and **BPP** values. I can see scheduling one or two cupcakes, but generating 20 percent of your entire season's win total from them is a tad excessive. That 2015 Alabama team played at least two more games than any of the other pre-playoff finalists. Recall that 1982 Penn State's **POTAB** is highest among all champions that played less than 13 games.

Let's assign a numeric value to where each of our 56 national champions rank according to our five schedule strength metrics (**SoS**, opponent win/loss percentage, **PAM, POTAB,** and **BPP**). For example a team would receive a 2 for second place, an 8 for eighth place, and so on, and then the cumulative results of all four metrics are averaged. We focused only on the games these teams played in the year they won their title. The results are below.

5 Mtrc Avg	Year	Team	SoS	Opp W/L Opp. W/L %	Rank	PAM PAM W/L %	Rank	POTAB % Of Bowl Opp.	Rank	BPP # Bowl Opp / Tot # Bowls	Rank	Away Games vs Top 15	Championship Season Top 15 Opp.	Top 10 Opp.	Top 5 Opp.	15 Game Data Top 15 Opp.	Top 10 Opp.	Top 5 Opp.
5.1	1982	Penn State	10.27	5	.629%	4	82.00%	2.5	58.3%	11	43.8%	3	**4**	**6**	**4**	**4**	**8**	**6**	**5**
8.0	2015	Alabama	7.46	15	.682%	1	84.06%	1	80.0%	2	29.3%	21	**4**	**6**	**5**	3	6	5	3
9.5	1978	USC	13.20	1	.638%	3	74.14%	11	46.2%	28.5	40.0%	4	2	4	3	2	4	3	2
9.6	2016	Clemson	6.54	21	.641%	2	75.00%	10	86.7%	1	31.7%	14	2	4	4	2	4	4	2
12.5	1975	Oklahoma	11.32	3	.562%	21	72.55%	14	50.0%	23.5	54.5%	1	1	4	3	3	5	4	3
15.2	2009	Alabama	6.62	20	.598%	10	77.05%	7	64.3%	5.5	26.5%	33.5	1	4	2	2	5	**6**	3

This grid also includes columns to the far right detailing the number of ranked opponents played both during a team's championship campaign as well as their extended 15-game season. Not only did 1982 Penn State play more teams ranked in the final AP top five than any other national champion in the modern era (four), but also when you extend their season to include their final three games from the previous year, they played more teams ranked in the top 15, top 10, and top 5 than any of the other teams...ever.

This weighted average exercise identified two teams (1982 Penn State and 2015 Alabama) that appear to have distanced themselves from the others. Since we also attempted to level the playing field with regards to the number of games played, we may now be able to achieve the near-impossible: a legitimate head-to-head comparison between two champions—one past, one present.

Let's examine the top 10 opponents these teams faced during their 15-game seasons which includes Penn State's final three games in 1981.

Year	Team	Date	Opponent	W/L	Score	Record	Game Rank	Record
1981	Penn State	11/28/1981	Pittsburgh	W	48-14	11-1-0	1/1	
1981	Penn State	1/1/1982	USC	W	26-10	9-3-0	8/7	
1982	Penn State	9/25/1982	Nebraska	W	27-24	12-1-0	2/2	
1982	Penn State	10/9/1982	Alabama	L	21-42	8-4-0	4/4	
1982	Penn State	11/26/1982	Pittsburgh	W	19-10	9-3-0	5/5	
1982	Penn State	1/1/1983	Georgia	W	27-23	11-1-0	1/1	5 - 1
2015	Alabama	10/3/2015	Georgia	W	38-10	10-3-0	8/6	
2015	Alabama	10/17/2015	Texas A&M	W	41-23	8-5-0	9/10	
2015	Alabama	11/7/2015	LSU	W	30-16	9-3-0	4/4	
2015	Alabama	12/31/2015	Michgan St.	W	38-0	12-2-0	3/4	
2015	Alabama	1/11/2016	Clemson	W	45-40	14-1-0	1/1	5 - 0

Penn State is 5–1 versus top 10 teams while Alabama is a perfect 5–0. But for their combined records of top 10 opponents, Penn State's equals 60–13–0 (82.2 percent) while 2015 Alabama's equals 53–14–0 (79.1 percent). Penn State also has more AP top five opponents (five) than Alabama (three) and better ranked opponent results. The 1982 Penn State team defeated teams ranked No. 1, No. 1, No. 2, No. 5, and No. 8 while 2015 Alabama beat teams ranked No. 1, No. 3, No. 4, No. 8, and No. 9

In the categories that pertain strictly to their national championship seasons, Alabama comes out ahead. But when you look at the extended 15-game season section, the scales seem to tip in Penn State's favor. Here is the complete head-to-head comparison:

	2015 Alabama	1982 Penn State
National Championship Season	14-1-0	11-1-0
Opponent Win / Loss Record	135-63-0	88-50-2
Opponent Win / Loss %	.682%	.629%
Strength of Schedule (SoS)	7.46	10.27
# of opponents ranked in Top 15	6	6
# of opponents ranked in Top 10	5	4
# of opponents ranked in Top 5	3	4
PAM (Final 6) Opponent W/L records	58-11-0	41-7-2
PAM (Final 6) Opponent W/L %	84.06%	82.00%
# of opponents who went to bowls	13	7
# of bowl games	41	16
POTAB (% Opp. That Appeared in Bowls)	80.00%	58.33%
BPP (Bowl Participation Percentage)	29.27%	43.75%
Extended 15 Game Season		
# of opponents ranked in Top 15	6	8
# of opponents ranked in Top 10	5	6
# of opponents ranked in Top 5	3	5

According to this data, there are only three schools in the history of college football that recorded three straight 10-win seasons against schedules rated among the most difficult in the county. Of those, Alabama and Penn State are the only programs to capture a national title in this scenario of facing extremely difficult schedules in consecutive years.

Year	School	W	L	T	SoS	Schedule Strength	AP Pre	AP Post	Coach	Bowl
2016	Alabama	14	1	0	7.29	1 / 128	1	2	Nick Saban	CFP Champ - L
2015	Alabama	14	1	0	7.46	1 / 128	3	1	Nick Saban	CFP Champ - W
2014	Alabama	12	2	0	7.26	5 / 128	2	4	Nick Saban	Sugar Bowl - L
1982	Penn State	11	1	0	10.27	3 / 113	8	1	Joe Paterno	Sugar Bowl - W
1981	Penn State	10	2	0	11.86	1 / 137	7	3	Joe Paterno	Fiesta Bowl - W
1980	Penn State	10	2	0	9.44	9 / 138	18	8	Joe Paterno	Fiesta Bowl - W
1973	Oklahoma	10	0	1	13.23	4 / 129	11	3	Barry Switzer	probation
1972	Oklahoma	11	1	0	9.57	15 / 127	6	2	Chuck Fairbanks	Sugar Bowl - W
1971	Oklahoma	11	1	0	10.07	7 / 128	10	2	Chuck Fairbanks	Sugar Bowl - W

Every rating service listed reflects unanimity in identifying 1982 Penn State and 2015 Alabama as playing the most difficult in the country in the year they won their titles. In addition, there have been only 10 teams since 1961 that have produced a 10-win season while facing the most difficult schedule in the nation, according to sports-reference.com's schedule strength metrics. Only four of those teams ('71 Alabama, '81 Penn State, '97 Tennessee, 2015 Alabama) followed that accomplishment up one year later with an encore performance of winning at least 10 games, while 1982 Penn State and 1998 Tennessee won the national championship. A complete listing of rating service results can be found at billcontzpsu.com.

Of all national championship teams since 1970, only six had a schedule rated at least the third toughest in the country, eight had opponent win/ loss percentages of more than .600, six had a **SoS** of more than 10, two had a **PAM** value of more than 81 percent, four had a **BPP** value of at least 40 percent, and three had a **POTAB** greater than 58 percent prior to 2000 (the year when bowls began to exceed the average number of games played). That's six different categories, and 1982 Penn State is in every single one of them.

Joe Versus the World

Miffed at being passed over for national recognition on three separate occasions, Joe Paterno took action. After his third undefeated team in six years (one that produced the school's only Heisman Trophy winner, John Cappelletti) finished no higher than fifth in any major poll in 1973, Paterno was convinced voter bias existed against eastern football schools. These suspicions were supported by the fact that no eastern team had won a national title since Syracuse in 1959.

In the ultimate put-up-or-shut-up move, Joe adopted the philosophy that—in order to be recognized as the best—his team had to play (and beat) the best. By the late 1970s, Joe's teams were playing top 10 programs virtually every other week...and winning. For the six-year span beginning in 1977, *USA TODAY* ranked Penn State's schedules as having the No. 1 top opponent record *four different times* (in 1977, 1979, 1981, and 1982). In addition *USA TODAY* recognized the 1980 Nittany Lions' as having the second highest Opponent Record (.647). The NCAA's Toughest Schedule Leaders also listed Penn State as its top team relative to schedule strength in 1981 and 1982.

During these six years, Paterno's teams went 11–1, 11–1, 8–4, 10–2,

10–2, and 11–1, an astounding 84.7 winning percentage (61–11–0) against what two different recognized sources agree were the toughest schedules in the county. This was not lost on NFL scouts as Linebacker U churned out pro-caliber talent at multiple positions. Over this six-year span, 49 Penn State players were selected in the draft, second only to USC (51). These results are remarkable given the school routinely graduated more than 90 percent of its players.

Joe rolled the dice with his own program and routinely came up with sevens and 11s. He convinced the most stubborn pollster that championship football was very much alive and being played in central Pennsylvania by producing no less than three straight 10-win seasons against what was a Murderer's Row of top-flight competition.

Penn State's sustained success enabled a Brooklyn-born, Ivy League-educated mad scientist with Coke bottle-thick glasses to prove his "Grand Experiment" could not only work, but also be a resounding success. The notion that a major college football program could simultaneously achieve athletic and academic supremacy with players who were accountable for going to class and graduating on time was refreshing in an era where program integrity was on the decline.

It also provided Paterno with the platform to lobby for two other radical concepts. He became an outspoken advocate for the formation of an eastern all-sports conference and a formal college football playoff system. Although his efforts for the former fell largely on deaf ears, the latter came to fruition three full decades later after other various methods were deemed flawed and inefficient.

Joe stood his ground with beliefs that athletics and academics could mutually exist while daring pollsters to recognize his program's success on the gridiron. He truly was a breed apart when it came to insisting his teams would successfully compete at the highest level while preparing them for a life outside of it. Lou Prato has authored several books on Penn State football and captures the essence of Paterno's intentions in *100 Things Penn State Fans Should Know & Do Before They Die*: "Even before he became Penn State's head coach in 1966, Joe Paterno began thinking about the kind of football team he wanted. Paterno believed he could build an outstanding football team composed of superior athletes who also were superior students. Paterno had nothing but disdain for the 'dumb jock' syndrome, a conviction held by much of the public—especially those in academics—that most athletes would not be in college if not for their physical abilities and skills. Even many coaches and administrators steered players toward degrees in physical education rather than the more demanding engineering, premedical, and business curriculums."

How the College Game Has Changed

Polls voted on by coaches and sportswriters all too often reflected regional bias, lack of consensus, and indecisiveness as evidenced by crowning co-champions eight different times over a 46-year span. Bowl alliances, coalitions, championship series, and now playoffs are all considered radical improvements over what was an obscenely antiquated poll system. Yet even this present format is not without fault since the scales still favor teams from the major conferences. The system will also on occasion omit a very worthy candidate. For proof just ask loyal TCU supporters to provide a valid reason why their Horned Frogs were denied a chance to participate in the four-team playoff in 2014 despite its only loss coming to fifth-ranked Baylor by three points on the road.

The current playoff format satisfies the demand to have college football's national champion determined on the field. The schools selected to participate in the playoff (along with the conferences they represent) reap huge financial windfalls at the expense of their players' health. Personally, I think a team having to play 15 games in order to determine an undisputed national champion borders on the absurd. A schedule that starts before Labor Day and ends the second week of January is an agonizing grind—yet another obstacle athletes must overcome in pursuit of their undergraduate degree.

Since grueling schedules are now the status quo for a chance to grasp the brass ring, Power Five conference teams will continue to populate their schedules with an occasional cupcake every few weeks to give their athletes a break, invariably diluting their overall strength of schedule. Look no further than the second week of the 2016 football season where the schedules in the SEC offered up these intriguing matchups involving SEC schools: Alabama-Western Kentucky, Georgia-Nicholls State, Ole Miss-Wofford, LSU-Jacksonville State, Auburn-Arkansas State, and Texas A&M-Prairie View. The average scores of these games was a decidedly non-competitive 42–12. These glorified scrimmages weren't limited to that conference as the ACC featured matchups such as Florida State-Charleston Southern, Georgia Tech-Mercer, and Clemson-Troy. Oddly every member of these major conferences played host to their opponents.

No disrespect to any of those lower-tier FBS and FCS schools, but to me it is hypocritical to pass off these contests as competitive events where fans pony up the full price of admission to witness what amounts to a dress rehearsal. (In the NFL these are known as preseason games.) The flip side here is that—save for Appalachian State and its stunning upset of mighty Michigan in Ann Arbor in 2007—smaller schools willingly offer themselves up as sacrificial lambs in return for a huge financial payday to foster the growth of their own programs.

Future national champions in this new playoff era will no doubt follow this blueprint and schedule multiple games against lower tier FBS and FCS schools so as to have enough gas left in the tank for the inevitable late-season single-elimination games that future national champions will routinely play. The national title is now a survival of the fittest, an exhausting last-man-standing war of attrition. These days a football scholarship is the equivalent of a four to five-year military commitment with players under daily scrutiny. Going home for the entire summer or even for the Christmas holiday is now no longer an option for college players.

My own aha moment as far as how radically things have changed since I left campus occurred in early June of 2010. It happened during a chance meeting with former Nittany Lions and current Philadelphia Eagles offensive lineman Stefan Wisniewski at a golf outing in suburban Pittsburgh. Our five-minute conversation pretty much provided me all I needed to know as far as how much the collegiate game has changed over the 25 years or so since I participated.

Stefan is the son of my former teammate and Penn State standout Leo Wisniewski. By 2010 Stefan had already been recognized for his stellar academic achievements. He was two months away from the start of his senior season, so I asked Stefan what his plans were for the rest of the summer. He explained that he was only home for a few more days before heading back to campus to take a summer class and resume his workout program.

I was stunned. I said, "Stefan, you've been a starter since your freshman year and carry a 3.95 GPA. Help me understand why you have to be back to campus a full six weeks before the start of preseason camp?" He told me matter-of-factly: "Well, Joe thinks it would be a good idea for me to be there to set the right example for the younger players." My conversation with Stefan reinforced the ridiculous demands placed on major college football players—even those who have nothing to prove academically or athletically.

The era in which a student-athlete has free time to enjoy different facets of college life, work a summer job, or even complete an internship away from campus may be long gone.

It is a sad reality that this ready-made farm system for the NFL, in conjunction with the NCAA, continues to tweak their definition of amateur athleticism. The Cost of Attendance stipend enacted in January of 2015 essentially now permits schools to "pay" their athletes. It is nothing more than a smokescreen, a convenient way for schools to keep their prized athletes on campus to train year round in return for what is—at best—modest compensation. Making matters worse, schools can offer varying amounts of stipends, which is likely being used as a bargaining chip during recruiting.

Blue-chip athletes now attract attention from college recruiters before they are issued driver's licenses. Once they sign with a school, the athlete is under intense pressure to enroll early so they can participate in spring practice, which means they sacrifice their final five months of their high school experience. Schools dismiss this as the collateral damage necessary to keep their 100,000-seat stadiums filled and win enough games to satisfy their influential, deep-pocketed alumni. But because of this trend, decreased emphasis on delivering well-rounded, educated athletes who go on to become productive members of society will continue.

Rebuttal

Use of the phrase "best ever" when comparing teams can be controversial as there are myriad underlying factors that come into play when using it. Members of the undefeated 1972 Miami Dolphins would no doubt cry foul if/when fans of the unbeaten 1948 Cleveland Browns made this claim. The '71-'72 Los Angeles Lakers won 33 straight games on their way to winning their NBA title, but Boston Celtics, Chicago Bulls, or Golden State Warriors fans would argue their teams' dominance enables them to make this best ever claim. Excellence in team sports are a matter of and subject to interpretation.

I believe best ever can only truly be determined in individual sports like golf, track and field, or tennis where the accomplishment is quantifiable and performed under similar circumstances. One example would be Jack Nicklaus who, in my opinion, is the best ever golfer since he not only won more major championships than anyone else, but also finished second in those events an incredible 19 times.

To those who dismiss my analysis as a tad simplistic due to the emphasis placed on schedule difficulty, then I am guilty as charged. It's hard to overlook dominant single seasons such as the undefeated 2013 Florida State Seminoles or 1995 Nebraska Cornhuskers, teams that beat opponents by an average of nearly 40 points per game. Generating sustained success like Oklahoma in 1973 that put together an incredible 28-game winning streak (a feat duplicated five years later by Alabama) or the USC Trojans that defeated 16 consecutive ranked opponents between 2002 and 2005 is also hard to argue against.

Mini-dynasties established by schools who won national titles in consecutive years such as 2011–12 Alabama, 2003–04 USC, and 1994–95 or 1970–71 Nebraska warrant serious consideration here as well. Active discussions also frequently center on other great college teams who, for a variety of reasons, did *not* win a national title. Tom Osborne's decision to go for a two-point conversion in the 1984 Orange Bowl offset a season where his Cornhuskers dominated every other opponent they played. A controversial pass interference penalty in the end zone in overtime cost 2002 Miami the chance at back-to-back titles, ending its 34-game win streak while an inflexible bowl system robbed fans of the chance to see a clash of the titans following the 1994 season between Penn State and Nebraska.

I expect naysayers outside of Pennsylvania to dismiss this assessment as sheer lunacy. I can already hear, "Well, Contz, if ifs and buts were candy and nuts" regarding the use of metrics that favor schedule strength. I also understand that these newly defined metrics (**PAM**, **POTAB**, and **BPP**) and the questionable decision to expand some teams' seasons by including games from the prior year to level the playing field is somewhat flawed and unconventional. My logic is that these new metrics allow us to look at things in a different light, and coming up with a similar number of opponents enables us to establish some common ground in our comparison of past and present champions.

This analysis supports a claim that the 1982 Penn State team may rank right up alongside some of the best college football teams in the modern era based on schedule strength. When you factor in that Paterno's program consistently produced extremely impressive graduation rates, the quote by former Houston Oilers head coach Bum Phillips used to describe his Hall of Fame running back Earl Campbell comes to mind: "I don't know if he's in a class by himself, but I do know that when that class gets together, it sure don't take long to call the roll." I feel the same way about the 1982 Penn State team, among the other greats.

CHAPTER 14

Reflections on Paterno

number of books chronicling Joe Paterno and what he stood for have already been written. All capture the essence of what he felt the ideal college experience should be for his players as well as what role sports should play in their lives. Undefeated teams in four different decades as well as an Orange Bowl win and No. 3 ranking in a fifth (at the tender age of 79, no less) speak to the man's coaching prowess. Consistently high graduation rates throughout his tenure confirm his "Grand Experiment" was an unprecedented success. From 1966 to 1986 *every one* of Joe Paterno's classes either played for an undefeated team or a national title, and that qualifies him as a pretty unique individual. You don't need another book to tell you that.

As I collected information for this project, it came as no surprise that virtually all former players and coaches I spoke with volunteered how they still practice at least one "Paternoism." I don't know a lot of people I can say that about. Joe was a breed apart because of his genuine interest in preparing his players for life outside of football. The 15-game stretch chronicled in this book somewhat understates the fact that Joe reached the pinnacle of his sport without compromising his ethics or principles.

His football program was no monastery, and his players weren't choirboys.

The majority of them did, however, respect the process, buying into the idea that academic and athletic success are not mutually exclusive. That both are achievable without cutting corners. Joe knew the kind of people he wanted to coach and the type of program he wanted to run. He advocated that his players be students first, embrace the college experience, and exit campus as better, more well-rounded people than when they arrived. "Other schools resented our image and what we stood for," said former assistant coach John Bove, who was part of Penn State's administrative staff for more than 35 years. "People perceived us as having some Goody Two-shoes attitude. We were gonna win with doctors, lawyers, and teachers. That rubbed a lot of people the wrong way."

Paterno set lofty goals and expectations, ones that would not be compromised. There were clearly stated rules you abided by and lines you simply did not cross. He was very consistent when it came to emphasizing his rules and ethics with his staff. His commitment to academics meant holding himself and his assistants to the highest standards when it came to the treatment of players regardless of status. "One time I'm in his office, and his secretary buzzes him to say, 'Coach, one of the professors is on the phone and would like a word with you.' Joe says, 'Okay, put him through,'" Tom Bradley said. "The next thing I hear is, 'Coach, it's Professor X, and I have a problem. I think I caught one of your players cheating on a test.' Without missing a beat, Joe goes, 'Professor, let me ask you a question. What would you do if you caught a *regular* student cheating?' Professor X says, 'Well, I'd flunk him.' Without any hesitation Joe says, 'Well, then *flunk* him' and hangs up the phone. He didn't mess around."

Bradley cited other examples regarding the ethics Paterno practiced. "Joe insisted we never use foul language or ever swear at a kid, no matter how upset we were at them," Bradley said. "Nowadays, it's commonplace where coaches do that. Joe never, ever swore. The strongest word I ever heard him use was Goddammit. For my first few years as a coach, I thought my first name was Goddammit because he'd get my attention in staff meetings by saying 'Goddammit Bradley, you gotta get these guys to do this.'

"When Penn State decided to build luxury skyboxes at Beaver Stadium,

Joe was 100 percent against the idea. He said to me, 'You know what those do? They create two classes of fans—one class that now looks down on the others who go to the games.'"

Scrap Bradley spent a total of 31 years on Paterno's staff, the last 11 as both defensive coordinator and Joe's top lieutenant—before being named interim head coach in 2011. His brief stint as head coach defined the word bittersweet because of how close he was with the man he replaced. "Joe was a guy's guy," Bradley said. "He also had a sense of humor that was off the charts. He once asked me why I never got married. I fired back with, 'Why should I get married?' He says, 'To give you a different perspective.' He's been gone almost five years now, and I still miss him."

Players changing positions at the college level was commonplace at most schools, and Penn State was no different. The goal was to field the best possible team from the existing rank and file. "Joe loved to take his roster home and move people around in an effort to get his best 22 players on the field," Dick Anderson said. "He'd come back the next day and out of the blue just throw different ideas at us. Depth at a particular position was not as important as getting the best players on the field. We went into almost every one of our meetings talking personnel. *How is this guy doing? Is he better suited for another position? Can he help elsewhere?* We would sit down, give our opinions to Joe, then figure out how to get them all on the field.

Mike Munchak, a fullback and defensive end in high school, was one shining example of what emerged from coaches' discussions as to where players best fit. "Initially, we were gonna use Mike on defense," Anderson said. "One day Joe says, 'We need to change him to offense.' He felt Mike was a good athlete that could have played defense for us but could become a *really* good offensive lineman. It took some coaxing, but he agreed to switch positions. I knew the minute Mike put his hand on the ground he would become a great player. I never saw a lineman with a stance that square, that balanced."

Munchak flourished after moving to guard, eventually becoming the eighth overall pick as well as the first offensive lineman selected in the 1982 NFL Draft. Mike played 12 seasons with the Houston Oilers, making the Pro Bowl nine times prior to his induction into the Pro Football Hall of Fame in

2001. He is widely considered one of the best guards of his generation.

Position switches were standard fare and they usually occurred early in a player's career. As Bove pointed out, "Heck, even John Cappelletti played defensive back as a sophomore. It was all about the team."

The 1982 squad had their fair share of players who switched positions. Joel Coles played tailback as a true freshman in 1978, started seven games at cornerback the following fall, and ran for 150 yards against N.C. State the year after that. Dave Opfar served as a backup tight end and linebacker before settling in at defensive tackle. Pete Speros was a reserve defensive tackle as a freshman before shifting over to the offensive line.

Probably the best example of Joe working to get his best players from the 1979 recruiting class on the field was East Stroudsburg's Dave Paffenroth. As a true freshman, Dave was a backup fullback to Matt Suhey, carrying the ball 10 times for 48 yards against Syracuse in the Meadowlands. In 1981 he played a significant amount of snaps at nose guard and was listed as a starting defensive tackle opposite Leo Wisniewski for the 48–14 game against Pitt. One month later he blocked a punt for a safety while playing special teams in the Fiesta Bowl against USC. As a senior Dave started all 12 games at inside linebacker, picking off a pass in our homecoming win against Syracuse and another the next week at Boston College. He ended up as the third leading tackler on the '82 defense with 56 stops.

Joe scrutinized the players he wanted at Penn State. He made it crystal clear to his assistants how they should be recruiting them. "At times Joe would accompany me in my territory, which was northern Pittsburgh, New Castle, Youngstown, Cleveland, and Buffalo," Bradley said. "I was a young coach, so when we recruited together he would use the opportunity to critique me. One time we're over in Youngstown, Ohio, trying to get Mike Zordich to commit. During the visit I made an off-handed negative comment about a rival school, and Joe let me know about it. Mike was from the same area as the Pelusi brothers, Matt Cavanaugh, some other guys all of whom went to Pitt. After I make my pitch to Mike and his family, we get back in the car. I start driving, and Joe says, 'Hey, I didn't appreciate what you said in there.' He then explains to me that, 'Recruiting is like trying to decide between a good-looking blonde and a brunette. There are no bad schools, just different ones. If you spend your time badmouthing other schools, it's just less time you can tell them about all the good things we have to offer.'"

Despite the late hour, Joe used the opportunity to deliver a lesson—as well as a subtle message about his own humble beginnings. "Joe makes me drive him from Youngstown all the way down to Oakland right in the heart of the Pitt campus," Bradley said. "Now it's already late, around 11 o'clock at night when we leave Youngstown. He tells me to take him right down to the front of the Cathedral of Learning. He then proceeds to tell me all about how great the academics were during the entire ride down there. After we leave the Pitt campus, he makes me drive him over to Homestead and when we get there he says, 'Now stop the car.' We both get out of the car, and he says to me, 'Tom, when I was a young assistant I had to hitchhike to Pittsburgh to go recruiting. The guy that gave me my very first ride dropped me off right here. Now drive me to the Pittsburgh airport.'"

The type of player Paterno sought for his program sometimes handicapped his assistants' ability to lure top talent to Happy Valley. "I recruited in northern New Jersey while Dick Anderson had South Jersey," Fran Ganter said. "There were guys in both areas that academically we just could not touch. That handcuffed us somewhat in recruiting because we couldn't go after just anybody. Joe had a rule that we could handle at most an average of two academic risks in each recruiting class. There was always a discussion as to who those two or three kids would be. You really had to plead your case to Joe regarding a kid like that. Joe also insisted on having a face-to-face meeting with those kids. He'd tell them, 'Hey, if you are gonna come here, you *will* go to class.' Either the kid responded by saying, 'Okay, Coach, you won't have to worry about me,' or the kid just walked out. If that happened then, you knew that kid wasn't coming to Penn State because of what would be expected of them."

Anderson confirmed Ganter's observations regarding recruiting limitations. "At times our hands were tied and we could not go after certain players," Anderson said. "It was not that different from recruiting for an Ivy League school. High school coaches would oftentimes try to oversell their player's qualities, and Joe was cautious in that regard. Joe wanted to be fair to players, and we were careful not to get [recruits] in a situation where they were in over their heads. He always wanted kids to graduate. Some players who were marginal academically turned out to work at it, be very conscientious, never give us any problems. You'd really have to go in and convince Joe this was a kid we should take a chance on. He wanted to get as many good students as possible. It translated to success in the classroom and learning on the field. The Grand Experiment was about recruiting quality individuals. That's where the whole success with honor thing began."

Bove felt Paterno's matter-of-fact style resonated with recruits and stood out in a process where rival coaches would not hesitate to stoop to low levels to get players to commit. "Joe was very up front and honest in what he was promoting to recruits," he said. "He never promised a kid how many carries he'd get each game or how we would promote them as an All-American. He would tell recruits, 'Look, if you come here and don't want to pursue your education, then you're not gonna like me, and I'm not gonna like you.' He didn't want to spend time in staff meetings talking more about the guys who were the academic risks when we should be talking about the other players."

Along with rigorous academics, difficult schedules were part of Penn State football. The schedules Penn State played in the early 1980s impacted the coaching staff as well as the players.

"The really big games were exciting for the coaches," Bove said. "It made them want to get in the office earlier. We never believed we couldn't win any football game. We would go out recruiting on Friday nights to watch high school games, and people would come up to us and recognize the game's importance."

Did playing tougher schedules put more pressure on the coaches? "Actually, no," Anderson said. "It made it more challenging, more fun. You want to play the best. It helped us recruiting. Joe was all about wanting to be the best, and in order to achieve that, he felt we had to play against the best. His, 'we-gotta-play-the-good-ones' outlook was the way he always approached things. There aren't very many coaches taking on that type of challenge these days. It's a big risk. You do that with the wrong administration, and they want to make changes."

Paterno showed a willingness to listen to others, acquiescing more than people thought.

"After we beat Georgia, I was disappointed to find out that student trainers would not be getting national championship rings," Tim Bream said. "Joe's stance was that our duties were considered an academic class, and that we were benefitting academically. I went to [Jim Hochberg] to plead my case, and he said, 'The old man ain't gonna give you one.' I said, 'Hoch, even the ball boys are getting one!' I then asked [Hoch] if I could talk to Joe about it, and he was okay with that. I decided I would present my case formally to him. I researched the amount of time I had invested and on the day of the meeting put on a coat and tie. I explained to Joe that I worked over 900 hours and was getting no credit for that. He listened to my argument very patiently, reviewed the information I presented to him, and concluded the meeting by saying, 'I never thought of it that way.' I got my ring later that spring. A lot of time people never saw or understood the benevolent side of Joe."

Although Joe was genuinely interested in helping people improve their lives, he employed different methods to get his points across. Various players from the '82 team offered examples of Paterno shaping their lives. Joe routinely pushed the envelope during practice, singling out individuals in front of the entire team to emphasize the standard of play he expected. His reprimands were usually about as subtle as a Metallica Christmas album.

Al Harris: "If Joe saw something he didn't like, he'd sprint over to show you how he wanted it done, and absolutely no one was exempt from his wrath. One day we were grinding it out, and Joe starts yelling at Sean Farrell. I mean, Farrell is an All-American, the team captain, one of the best players on the team. Joe yells, 'Farrell! Your dad's a doctor, your mother's a lawyer, but you? You're an *idiot*.' I still hear his voice to this day, sometimes when I am working on a patient's tooth. 'C'mon Harris, get it there! Get it done!'"

Gregg Garrity: "My sophomore year we were using both practice fields, and Joe was with the defense way down at the other end of their side of the field. We ran a crossing pattern, and I just dropped it. I came back to the huddle, and Joe was about 100 yards away. As he got closer, you could hear he was yelling stuff, and I'm laughing, thinking, *Oh man, someone's in trouble.* He kept approaching, and the next thing I hear is, 'Garrity! Why did you drop that ball? Your dad was better than you! He'd *never* drop that ball!' At that point I took things a little more seriously because I always prided myself on never dropping any pass. He was like the old TV show *Columbo.* He'd say something to you, he'd walk away for two steps, and then he'd come back and say, 'And another thing…' You just knew there was always more, that he was always going to turn around and say something else."

Jon Williams: "We were doing a drill one day on the offense's side of the field. There was no tackling, just upper-body thud. One play I carry the ball, break into the clear, then turn around, and start running back to the huddle. Harry Hamilton comes over and knocks the ball out of my hand. Paterno is on the defensive side of the field, sees this, comes running over, and starts screaming, 'Get on the ball! Get on the ball!' I have no idea what he's talking about because the play is over. Then I realize he's yelling at me. I go get the ball from Harry, bring the ball back, and Joe grabs it from me, then he throws it about 20 yards down the field, and yells, 'Get on the ball' again, so I go after it, bring it back, and hold on to it. He wanted me to recover it like it was a fumble. From that point on, he was riding everybody hard for the rest of that practice. Various players start coming up to me going, 'Thanks for getting Joe all riled up, Williams.' The lesson Joe was teaching me was that it was always a game situation, even in practice, and to never let your guard down."

Grades

Curt Warner: "Joe wasted no time illustrating his point about the importance of academics. At our very first squad meeting, Joe told us Karl McCoy and Pete Harris didn't make grades and were off the team. These were two guys going into their senior seasons who started against Alabama in the Sugar Bowl! His message was clear: if you don't go to class, we're gonna have a problem. We knew right then Joe wasn't messing around, someone who would not compromise his principles. He got his point across."

Greg Gattuso: "The only time I was ever in Joe's office was about my grades. I was humiliated and embarrassed for my family. He made sure he held me accountable to that. I started poorly academically because I played gin with my roommate, Nick Haden, all night, every night during my freshman fall semester. I really had to dig myself out of a hole. Joe reinforced his expectation that no one would do this for you. The way he handled that with me was masterful. If he doesn't do that, I could never have achieved anything. Had he not cared enough to discuss this with me, I would have definitely flunked out or transferred."

Mike Meade: "It was early into the second semester of my freshman year. We were preparing to play for the national title against Alabama, and I get a call from Joe's secretary stating, 'Coach would like to see you.' I'm just a freshman, so a thousand things crept into my mind, all football-related stuff. Was I being moved to a different position? Was he renouncing my scholarship? I go into Joe's office, and he peers out at me through those glasses and says, "Mike, I just reviewed all the players' fall semester grades. You only got a 2.75 GPA and can do better than that. I think you could be an Academic All-American.' I was blown away. Here's a guy about to coach in the single biggest game of his career, and he's taking the time to schedule an individual meeting with some lowly freshman buried on the depth chart to discuss me improving academically? Hell, I was proud I had a 2.75 GPA, which at the time may have been the second highest among all the guys in my recruiting class."

Life Lessons

Ron Heller: "As I began coaching in the NFL, I would evaluate players based on what a guy did when [he] got beat. I remember Joe suggested we 'Go to a Penn State wrestling match and watch our best wrestler, Carl DeStefanis. Whenever he gets taken down, he's already working on ways to get back up off the mat.' Being very familiar with that sport, I thought Joe brought up wrestlers as an indirect reference to situations where you have to do it all on your own. I always wondered if he was appealing to all the football players who were former wrestlers like me, Steve Sefter, others."

Al Harris: "Joe was part father-figure, part taskmaster, part motivator. He didn't sell you a bill of goods during recruiting; he only promised an opportunity to get a quality education with a great campus setting and an opportunity to play top-flight football. It's up to you to take advantage of that. He made no promises regarding playing time or becoming an All-American. He set the tone for dedicated learning and ensuring his players would achieve academic success—not just athletic success. People ask me all the time what Joe was like. I tell him he was a sincere hard-working, detail-oriented guy. His goal was to mold young people into responsible citizens, to guide young people during their formative years."

Jon Williams: "My freshman year I had a good game and ended up appearing on *TV Quarterbacks*. I kept saying, 'um' or 'and um,' really stuttering through it. During breaks Joe would say, 'Calm down, take your time, think about what you want to say. After the show he suggested I sign up for a linguistics class. Taking that course changed my life. It taught me how to articulate, to communicate better, how to pause, using the correct wording, to use the right words in the right context. Joe helped me grow as a person. He helped you understand the things you need to be successful in life. I share that story with people to this day."

Squad meetings would commence with Joe checking his wristwatch to ensure we began exactly at the scheduled time while quickly scanning a piece of paper that listed his agenda items. Joe's attire for these meetings was maddeningly predictable. He would wear the same navy blue polo shirt and tan khakis during practice, adding another layer, usually a plain gray sweatshirt, if the weather got a tad chilly.

Depending upon the mood he was in, any late arrivals would incur Paterno's full wrath, and that player would be dressed down in front of the entire team. Joe would glare menacingly at any player who wandered in 15 or 30 seconds after the meeting started and demand a valid reason for the egregious oversight. Arriving on time meant you were already late. To this day most former Penn State players exhibit near-obsessive behavior when it comes to arriving to meetings a few minutes before the designated start time. "Every single timepiece I own—my alarm clock, the one in my car, in my office, my wristwatch—are all set five minutes ahead of the current time," Mark Battaglia said. "He ran a tight ship and was constantly enforcing his own standards. Stuff we would ordinarily take for granted but would help us later in life, the it's-all-in the-details mind-set."

Joe continually harped on concepts that had bigger picture implications. Here are some of the many "Paternoisms" he regularly reinforced.

Tim Bream: "Jerry Slagle and I were late getting back to the training room, walking on the sidewalk and we decided to take a shortcut across the grass. Unbeknownst to us, Joe is right behind us and yells out in that high-pitched voice of his, 'Heywhaddyathink they make sidewalks for? Get off the grass!' I learned as much just standing on the football field at practice as I learned in the classroom probably because of who the message was coming from and the examples he would use delivering it."

Mark Robinson: "One day Joe comes into a squad meeting and says, 'On my way over here, I watched these kids cutting across the grass when there was a sidewalk there, and you know what I did? I yelled at 'em!' I said, 'Hey, stay off the grass! At Penn State we don't take shortcuts!' I mean he's not just yelling at his players. He's giving students the business, too. To this day I can't ever cut across a lawn. I stay on the sidewalk. It was his way of expressing that there are no shortcuts in life, that you gotta earn it, that nothing is ever given to you, and you can't take the easy way out. We have patterned our lives around simple concepts like that."

Jon Williams: "His open-step-then-go message still sticks in my mind. There was one time where Joe yells at me because I took two hop steps. He says, 'Hey Williams, whaddyathinkyadoin? We don't have a play where you take two hop steps!' Then he starts yelling at Frannie for not correcting me. It was a very direct, this-is-the-way-we-want-it-done message. I didn't realize until much later that you took that open step to freeze the linebacker. We used that on the 6 series in the passing game, the very same play Blackledge threw to Garrity in the Sugar Bowl. Joe's attention to detail was amazing."

Scott Radecic: "We were conditioned to never talk about how well we were doing. Joe instructed us to be humble in the ways we addressed things publicly. We still tell our stories usually in a self-deprecating manner because of that. Joe always told us, 'You either get better or you get worse.' He also felt that no matter how good you did, he always felt you could be better. I'm a 53-year old man and I still think about that every day."

Dan Biondi: "Joe liked to quote Winston Churchill or George S. Patton. I remember him always saying you are either good enough, or you're not, so enjoy the challenge, enjoy the moment."

After we won the 1983 Sugar Bowl, Todd Blackledge saw a more relaxed side of Joe on their travel to New York for an appearance on *Good Morning America*. Other players had similar experiences albeit in different situations.

Al Harris: "You saw another side of Joe after you graduated. At our 10-year reunion, Joe sat down and just started telling stories about guys, some of whom we had never heard of, some scout-team guys. After a few stories, I stop him and ask, 'How can you remember all these stories?' Joe then said something I thought was very sincere and very touching. He says, 'For the time when you guys are here, you are like my kids. You guys are what make up my life.' It amazed me that, as dedicated as he was to what he was doing, he could have that type of total recall along with that type of perspective and be willing to share both with his former players."

Jeff Butya, a former walk-on, said Joe didn't just remember those who started or played regularly for him. "Ten years after we left school, Joe came down to Pittsburgh as part of some PSU coaches caravan. He comes up from behind, grabbed me by the back of my hair, and goes, 'Butya! You need a haircut' in that high voice," said Butya, who owns the All-Star Sports & Grill in Pittsburgh, Pennsylvania. "The next thing he says is how was my bar doing? It seemed like Joe knew everything about everybody."

Battaglia is equally astonished at Paterno's memory. "His most remarkable quality was his ability to remember detailed information about your family, things that are important to you as a person," Battaglia said. "If I had a penny for every time somebody said, 'Joe remembered my daughter, my son, and asked how they are doing in school,' I would be a rich man. One time I picked him up at the Butler County Airport, and he says, 'How's your dad, the Lehigh guy?' Now Joe had met my dad exactly *one* time, when I was being recruited. I said, 'He's great, do you wanna talk to him?'" I call my dad from my car, hand Joe the phone, and he goes, 'I remember we used to run up and down the field against Lehigh.' He's talking smack on my dad! Those two are chatting it up like they're the best of friends. That to me is how I will remember Joe—his memory and the way he bonded with people."

After Penn State beat Rutgers in 1982, Williams found out how easily Joe bonded with players' family members and how accessible he was to them. "It's my state university so it's special for me, and I had a good game," said Williams, a Somerville, New Jersey, native. "My future wife's family are all visiting from New Jersey and we all go out to dinner afterward. This is a big entourage. We are all sitting around after dinner having a few drinks. I may have had one too many and blurt out, 'Hey, do you guys wanna go over to Joe's house?' Usually after a game Joe is entertaining the president of the university or other big boosters at his house. Of course they all say, 'Yes!' So we get in the car and drive down Joe's street. I park the car and say to my family, 'Wait here.' I go up to Joe's house, knock on the door. Sue comes to the door, and I say, 'Hey, I want Joe to meet my family.' She explains, 'Well, he's got people over, but I'll let him know you're here.' After a few minutes, Joe comes to the door, and my family gets out of the car to come to the door to meet him. He spends about 10 minutes talking to them. He even signed autographs for them! Man, they loved it. They're all excited. As we are leaving, he says, 'Hey don't be late for practice tomorrow.'"

As the evening wound down, sobriety eventually returned and brought with it a healthy dose of paranoia. "Later on that night, I start thinking bad thoughts like, *Did he notice I had been drinking? What was I doing? Why did I take people to his house?* I am *really, really* nervous about seeing him the next day," Williams said. "I am getting ready for the squad meeting, which always starts on Paterno Time, so I was in my seat five minutes before it starts. I'm on pins and needles worrying. Before the meeting he comes over and says, 'Hey, you got a very nice family, really nice people,' and that's all he said. I was expecting him to tear into me, to say things like, 'Whaddya doing? Don't you know I'm entertaining? Don't come to my house! Don't ever do that again!' I always wondered if he knew I was drinking, but he was too classy to embarrass you in front of your family. It made you want to go out and play harder for him because of how he treated your family. Out of all the other stuff he wanted to speak to about the previous game, he comes up to me and compliments me on my family. He didn't have to do it, but he did anyway. My wife's family still talks about that to this day. It was a special moment, a really big deal for them to meet Paterno. It really meant something to them. He could have told Sue, 'Hey, I'm too busy,' but he didn't. That's how Joe was. He would make time for you, especially if it involved your family. His gesture not only made their day; he made the rest of their life."

Years after he left the program, Chet Parlavecchio approached Joe with what he felt was an egregious oversight regarding his family. "I told Joe, 'You know, out of all the guys you recruited in my class, I was the only one you never came to the house of. That was a little disrespectful to my mom and dad,'" Parlavecchio said. "That must have resonated with him because I get a call one day, and it's Joe. He and Frannie Ganter are out recruiting in the area where I grew up and asked if they could stop at my mom Josephine's house to visit. They ended up staying for dinner."

Fran Ganter cited a valid reason why Joe didn't visit the Parlavecchio residence when Penn State was recruiting him. "Chet had already committed very early," Ganter said. "And we knew he wouldn't change his mind, so we focused our efforts on recruiting the guys we were still battling for. But we did go back years later to eat a fantastic Italian meal at Casa di Parlavecchio."

Countless former players have shared their observations about playing for Joe Paterno. I don't consider mine all that significant or enlightening because I never developed a really close, personal relationship with him. I am not sure many players ever do while on campus. That is okay because it didn't impact my overall college experience very much. I never looked at Joe as a father figure probably because I was fortunate to grow up in a very caring, two-parent household. That said, I certainly respected what Joe stood for and how he ran his program. My goal was to secure a quality college education. I was fortunate to stay out of Joe's doghouse and avoid any major injury during my four years there. When given the opportunity to play, my main goal was not to embarrass myself or let my teammates down.

Don't get me wrong: I was grateful for the occasional words of encouragement Joe gave me during my four years, but he had a business to run. Penn State football was an organization with a ton of moving parts to manage and lead. Like most of his former players, I am much more appreciative of the direction, the proper tone, and example he set in terms of punctuality and preparedness. Those are the life lessons I carry with me to this day.

Joe Paterno did a lot of things. As a former player who has been in his fair share of other football locker rooms, I can tell you seven things he *didn't* do. Joe never:

- shattered a chalkboard during a halftime rant or swore at his players
- grabbed a kids face mask to get his attention
- embarrassed a kid publicly for his own personal gain
- punched an opposing player or slammed his glasses to the ground in a rage
- tolerated his players taunting any opponent
- showed blatant favoritism toward star players

The controversy regarding the Paterno statue—it was erected more than a decade ago outside Beaver Stadium then removed in 2012— remains an extremely sensitive subject. My thought is this: I don't know any other coaches who have libraries named after them. To me, that is where his statue should go.

CHAPTER 15

Where Are They Now?

ach year when a school wins the national championship, it brings back fond memories of what I experienced back in 1982. To me it's a little like the final scene of the animated Christmas movie *The Polar Express*. I still hear that bell ring. I can still visualize running out of the tunnel in Beaver Stadium before kickoff, the smell of the practice field grass, the on-field chaos after the Nebraska game, the total exhaustion offset by the utter and complete satisfaction of walking off the Superdome floor after securing Penn State's first national title.

Some of our teammates are no longer with us, having passed on and left this Earth way too soon. Most of the surviving members of the '82 team now confess to various aches and pains, the permanent battle scars from Paterno's always enjoyable Bloody Tuesday practices. The trade-off is that most of us have raised families incorporating at least one (or more) Paternoism into their lives and those of our family members.

I think most of the players from that team can still recall either the lights going out against Nebraska, the energy-sapping heat in Birmingham, the brisk chilly air that greeted us upon our arrival in South Bend, or the first-night haze in the nether reaches of the Louisiana Superdome. This book exists because it's evident that—after soliciting their many stories—the majority of my former teammates also still hear their own version of that same bell. Here (in their own words) is what they are doing now:

Anderson, Dick—I retired from Penn State in 2012 after coaching football for almost 50 years. My wife, Kathy, and I live in State College, enjoyed raising four children here, and now have 10 grandchildren, two of whom are football players so far. Grandson Matt played for Lafayette College (Class of 2016), and Ryan starts at right tackle for Wake Forest (Class of 2018). We have 12 Penn State degrees in our immediate family so far and still love the Nittany Lions.

Allen, Pete—I reside in Dallas, Texas, with my wife Gloria and five Penn State loving children. I am an executive vice president at Vizient, a healthcare performance improvement company. Even with all of that chaos, I never miss a Penn State football game.

Battaglia, Mark—I live in my hometown of Pittsburgh with my wife Diane (PSU '84). We have three daughters—Amanda, Andrea, and Alyssa—all of whom are Penn Staters as well. I have been in the financial services industry for more than 30 years, including the last 15-plus years at Merrill Lynch where I manage the South Hills, Pennsylvania, office as well as help my clients reach their financial goals.

Bellaman, Michael—Carolann and I reside in the Washington, D.C., area and are blessed with three awesome children—Colby, Campbell, and Connor. My PSU architectural engineering degree has enabled me to enjoy a successful career in the construction industry. Fingers crossed, we hope to be visiting our children on many PSU sports weekends in the future.

Blackledge, Todd—I live in Canton, Ohio, with my wife, Cherie, and we have four boys. The two oldest are in college, and the other two are 16 and 14. I am a college football analyst for ESPN during the fall and a varsity basketball coach at my alma mater in the offseason.

Bove, John—Anna, my better half, worked 26 years for Penn State. My three children are Penn State products. Our son wrestled, was an NCAA qualifier, became an Eastern Intercollegiate Wrestling Association champion, and won three gold medals for PSU in freestyle. Our oldest child was a Pennsylvania and *USA TODAY* Teacher of the Year. Our three grandchildren are all PSU graduates; one grandson played soccer at PSU.

Bowman, Kirk—I live outside of Fort Worth, Texas, with my wife, Nancy (PSU '86). One daughter, Emily, played soccer and is now in med school at Oklahoma. Another daughter, Tori, is a junior playing soccer at Oklahoma while my youngest is a junior playing quarterback for Grapevine High School. I am working in corporate account sales for Smiths Medical, managing the Vizient relationship.

Bradley, Tom—I live in Santa Monica, California, but still keep my home in Pittsburgh, Pennsylvania. I am the defensive coordinator for UCLA football.

Bream, Tim—I graduated from Penn State with a bachelor's degree in health and physical education prior to earning my master's degree in physical education from West Virginia. I spent 19 years with the NFL's Chicago Bears and was the head athletic trainer with that organization from 1997 to 2011 before returning to PSU in 2012. I am an assistant athletic director for sports medicine support services and am responsible for overseeing sports medicine support and athletic training services for all 31 varsity sports as well as approximately 900 Penn State student-athletes. I have two daughters, Rebecca and Elizabeth.

Brooks, Booker—I am "retired" now after coaching football almost non-stop since 1963 at the high school, major college, and professional level over 50 years. I have one son, Aaron, a lawyer at PSU; two wonderful grandchildren, Alia and Tiberius; and a most gracious and beautiful wife, Cynthia Plecity Brooks.

D'Amico, Rick—I reside in Allison Park, Pennsylvania, with my lovely wife, Michelle (Porter) D'Amico. We have three beautiful children—Mia Isabella, Nicolas Edward, and Sophia Geraldine. I am currently a senior regional vice president with Deutsche Asset Management in Pittsburgh, Pennsylvania.

Dunlay, Michael—After residing in my hometown of Oakmont, Pennsylvania, for 41 years, I moved to Chicago, Illinois, to open one restaurant. Now, I am the CFO of the 4 Star Restaurant Group that I run with three partners, and we operate 10 restaurants in the Chicagoland area. I still attend three to six Penn State games every fall and have been a season ticketholder since 1983. Please look me up when in Chicago at www.4SRG. com. I plan to retire in 2020(ish) and move to Ireland or Napa.

Fuhrman, Chet—I have been blessed to have coached a No. 1 team at all three levels—the Pittsburgh Steelers to a Super Bowl title, Penn State University to two Division I collegiate national championships, and Steelton-Highspire to a Pennsylvania high school No. 1 ranking. I am a native of Harrisburg, Pennsylvania, and have coached 35 years in the field of strength and conditioning. I presently live in Pittsburgh, am married to Lisa (Penn State '83), and have three children: Erica, Mike (Penn State football letterman 2012), and Maria (Penn State student).

Ganter, Fran—After 45 years at Penn State as a player, coach, and administrator, I retired in 2012. I continue to reside in State College and have four sons, all of whom played college football—two at Penn State, one at Princeton, and one at Cornell. Two of my sons married Penn Staters in 2016. All of the Ganters continue to gather in State College on football Saturdays and will always bleed Blue and White.

Garrity, Gregg—I live in Bradford Woods, Pennsylvania, married to my Linda, and have two children. Samantha teaches third graders in the North Allegheny School District, and Gregg Jr. (aka Pook) just graduated from Penn State with a communications degree and is a member of the 2016 B1G Ten champions football team.

Gattuso, Greg—My wife, Colleen, and I have relocated to Albany, New York, where I am the head football coach of the Albany Great Danes. I have spent the past 20-plus years as a college football coach heavily influenced by Coach Paterno. Our two daughters, Jacqueline and Kaitlin, are doing great and have successful careers.

Giacomarro, Ralph—I was drafted by the Atlanta Falcons and played three years in Atlanta and another with the Denver Broncos. I have lived in the suburbs of northern Atlanta for more than 30 years. I am a licensed professional engineer in the state of Georgia specializing in structural engineering. I have three children: Charlie, Chrissy, and Eddie who all reside in the Atlanta area. I also have four grandchildren: Kaylee, Cameron, McKenzie, Cavin, and son-in-law Mike. I enjoy weightlifting and running as my hobbies and also compete in several half marathons each year to keep in shape.

Harris, Al—I graduated the University of Pennsylvania School of Dental Medicine in 1987 and I have lived and practiced dentistry in South Jersey since then. My wife, Alisa, and I met at Penn State. We have two sons, and I am very grateful to be a product of "The Grand Experiment!"

Heller, Ron—My wife, Heidi, and I currently split time between Red Lodge, Montana, and Ponte Vedra Beach, Florida. We have one child, Hollyann, who is a senior at University of North Florida studying logistics. After my NFL playing career, I was involved in several businesses but ultimately became a football coach and spent the last five years coaching with the New York Jets and the Jacksonville Jaguars.

Kelley, Ken—I have two beautiful, successful daughters, Lyndsy and Erin. Lyndsy is a 2010 Penn State graduate, and Erin graduated from Rowan University in 2012. I'm a lifelong South Jersey resident and recently retired after 30 years in medical sales.

Laube, David P.—I reside in Saddle Brook New Jersey, with my wife, Jolene, who is the groups manager of Perillo Tours Learning Journeys. We have two sons, David Sean and Jonathan Matthew. David lives in Louisiana, and Jonathan lives with us. I have been employed by Mathusek, Inc. for more than 30 years. I am the vice president of the construction/synthetic division. We are PSU through and through!

McCann, Brian—I live in Doylestown, Pennsylvania, with my wife, Nancy (PSU '83). We have two boys, Connor and Colin. I am the east coast vice president of sales for Hanger Clinic, a national company that provides prosthetics and orthotics. The McCann family bleeds Blue and White. I am blessed. Thanks Joe for your influence on and off the field.

McCloskey, Mike—I currently reside in Lower Gwynedd Township, Pennsylvania, with my wife Mimi (PSU '85). We have three great kids, Kiernan (Lehigh '17), Megan (PSU '18), and Kyle (Villanova '21). I am a managing partner at Chartwell Investment Partners, which is located in Berwyn, Pennsylvania.

Parlavecchio, Chet—I currently live in Florham Park, New Jersey, with Jean, my wife. We have two children, Chet and Nicole. After coaching in the NFL with dear friend and former teammate, Mike Munchak, I was appointed dean of students and head football coach at Passaic Valley Regional High School in Little Falls, New Jersey. My son, Chet, is a teacher and is a football coach at Delbarton School and also coaches lacrosse. My daughter Nicole is a teacher in the inner city of Newark, New Jersey, and coaches softball and basketball.

Radecic, Scott—I reside in Mission Hills, Kansas. My son, Matt, played lacrosse at Penn State and graduated with a degree in computer engineering. My daughter, Taylor, played lacrosse at Virginia Tech and graduated with a degree in business/marketing. Both are married and have blessed me with three amazing grandchildren, with No. 4 on the way. I am an owner and senior principal at Populous, the world's largest architecture firm dedicated solely to the design of sports facilities.

Robinson, Mark—I live in Palm Harbor, Florida, with Melinda, my wife. We have three beautiful daughters—Jordan, Jasmine, and Haley. We own and operate a private Montessori School in Clearwater. I also have been the color analyst for University of South Florida (USF) for the past 20 years. I miss coming to Penn State football games due to my broadcast commitments.

Sefter, Steve—I have been living in Cary, North Carolina, for the past decade. My wife, Mary Rose, works as a teacher in the Wake County/North Carolina school system. My daughter, Rebecca, is at East Carolina University majoring in communications and political science. I am currently a territory manager with ExxonMobil in their fuels and lubricants marketing company. I have been employed by ExxonMobil for more than 30 years. I continue to follow the Penn State football and wrestling teams and wish them all the success possible.

Speros, Pete—I reside in Great Falls, Virginia, with my wife, Jessica. We have four wonderful children: Chris (Richmond '13), Will (Fordham '14), Kayla (Miami University '18), and Avery. I am a co-founder and partner at Sullivan, Bruyette, Speros & Blayney, a registered investment advisory firm in McLean, Virginia, which was established in 1990.

Suter, Mike—I live in Cincinnati, Ohio, with Shirley, my wife of 31-plus years. She is a Penn Stater (1985) and was a member of the swim team for four years in Happy Valley. We have two boys. My youngest son, Troy, is a Notre Dame grad who lives and works in Madison, Wisconsin, while my oldest, Brent, graduated from Harvard and is currently a pitcher for the Milwaukee Brewers. He made his MLB debut in August of 2016 and got married that same year. I am in marketing for Regal Beloit Corporation and have been working for this division in a variety of sales and marketing roles for nearly 33 years all over the U.S.A. Shirley and I remain avid Penn State fans and have been very blessed.

Warner, Curt—After graduation I was drafted third overall by the Seattle Seahawks. I led the AFC in rushing my rookie season with 1,449 yards on 335 carries and scored 13 touchdowns in helping the Seattle Seahawks reach their first ever AFC Championship Game. I suffered a torn ACL in the 1984 opener and missed the rest of the season but came back in 1986 to post a career-best 1,481 yards rushing. I earned Pro Bowl selections and was named All-Pro in 1983, 1986, and 1987. I presently reside in Camas, Washington, with my wife, Ana. We have four children. Our eldest son, Jonathan, graduated from Penn State in 2016. We also have twin sons (Austin and Christian) and a daughter Isabella.

Williams, Jon—I have lived in Massachusetts since 1984 and been married to my lovely wife, Diane, for more than 30 years. We have three beautiful daughters (Laurenn, Courtney, and Brooke-Lynn) and two grandchildren (Emri, Mia). Brooke-Lynn is attending PSU on a full track scholarship. I have worked at FedEx, handling corporate accounts and have a tattoo of the Nittany Lion on my left arm. I will always cheer PSU football and now track. (My wife and I can't wait to make those six-hour drives.)

Zordich, Michael—I split time between Ypsilanti, Michigan, and Youngstown, Ohio. I am currently coaching for the Michigan Wolverines after my great experiences with coaching at University of Youngstown and the Philadelphia Eagles. I have a beautiful wife, Cindy, and three awesome children, two of whom are PSU alums. Although they say "Go Blue" here, my heart is never far from the Blue and White in Happy Valley.

Gone But Not Forgotten

This book is in memory of our former '81 and '82 teammates, coaches, and trainers who have passed on before us, including Matt Bradley, Dick Maginnis, Gene Lyons, John Bruno, Dr. Stuart McMunn, John "Hubba" Fee, Tim Robinson, Kevin Baugh, Scott Carraher, Joe Paterno, and Jim Hochberg.

Acknowledgments

The earliest working title of this project was *Six Minutes in Birmingham*, something I came up with shortly before Mark Battaglia decided to chug what remained of my second Moscow Mule I was apparently nursing after a round of golf at St. Clair Country Club. The intent was to focus on the strange circumstances resulting in Penn State's lone blemish in an otherwise improbable 15-game stretch where David routinely took on Goliath and slayed college football's giants seemingly every week. Mark and all of my former teammates helped me turn this into something much more. I am extremely grateful for their help doing that.

The idea for this project was born out of a hunch that very few college football teams had accomplished what Penn State managed to pull off back in 1982. It was my proverbial itch requiring the occasional scratch. Years ago I originally stumbled across strength of schedule data buried in a 10-inch thick NCAA record book accessed via the local library. Since then I would periodically revisit the topic by checking other random data sources, fully expecting to see other schools post 10-win seasons or secure national titles while playing one of the nation's toughest schedules. To my surprise, very few ever did.

Having the good fortune to be around some of the funniest people anyone has a right to meet inside a never-a-dull-moment Penn State locker room, my goal was to document these folks' experiences and capture the pulse of the characters responsible for events that transpired over a 14-month,

15-game period while attempting to shed light on how unique that team's achievements were through using detailed statistical analysis.

This project chronicles what may have been the ultimate litmus test of Joe Paterno's Grand Experiment, when a confluence of academic and athletic excellence proved that true student-athletes could pursue higher education while reaching heights rarely achieved in college football.

My rather abrupt departure from corporate life in October of 2013 also proved to be pivotal in bringing this to fruition since it afforded me the free time necessary to do so. My displacement was explained to me as "a difficult business decision" and "not performance-related." I would have appreciated a more direct approach like, "Hey pal, take a hike. We gotta downsize here, so we're canning your 53-year old ass."

I spent the next few months addressing minor health issues. After rehabbing my way through three different arthroscopic procedures (all performed by an orthopedic magician named Dr. Volker Musahl), I began giving very serious thought to marrying the obscure statistical quirk about schedule strength to my teammates' recollections of the 1982 season. Reluctantly, I concluded this may be what I was called to do at this point in my life.

I took the stance that if somebody didn't get around to writing this thing then it's likely no one ever would. The sad truth is the mortality of my teammates and I is now a sobering reality. In the brief span of time I began doing this research, I lost two former NFL teammates (Tom DeLeone of the Cleveland Browns and Hokie Gajan of the New Orleans Saints) to cancer. When you receive news like that, you tend to view it as a wake-up call to savor the moment, to hug family members every chance you get, and to actually start *doing* some of the things on your bucket list (please start one today if you haven't yet created one) instead of simply just adding items to it. Members of this '82 team are now in their mid-50s, and most are in varying stages of mildly-to-moderately declining health. When our team returns to campus in the fall of 2017 to celebrate its 35-year reunion, it could very well be the last time we all see each other.

To convince myself my hunch was indeed valid, I started off working backward by first examining a wealth of data on such popular topics like opponent win/loss percentages. Once I had sufficient evidence that what I discovered was uncommon ground, I summoned the nerve to contact the people who published Jay Paterno's well-written book, *Paterno Legacy*, which I received as a Christmas gift. Once I sold the publisher on the concept, I set out to reconnect with my former teammates, several of whom I had not spoken with in over a decade.

At the outset I felt a little like the Terrance Mann character in *Field Of Dreams* as he stepped into the cornfield to witness members of the 1919 Black Sox to get their side of the story. I had little to no idea of what I was getting in to yet knew it had the potential to be an enlightening experience.

At times I found the work frustrating, utterly exhausting, yet oddly galvanizing. Already keenly aware of my own versions of the circumstances involving the talented team I played on, I came away impressed at how lucid some of my teammates' memories were and how their own versions of similar events differed from mine. Securing content from my teammates required some initial coaxing. That's no real surprise since I'm not inclined to blind-side people I haven't talked to in years with a request to provide details of events that occurred nearly 35 years ago. When a teammate would say, "I don't remember much about…" I acquainted that to the elderly bar patron struggling to recall the name of a long-forgotten tune by explaining to Billy Joel's *Piano Man* that he "knew it complete when (he) wore a younger man's clothes." Some teammates, who were previously able to recite stories with great precision so as to include exact quotes verbatim, were victimized by the time that passed between when they last told their tale.

A few guys simply forgot about some of the games from that season. (Scott Radecic, of all people, was surprised to hear we even *played* Temple in 1982.) Most, however, could easily recall the marquee wins over Nebraska, Pitt, and Georgia. To me, it was no different than looking up in the sky at night but only seeing the closest and brightest stars versus those in some faraway galaxy.

Collecting the raw content became more enjoyable when it was apparent that many former teammates possessed both a wealth of information and a willingness to share it with crystal clarity. Their own unique versions of little-known events had been kept under mental lock and key only to be dusted off if someone came looking for them. The conversational interviews ended up being one of the most pleasurable aspects of this project.

I uncovered fantastically detailed answers and explanations, some from the most unlikely of sources. It was encouraging to hear details with pinpoint accuracy in such matter-of-fact fashion from teammates as if the events happened last week. A few are actually in possession of some pretty rare keepsakes (gameballs, coins, photos, etc.) that would no doubt qualify as invaluable memorabilia to hardcore Penn State fans.

This project was in some respects therapeutic for me. What former athletes (military personnel too, I think) miss most when their active participation ends is the camaraderie, that unique alliance forged out of the sacrifice, determination, and dedication necessary to achieve team objectives. Dr. Al Harris probably said it the best when he offered that "the bond that forms in a football locker room exists because you see guys at their absolute best as well as their worst, their most vulnerable moments."

It should surprise no one that my first published writing effort is a subject I know like the back of my hand. I take immense pride in sharing details about what I, along with my teammates, experienced in a magical season. The task of determining exactly where our results rank in the annals of college football is a slightly taller order.

I am cautious in that I hope this does not leave members of our Nittany Lion fraternity with the impression that the 1982 team was the best ever in school history. As mentioned earlier, that phrase is difficult to use in any team sport, but I also think doing so would insult anyone who has ever had the privilege to don our classic, no frills, blue and white Penn State uniform.

The 14 victories detailed in this book account for a very small percentage of Joe Paterno's NCAA-record 409 victories. By drawing attention to them, I run the risk of ruffling the feathers of the many other former Penn State players whose contributions to their own great teams helped forge our reputation as a clean program that competed with the absolute best college football had to offer.

My goal with this project was to point out that Penn State's 1982 achievements were noteworthy since winning a national title while playing a schedule recognized by multiple sources as one of, if not *the*, most difficult in the country, doesn't happen all that often. Hopefully enough statistical data was provided to enable the reader to conduct their own educated and thorough review of the information so as to arrive at their own conclusion as far as where this particular team may rank among other great national championship teams in the modern era.

Those closest to me would refer to me as a bit of a "smart aleck" (my dad's term, not mine), and I cannot disagree with that assessment. I tend to think of myself more as a seasoned conversationalist—someone expertly skilled at spin doctoring a variety of topics while being proficient at causing mild uproars by making fairly well-timed, quasi-outrageous assertions. (I prefer the term "thought-provoking.") Initiating these types of conversations promotes spirited dialogue, and I am quite content to sit back and gauge people's reaction. My father used to say I was "a card that needed to be dealt with." I polish that up by explaining to anyone willing to listen that "in a prior life, I was a washing machine stuck on the agitate cycle."

I do try to find the lighter side in most everything I do. Humor seems to be an escape for me. That doesn't mean I don't take things seriously when I have to; it's just that I seem to derive a fair amount of pleasure putting a smile on someone's face. Hopefully, this book does that for Penn State football fans while stirring debate with my contention that the 1982 Nittany Lions should go down as one of the greatest national champions in college football history.

I would be remiss without thanking the following people for providing me the many and varied forms of inspiration and information for this project.

There is no way this thing ever comes to fruition without my former Penn State teammates and coaches taking time out of their lives to go on the record and provide me with amazingly detailed recollections of events that transpired a long, long time ago. Without their observations, wit, and intellect, this would have been a pretty mundane grind.

Books written about Penn State football by people like Lou Prato, Jay Paterno, Ken Rappaport, and Joe Posnanski all served as not only invaluable resources, but also motivation to follow through with this project. Each

WHEN THE LIONS ROARED

found their own ways to effectively communicate their passion on this topic and convert it into periodicals I found both insightful and interesting. Lou provided me with keen insight throughout this process and indirectly served as my mentor. For that I am grateful.

I recognize both Tom Bast and Jeff Fedotin at Triumph Books. Tom took a flyer on an ex-jock with a ludicrous notion that the world needed another book about a championship season while Jeff withstood several of my spirited objections to nail down a catchy title. I am grateful of their show of faith in someone they have only met electronically.

Triumph assigned veteran journalist Scott Brown to be this book's ghostwriter. One can only imagine how thrilled he must have been to find out he had to work with some 55-year old ex-jock attempting to write his very first book. Turns out Scott was a fellow Penn State alum with a great passion for sports and zero tolerance for mediocre journalism. Scott taught me the art of the transition sentence, proper use of punctuation, and how to stay on point. I am extremely appreciative for his patience, candid feedback, and bluntly accurate observations regarding flow and writing style. Mostly, I am grateful for his many positive words of encouragement throughout this entire ordeal.

Two former colleagues from prior employs, Don Edwards and Charlie Rapp, merit recognition. Shortly after being displaced back in 2013, I met Don over coffee at a local Panera to do a little networking. At one point during our first face-to-face conversation in over 10 years, he looks me square in the eye and says, "You could pretty much do whatever you want and be successful at it." I don't know why it took me so long to realize that. A very sincere thank you for that encouragement, Big Boy.

Charlie Rapp took a chance on hiring someone with absolutely zero sales training or experience and less than three years later was onstage in a ballroom in Orlando, Florida, congratulating me in front of 1,000 people as I accepted the national sales rep of the year award. Charlie received the very first rough draft of this book in July 2015 and has been encouraging me to complete it ever since. He has been a confidant, a trusted source of both valuable guidance and honest feedback.

Mark Lehew and Jon Perry are two close friends who also deserve mention. When not masquerading as a senior vice president at German software giant SAP, Mark is my rotisserie league foil and music trivia antagonist. Jon Perry, to my knowledge, is the youngest lawyer to ever make partner in the western hemisphere while simultaneously founding his own successful charity, Pennies From Heaven, which is affiliated with Children's Hospital of Pittsburgh and has raised over $2.3 million to date.

Summoning bravery the likes of which few have ever seen from him, Mark approached me in a vodka-infused haze at Perry's 2015 Christmas office party to offer up what may be the only compliment he has ever paid me by proclaiming, "Hey, you're not a bad author. You ought to write something." Mark obviously felt compelled to say this in response to my near Contz-tant skewering of his hideously managed fantasy football team on the league's message board. As much as I hate to admit it, Lehew may have indirectly provoked me into doing this. Perry meanwhile remains arguably the single biggest supporter of Penn State athletics this side of my brother-in-law. In addition to his charity work, Jon is a very decorated and accomplished attorney who regularly hosts people at "Perrydise," the aptly named bar area in his expansive Wexford, Pennsylvania, home.

I once promised my older sister, Anita, to someday write a follow-up to my very first literary work, a one paragraph, never-published effort titled *Shoes and Shocks*. Pundits no doubt recall the story of the confused adolescent who removed his shoes on the bus ride home on the last day of school and then got off before realizing his gaffe. The topic remains something she finds funnier than it really is, but her occasional prodding to try my hand at writing may have produced the desired effect, albeit nearly 45 or so years later.

I am grateful to Mike Lynch and his colleagues at sports-reference.com for taking the time to help me better understand their website's various schedule strength metrics. The site contains an insane amount of information for sports data junkies like me and was my single most utilized point of reference for the data provided in this book.

Last but certainly not least, my wife, Melanie, has been my primary inspiration ever since the first time I set eyes on her in high school back in

1979. Her continued encouragement and support of my decision to suspend my medical sales career indefinitely to pursue this endeavor was a critical factor in seeing this through. Despite my many character flaws and stubbornness, she continues to put up with me. She has been and will always remain the love of my life.

Sources

Personal Interviews

Dick Anderson

Pete Allen

Patrick Allen

Mark Battaglia

Mike Bellaman

Dan Biondi

Todd Blackledge

Booker Brooks

John Bove

Kirk Bowman

Tom Bradley

Tim Bream

Jeff Butya

Joel Coles

Rick D'Amico

Mike Dunlay

Chet Fuhrman

Fran Ganter

Gregg Garrity

Greg Gattuso

Dr. Al Harris

Ron Heller
Steve Sefter
Pete Speros
Mike Suter
Curt Warner
Jon Williams
Leo Wisniweski
Mike Zordich

Newspapers
The Daily Collegian
Altoona Mirror
Pittsburgh Post-Gazette
The Pittsburgh Press
Center Daily Times
Philadelphia Daily News
The Philadelphia Inquirer
Miami Herald
The Times-Picayune
Orlando Sentinel
Harrisburg Patriot

Websites
bcinterruption.com
wrestlingstats.com
wilson.engr.wisc.edu (College Football Researchers Association)
si.com
dunkelindex.com (Dunkel Index)
sports-reference.com
miami.edu
blackshoediaries.com
espn.com
bcshof.org

archives.nd.edu
democratandchronicle.com
Usatoday.com (Jeff Sagarin ratings)
phys.utk.edu (Soren Sorensen Data)
texas.247sports.com (National 100— Dr. Charles Howell)
tiptop25.com (James Vautravers)

Books
Boyles, Bob; Guido, Paul. *The USA TODAY College Football Encyclopedia 2009–2010* Skyhorse Publishing

National Collegiate Athletic Association Official *NCAA Football Record & Fact Book*

Fitzpatrick, Frank. *Pride of the Lions: The Biography of Joe Paterno* Triumph Books

Paterno, Jay. *Paterno Legacy* Triumph Books

Prato, Lou. *100 Things Penn State Fans Should Know & Do Before They Die* Triumph Books

Other
Associated Press
Penn State football videotapes/TCN Sports
The Penn State Football Newsletter—John Black
Penn State Sports Information Department
NCAAction Official Football Statistics